INTERNATIONAL IDEA INSTITUTE FOR DEMOCRACY AND ELECTORAL ASSISTANCE

MW01701279

Electoral Justice:

The International IDEA Handbook

INTERNATIONAL IDEA INSTITUTE FOR DEMOCRACY AND ELECTORAL ASSISTANCE

Electoral Justice:

The International IDEA Handbook

Lead Author
Jesús Orozco-Henríquez

Editors
Ayman Ayoub
Andrew Ellis

Contributors
Adhy Aman
Tracy Campbell
Avery Davis-Roberts
Zoran Dokovic
Andrew Ellis
Sergueï Kouznetsov
Ralf Lindner
Augustin Loada
Deki Pema
Joram Rukambe
Maiko Shimizu
Denis Truesdell
Domenico Tuccinardi

Electoral Processes

Handbook Series

The International IDEA Handbook Series seeks to present comparative analysis, information and insights on a range of democratic institutions and processes. Handbooks are aimed primarily at policymakers, politicians, civil society actors and practitioners in the field. They are also of interest to academia, the democracy assistance community and other bodies.

International IDEA
SE-103 34 Stockholm
Sweden

Graphic design by: Santángelo Diseño
Cover Design by: Santángelo Diseño
Cover illustration: © Mariano Valerio
Printed by: Bulls Graphics, Sweden
ISBN: 978-91-85724-96-3

Foreword

Electoral justice is at the cornerstone of democracy in that it safeguards both the legality of the electoral process and the political rights of citizens. It has a fundamental role in the continual process of democratization and catalyses the transition from the use of violence as a means for resolving political conflict to the use of lawful means to arrive at a fair solution.

An electoral justice system that resolves political conflict through different legal mechanisms, guaranteeing full compliance with the law, enables democracy to thrive. This deepens the importance of strong electoral bodies, and improving the framework within which political, administrative and judicial institutions coexist. In consequence, it provides cognitive elements that will assure social stability.

Electoral Justice: The International IDEA Handbook combines a profound analysis of the concept of electoral justice with a prevailing pragmatic viewpoint that serves both academics and electoral officers within administrative and judicial institutions. Moreover, the Handbook offers a highly structured study of all that encompasses electoral dispute resolution, ranging from prevention to resolution.

The Handbook illustrates the importance of political culture and civic education in the prevention of electoral disputes, but these factors are also central to determining the manner in which such conflicts are resolved.

At the same time, this Handbook provides a thought-provoking classification of electoral dispute resolution systems, which sets out a series of structural principles and procedural guarantees that are of critical importance for electoral justice as a whole. This is especially relevant due to the short periods of time that electoral dispute resolution bodies (EDRBs) have to make their decisions. Thus, the performance and professionalism of electoral officers are key to a functional electoral dispute resolution system. Logically, an efficient EDRB is a compelling factor in a successful and rounded electoral system.

The Handbook emphasizes how crucial it is for institutions in charge of administrating electoral justice to be legitimized by the citizens. It draws attention to some key variables of legitimacy, such as the importance of political consensus in defining the structure and composition of the electoral body, the essential character of transparency and the imperative of the independence of the institution in charge of resolving electoral disputes.

The fact that the EDRB should be a permanent institution is also a legitimizing factor, as the Handbook mentions, and although its cost and sustainability may be a financial burden, the cost of a weak institution is much greater. Strong electoral institutions that are properly funded, are autonomous and have functional budgetary independence should be seen as an investment in the quality of democracy. This rings true because of the importance of the decisions that the EDRB has to make for the political future of a country. These decisions can imply ratifying, modifying or voiding electoral results as well as protecting the political rights of citizens.

Political parties and citizens have opted for lawful and just solutions as means to resolve political disputes. As a consequence, EDRBs are taking a more important role, providing solutions for equality, freedom of speech, disenfranchisement and illicit campaign financing, among other issues which confront democracy.

Without a doubt, this Handbook, elaborated by an outstanding group of scholars, will prove extremely useful to electoral judges around the world. International IDEA supplies groundbreaking material that enriches our comprehension of electoral justice and awakens the curiosity of the reader to continue further studies of this fundamental element of democracy.

María del Carmen Alanis Figueroa
Chief Justice of the Federal Electoral
Court of Mexico

Preface

Elections are at the core of the democratic process. The competitive and politically divisive nature of elections and their technical complexity make them vulnerable to abuse, fraud or perceptions thereof. At the same time, elections are able to achieve their key purpose of providing legitimacy to the government only if they are fully trusted and perceived to be impartial and fair. Hence the need for an effective mechanism to prevent, mitigate or resolve disputes that are likely to arise in every electoral process, and to preserve and when necessary restore the real and perceived equality of citizens and their representatives.

An efficient and effective electoral justice system is fundamental to securing these objectives. Without a system to mitigate and manage inequality or perceptions of inequality, even the best management of an electoral process may lead to mistrust in the legitimacy of a democracy.

International IDEA has developed this first global Handbook on electoral justice in order to increase understanding of the importance of robust, contextually sensitive and nationally embraced systems and to examine how a variety of electoral justice mechanisms and bodies are used to defend electoral rights.

While ongoing initiatives within International IDEA seek to address the causes of violence or conflict related to electoral processes, this Handbook explores the necessary technical and legal considerations and architecture needed in order to prevent such disputes and potential conflicts from arising. The Handbook explores a variety of the electoral dispute resolution (EDR) mechanisms currently employed around the world; how such EDR systems are classified and the elements, principles and guarantees that should govern them; and considers alternative dispute resolution mechanisms that are currently being used within the confines of an electoral justice system.

Examples of electoral justice systems have been incorporated throughout the Handbook, to explore the potential uses and benefits of a variety of methods in order to assist practitioners in developing a system that is suitable for their own context and reality. The comparative knowledge gathered in the Handbook is further expanded in International IDEA's online Unified Database (http://www.idea.int/uid), where users can continually update information using a wiki-style editing approach that will help to sustain the accuracy of the information provided.

International IDEA intends to bring the wealth of knowledge produced in this Handbook into the Building Resources for Democracy, Governance and Elections (BRIDGE) training curriculum (http://www.bridge-project.org) and to continue its development through the ACE Electoral Knowledge Network (http://www.aceproject.org).

Vidar Helgesen
Secretary-General
International IDEA

Acknowledgements

A great number of organizations and individuals have contributed to this work. Without the able hands of the management team, Paul Guerin, Adhy Aman, Shana Kaiser and Rushdi Nackerdien, this Handbook would not have been produced. In addition to the lead writer, editors and contributors we would like to extend our warmest appreciation to the expert group who contributed to the development of the publication: Diane Acha-Morfaw, Raúl Avila, Zsolt Bártfai, Francesca Binda, Krystian Complak, Peta Dawson, Manohar Singh Gill, Peter Harris, Jau-Yuan Hwang, Serguei Kouznetsov, Vishakan Krishnadasan, Ralf Lindner, Ismail Mohamed, Isabelle Ribot, Ali Sawi, Kate Sullivan, José Thompson, Saumura Tioulong, Domenico Tuccinardi and Yuri Zuckermann. Many experts also went the extra mile in contributing to the improvement of the publication and added great depth through their expertise and personal experience, including Ayman Ayoub, Andrew Ellis, Maarten Halff, Joram Rukambe and Gilles Saphy.

Special thanks go to our language editor Andrew Mash and copy editor Eve Johansson as well as the translator Charlie Roberts for their excellent work. The research and support team – Melanie Allen, Erika Beckman, Virginia Beramendi, Ingrid Bäckström-Vose, Luca Di Ruggiero, Henrik Domingo, Maria Gratschew, Erik Grunde, Mélida Jiménez, Stina Larserud, Nadim Mar'I, Maiko Shimizu and Sara Staino – have tirelessly supported the management team in making this Handbook more valuable to its readers. Our gratitude also goes to Antonio Spinelli for his advice and support.

We also acknowledge with gratitude the valuable contribution of the numerous electoral management bodies worldwide that took the time to answer our surveys and contribute to the online database created as an extension of this Handbook, and the ACE Regional Centres which have worked with International IDEA in gathering the comparative country information:

Association of Central and Eastern European Election Officials (ACEEEO), Hungary
Centre for Electoral Reform (CETRO), Indonesia
Commission Electorale Indépendante (CENI), Democratic Republic of the Congo
Electoral Institute for the Sustainability of Democracy in Africa (EISA), South Africa
Institute for Education in Democracy (IED), Kenya

Instituto Federal Electoral (IFE), Mexico
National Jury of Elections (JNE), Peru
Resource Building Institute in Democracy Governance and Elections (RBI), Armenia.

Additional thanks also go to IDEA's publications team, in particular Lisa Hagman, Nadia Handal Zander and Lucy Smith.

Contents

Tables

Figures

Boxes

Annexes

Acronyms and abbreviations

ADR	alternative dispute resolution
AEDR	alternative electoral dispute resolution
CEC	Commune Election Commission (Cambodia)
DRE	direct recording equipment
ECC	Electoral Complaints Commission
EDR	electoral dispute resolution
EDRB	electoral dispute resolution body
EDRM	electoral dispute resolution mechanism
EDRS	electoral dispute resolution system
EJS	electoral justice system
EMB	electoral management body
HAVA	Help America Vote Act
ICT	information and communications technology
IDEA	International Institute for Democracy and Electoral Assistance
NEC	National Election Commission (Cambodia)
NGO	non-governmental organization
OAS	Organization of American States
OSCE	Organization for Security and Co-operation in Europe
PEC	Provincial Election Commission (Cambodia)
SADC	Southern Africa Development Community
SoS	Secretary of State
TSE	Tribunal Superior Eleitoral
UK	United Kingdom
USA	United States of America

CHAPTER 1

CHAPTER 1

Introduction

1. The importance and role of electoral justice

1. Electoral justice, in general terms, involves the means and mechanisms:

- for ensuring that each action, procedure and decision related to the electoral process is in line with the law (the constitution, statute law, international instruments and treaties, and all other provisions); and
- for protecting or restoring the enjoyment of electoral rights, giving people who believe their electoral rights have been violated the ability to make a complaint, get a hearing and receive an adjudication.

2. In this Handbook, the notion of electoral justice further encompasses the means and mechanisms for ensuring that electoral processes are not marred by irregularities, and for *defending electoral rights*. Electoral justice mechanisms include all the means in place for preventing electoral disputes, as well as the formal mechanisms for resolving them by institutional means and the informal mechanisms or alternative means for their resolution. Any irregularity in the electoral process may give rise to a dispute. Among the mechanisms for resolving electoral disputes, a distinction should be made between:

a. those that provide a formal remedy or are corrective in nature, such as the means of bringing electoral challenges, which annul, modify or acknowledge the irregularity;
b. those that are punitive in nature, which impose a penalty on the perpetrator, entity or person responsible for the irregularity, such as election-related administrative and criminal liabilities; and
c. those alternative mechanisms for electoral dispute resolution which are voluntary for the parties in dispute and frequently informal.

3. In this respect, along with other elements of the electoral framework, electoral justice represents the ultimate guarantee of free, fair and genuine elections (and referendums) in keeping with the established electoral law. Accordingly, the design of an appropriate electoral justice system (EJS) is fundamental to democratic legitimacy and the credibility of electoral processes.

4. In democracies, electoral justice plays a decisive role in ensuring the stability of the political system and adherence to the legal framework, and thus also contributes to the consolidation of democratic governance. The role of electoral justice, although not new, has become recognized as a crucial factor in all democracies, whether emerging or established. Table 1.1 lists some relevant examples where the presence or absence of a robust EJS has been critical.

Table 1.1. Some critical rulings by electoral justice systems

Country	Year	Ruling/decision by	Outcome of ruling
United States	2000	Supreme Court	Final suspension of manual recount of votes in some districts of the state of Florida
Spain	2003	Constitutional Court	Declared certain political parties illegal due to possible ties with terrorism
Ukraine	2004	Supreme Court	Annulment of presidential election
Taiwan	2004	Supreme Court	Validated total recount of the national vote ordered by the Taipei High (appellate) Court
United Kingdom	2005	European Court of Human Rights	General prohibition preventing persons serving prison sentences from voting in parliamentary and local elections in the UK was in violation of the European Convention on Human Rights
Nicaragua	2005	Inter-American Court of Human Rights	Limitations in the electoral law whereby only those candidates nominated by political parties can participate in municipal elections held in indigenous communities is in violation of the American Convention on Human Rights
Costa Rica	2006	Supreme Elections Court	Total recount of votes for all presidential elections as mandated by law
Mexico	2006	Electoral Court of the Judicial Branch of the Federation of Mexico	Recount of votes ordered in presidential election for more than half of the polling stations for which it was requested
Turkey	2007	Constitutional Court	Annulment of the presidential election results
Colombia	2009	Council of State	Annulment of the 2006 Senate election due to irregularities in the counting of votes, and the ordering of a new count
Thailand	2007	Constitutional Court	Dissolution of Thaksin Shinawatra's party (Thai Rak Thai)

(cont.)

Country	Year	Ruling/decision by	Outcome of ruling
Germany	2008	Constitutional Court	Declared some provisions of the Federal Electoral Act establishing the effect of 'negative voting weight' in the electoral system unconstitutional, obliging the legislature to formulate a new constitutional provision by June 2011 at the latest
Moldova	2009	Constitutional Court	Recount of votes for parliamentary elections

5. Challenges may arise in any part of the electoral cycle. Challenges should be perceived not as a reflection of the weakness of a political system or a symptom of deficient or manipulated electoral procedures, but as a test of the strength, vitality and openness of the system and its procedures. While greater access to and understanding of the EJS may result in a larger number of challenges, it may also help to ensure that electoral conflict is dealt with and resolved by institutional means, thereby contributing to stability and peace and thus reducing potential conflicts of any other kind.

6. A wide array of means and mechanisms can be drawn on to prevent or resolve electoral disputes. This variety is a positive factor, as there is no single or magic formula for ensuring that the electoral process complies with the legal framework or for defending electoral rights.

7. Even though the existence of a robust electoral justice system alone does not guarantee the holding of free, fair and genuine elections, its absence may contribute to deepening or aggravating conflicts. If elections are held without an appropriate, comprehensive and consensus-based legal framework that is committed to democratic principles and values, if they are not well organized, or if there are no specific electoral justice mechanisms in place, electoral processes may aggravate existing frictions or even lead to armed or violent conflict, as occurred during the presidential election in Kenya in December 2007.

8. Electoral justice is not just about proceedings to enforce electoral rules. It is integral to the design and conduct of electoral processes, and influences the actions of all stakeholders. In addition to the influence of the law or the legal framework governing the electoral processes themselves, an electoral justice system is heavily influenced by the socio-cultural, historical and political context in which it operates. Hence diverse electoral justice practices and systems exist in different national and regional contexts around the world.

9. An electoral justice system needs to operate efficiently in a technical sense. It should also act effectively, which means independently and impartially, and should promote justice as well as transparency, accessibility, inclusiveness and equal opportunity. It should communicate that it operates well, so that all

interested persons perceive it as sound. Only in this way will it meet its aim of conferring credibility and democratic legitimacy on electoral procedures and their results.

2. The need to design an appropriate electoral justice system

10. The design of an electoral justice system is one of the most important institutional decisions any country must make when the time comes for its electoral regime to be established or reformed. The constitutional, statutory and institutional design of electoral processes in a particular country requires an integrated and all-encompassing approach that incorporates the EJS as one of its key components.

Figure 1.1. Important factors for an electoral justice system

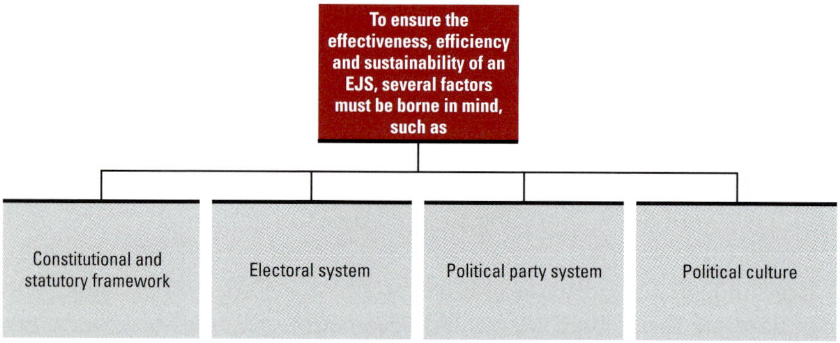

11. An electoral justice system should be reviewed periodically to ensure that it fulfils its function of guaranteeing the holding of free, fair and genuine elections in keeping with the provisions of law. At times the aspiration to obtain political power leads to the use of unlawful or unjustified means. A properly designed EJS needs to be positively geared to achieving two objectives:

- Preventing and identifying irregularities
- Providing appropriate means and mechanisms for correcting irregularities and/or punishing their perpetrators.

12. Both newly established electoral legal frameworks and reformed versions of some existing frameworks are currently paying increased attention to electoral justice, focusing, for example, on the procedures applicable to certain parts of the electoral process, such as the nomination of candidates, the conduct of campaigns or how the results are certified. There is growing awareness of the need to establish comprehensive and integrated legal and institutional

frameworks, and the EJS is often the key element of the electoral reform agenda. The lack of credibility of some electoral processes may lead electors to question the need to participate in elections or to reject their results. Effective and timely electoral justice becomes the key element in addressing this lack of credibility.

13. An emerging democracy either designs or inherits an electoral justice system. A country's legal and political tradition, along with the inheritances of colonialism or, on occasion, the influence of a neighbouring country may be decisive; so may the specific claims of society and short-term agreements among different dominant political forces. A political crisis in an established democracy stemming from a large-scale electoral conflict may provide an incentive to modify the EJS. In addition, those who promote democratic political reform may try to put changing the EJS on the political agenda in order to confer greater democratic legitimacy, more effectively protect electoral rights, or ensure free, fair and genuine elections.

14. The decisions made in relation to the design of an electoral justice system may have unintended consequences. They may prove not to be beneficial in the long term and may even on occasion have disastrous effects for the prospects for democracy. For example, in a country in which the judiciary lacks independence and prestige, if an EJS is modified in such a way as to transfer the final decision on challenges to an election result to a court which is part of the judiciary, the result could be worse than the previous system.

15. This Handbook recognizes that the design of an EJS, in terms of a supposed 'best system', is not something for which a group of independent technical specialists can come up with a single correct answer. It focuses on system design in a holistic manner. Since technical issues are involved, it is essential to have corresponding technical assistance, although it is rarely appropriate to export templates or models to different historical and political contexts. A comparative approach to the study of EJSs shows that there is no perfect system. But it also makes it possible to assess the strengths and weaknesses of different systems, identify trends, offer additional elements of analysis and identify successful experiences or practices.

3. The objectives of *Electoral Justice: The International IDEA Handbook*

16. In analysing existing electoral justice systems and their implications, and showing how they have worked in the diverse democracies around the world, this Handbook has two general objectives:

a. to expand knowledge and enlighten political debate on the concept, design and workings of EJSs and mechanisms; and

b. to offer tools to the framers of constitutions, political and judicial institutions, and electoral and procedural laws to help them make informed decisions when designing new EJSs or reforming existing ones.

17. The specific objectives of this Handbook are thus:

- to increase knowledge and encourage learning about EJSs, including conflict prevention mechanisms and procedures for resolving conflicts when they arise;
- to identify the various contemporary models of EJSs and how they are structured and perform in the light of the various institutional guarantees and international principles that uphold the obligations that govern them;
- to provide frames of reference and guidelines for those who seek to design, establish, reform or strengthen an EJS; and
- to provide tools that will help to ensure that all electoral actions, procedures and decisions are in line with the law and with democratic principles and values, safeguarding electoral rights.

18. The Handbook addresses the likely concerns of those who intend to design or redesign an electoral justice system, such as those who are drafting constitutional and statutory texts, political negotiators, electoral advisors and officials. To this end, it analyses some of the most complex issues, taking into account the key points of the relevant professional and academic literature. It is written to be accessible to political reformers, but is inevitably 'heavy' in its legal content because of the legal nature of many of the issues discussed.

19. The electoral justice system is an integral part of the electoral framework. To be fully effective, electoral assistance and observation thus need to consider the design, establishment and functioning of the EJS throughout the electoral cycle in framing their activities and assessments.

20. This Handbook focuses on electoral justice systems at the national level, but the alternatives examined are appropriate for any community that wishes to resolve the possible conflicts that may arise in relation to electoral processes, both of representative democracy and of direct democracy through a referendum or recall vote. The Handbook will also be useful for those who design institutions for local or supranational electoral processes; for internal political party elections, traditional and communal systems; and for trade unions, associations of professionals, or organized civil society groups. As many electoral justice systems are unique, the means for preventing conflict and alternative dispute resolution mechanisms will naturally be context specific and will require more analysis of the local conditions.

21. Chapter 2 addresses the notion of electoral justice and other related concepts, such as electoral rights and their defence, and the challenges that can arise in the different stages of the electoral cycle, as well as the elements that constitute EJ. Chapter 3 introduces various means for preventing conflicts, and chapter 4 studies the principal electoral dispute resolution (EDR) mechanisms. Chapter 5 puts forward a global classification of EDR systems. Chapter 6 outlines the main principles and guarantees of EDR systems and chapter 7 examines their basic characteristics. Finally, chapter 8 gives an overview of alternative methods of resolving electoral disputes.

Table 1.2. The contents and organization of this Handbook

	National level						
Topic	Electoral justice; electoral rights; kinds of challenges; elements of electoral justice	Means for preventing conflicts	Principal EDR mechanisms	Global classification of EDR systems	Main principles and guarantees of an EDR system	Basic characteristics of EDR systems	Alternative dispute resolution mechanisms
Resolution			Formal resolution processes	Resolution of electoral challenges			Informal resolution processes
Measure		Preventive measures	Corrective and punitive measures			Corrective measures	Voluntary measures
Chapter	**Chapter 2**	**Chapter 3**	**Chapter 4**	**Chapter 5**	**Chapter 6**	**Chapter 7**	**Chapter 8**

CHAPTER 2

CHAPTER 2

Electoral justice and other related concepts

1. The notion of electoral justice

22. The expression 'electoral justice' has various meanings. In a broad sense, and for the purposes of this Handbook, it means ensuring that every action, procedure and decision related to the electoral process is in line with the law (the constitution, statute law, international instruments or treaties and all other provisions in force in a country), and that the enjoyment of electoral rights is protected and restored, giving people who believe their electoral rights have been violated the ability to make a complaint, get a hearing and receive an adjudication.

23. A procedural act may be performed or an electoral decision adopted in any of the three periods of the electoral cycle (pre-electoral, electoral, or post-electoral: see paragraphs 44–53 and figure 2.4), and it is up to the electoral justice system to ensure that it is in keeping with the provisions of law.

24. Electoral justice encompasses both the means for *preventing* violations of the electoral legal framework, and those mechanisms that are aimed at *resolving* electoral disputes that arise from the non-observance or breach of the provisions of the electoral law. In this regard, it includes both formal mechanisms for EDR by institutional means and informal ones, such as alternative electoral dispute resolution (AEDR) mechanisms.

25. The electoral justice system is the set of means or mechanisms available in a specific country (sometimes in a specific local community or even in a regional or international context) to ensure and verify that electoral actions, procedures and decisions comply with the legal framework, and to protect or restore the enjoyment of electoral rights. An EJS is a key instrument of the rule of law and the ultimate guarantee of compliance with the democratic principle of holding free, fair and genuine elections.

26. The essential purpose of an electoral justice system is the genuine and effective protection of the right

- to either elect or be elected as a representative to hold a public or government position – national, local, or even supranational; or
- to participate directly in a direct democracy process or procedure by means of voting in a referendum or recall vote.

27. When a given action, procedure or decision related to the electoral process is not in keeping with the provisions of the law, it is said to be an irregularity, and a conflict or dispute arises between the person or entity who committed the irregularity and the person or entity who considers himself or herself to have been harmed by a violation of their electoral rights.

28. Among the formal electoral dispute resolution mechanisms, a distinction can be made between those that are corrective in nature and those that are punitive in nature. Electoral challenges (see chapter 7) are corrective. They annul, modify or acknowledge the irregularity and, as the case may be, protect or restore the enjoyment of electoral rights. Mechanisms which are punitive punish the entity or person responsible, for example, through procedures for assigning administrative (civil) and criminal liability in electoral matters (see chapter 4, section 3). There are also AEDR mechanisms, which are characterized by their voluntary nature for the parties to a dispute and are frequently informal (see chapter 8).

Figure 2.1. The elements of electoral justice

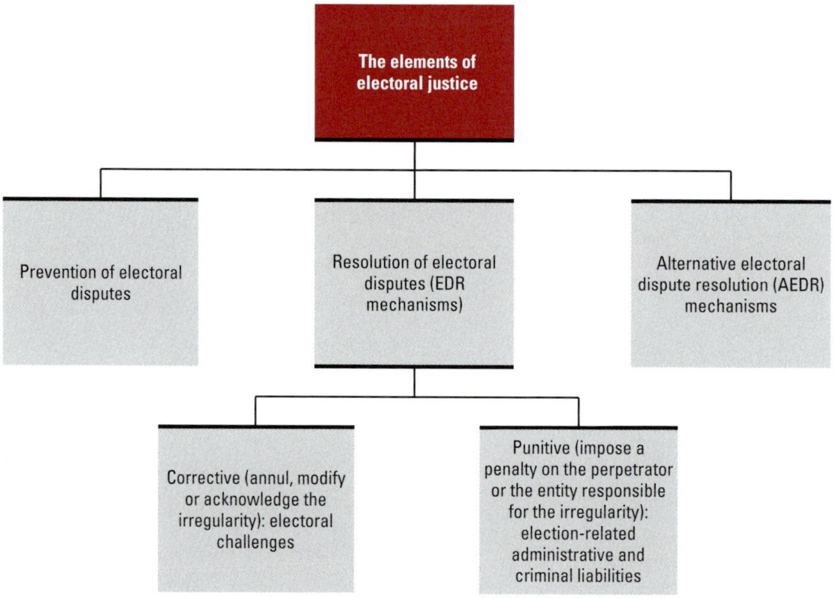

29. In this regard, when an electoral conflict or dispute arises (e.g. if it is alleged that a candidate has won an election as the result of vote-buying), the electoral justice system generally provides for EDR mechanisms by which the party affected may file:

a. an electoral challenge before a competent electoral dispute resolution body (EDRB) asking it to grant a remedy consisting of the annulment of the election or the modification of the result to find a different candidate to be the winner. This must be presented in accordance with the procedure laid down in the electoral or procedural law through a claim, complaint or petition as a trial or an appeal, the different characteristics of which are analysed in section 1 of chapter 7; and/or
b. a complaint before the competent authority, which may be an authority in charge of criminal investigation or, in some EJSs, the electoral management body (EMB).
    i. If the authority in charge of investigating the possible commission of crimes concludes that criminal offences may have been committed, it may prosecute the person liable before a judge in a criminal court, seeking the imposition of a criminal sanction of either imprisonment or a fine. It should be noted that in some EJSs, the same electoral justice body that hears the challenge that may be grounds for annulment of the election or modification of the outcome also has jurisdiction to rule on criminal liability.
    ii. In some EJSs the EMB may undertake the investigation. If, after an administrative procedure in the form of a trial or hearing, it is concluded that a political party or candidate is responsible for an administrative infraction (a violation or breach of the law which is not a crime), the EMB may then impose an administrative sanction, for example a fine, which it is then often possible to appeal against before a court. However, in certain EJSs the sanction is imposed subsequently by a civil court, an administrative court of law or even a criminal court, as is often the case in countries with a common law tradition where no distinction is made between criminal and administrative liability.

30. It is therefore important to distinguish between:

a. challenges, which offer a remedy (the means of enforcing a right or redressing a wrong) and have as their purpose to annul, modify or recognize the irregular act;
b. procedures for determining administrative or criminal liability in the electoral area, the purpose of which is to sanction the person responsible for an irregularity which constitutes a criminal offence, gives rise to criminal liability and is adjudicated by criminal courts; and
c. action to deal with administrative infractions (violations or breaches of the law that are not crimes), which give rise to an administrative

liability that may be imposed by the EMB or an administrative agency after proceedings in the form of a trial, or by a civil court or an administrative law court.

31. This Handbook discusses the means for *preventing* electoral disputes (chapter 3) and formal mechanisms for *resolving* them (chapter 4) as well as AEDR mechanisms (chapter 8). In chapters 5, 6 and 7 the Handbook emphasizes those mechanisms established in different legal systems for resolving such disputes as they arise – electoral dispute resolution systems (EDRSs) – with special reference to the means for bringing electoral challenges and the organs in charge of resolving them.

2. Upholding electoral rights

a) What are electoral rights and where are they established?

32. Electoral rights are political rights, which are in turn a category of human rights. Electoral rights are enshrined in the basic or fundamental provisions of a particular legal order (generally in the constitution and the relevant statutes of a country) and in various international human rights instruments, although on occasion they also stem from case law.

33. Among the most important international human rights instruments that provide for electoral rights are several universal and regional declarations and conventions which are binding in the countries that have ratified them (see figure 2.2).

34. Even where a particular country is not a party to these international human rights instruments, the international commitments on electoral rights that they contain, such as the commitment to holding free, fair and genuine elections by universal, free, secret and direct suffrage, have an important persuasive value. The democratic legitimacy of the government of such a country and the credibility of that country's electoral processes depend on whether it observes such commitments.

Figure 2.2. Examples of international human rights instruments that establish electoral rights

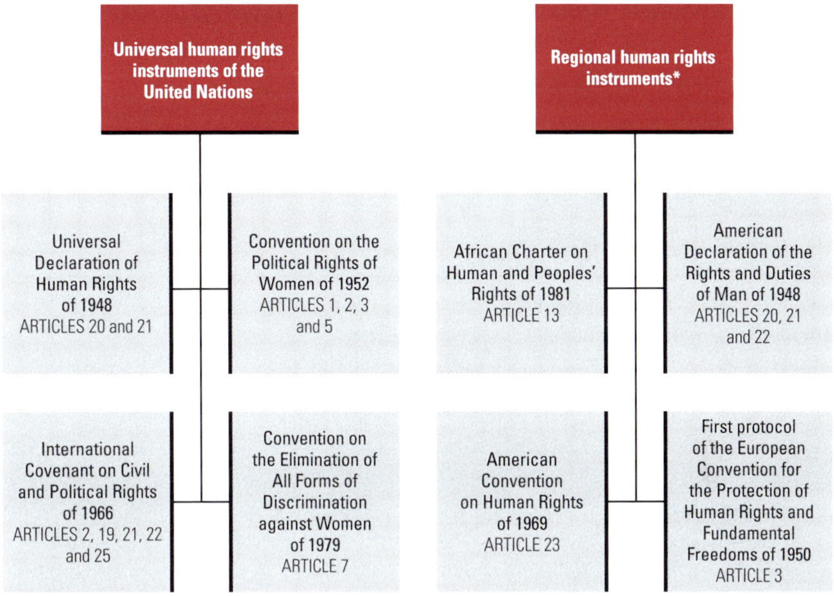

* In addition, mention should be made of other regional instruments, such as the Charter of Paris for a New Europe of 1990; articles 15 and 16 of the American Convention on Human Rights of 1969 (article 15 on the Right of Assembly and article 16 on Freedom of Association); sections 5, 6, 7 and 8 of the Document of the Copenhagen Meeting of the Conference on the Human Dimension of the Conference on Security and Co-operation in Europe of 1990 (CSCE, although it is not binding); and other instruments that have emanated from international and intergovernmental organizations, such as the Inter-Parliamentary Union's Declaration on Criteria for Free and Fair Elections of 1994, and the Harare Commonwealth Declaration of 1991.

35. Among the main electoral rights are the right to vote and to run for elective office in free, fair, genuine and periodic elections conducted by universal, free, secret and direct vote; the right to gain access, in equal conditions, to elective public office; the right to political association for electoral purposes (e.g. the right to establish or join or not join a political party or any other grouping with electoral aims); and other rights intimately related to these, such as the right to freedom of expression, freedom of assembly and petition, and access to information on political-electoral matters. In general, electoral rights realize the political right to participate in the conduct of public affairs, directly or by means of freely elected representatives (see figure 2.3).

36. Electoral rights can be distinguished from other political rights that do not refer to electoral matters. These include, for example:

- the right to participation in political affairs through a process which does not involve electoral issues (for example appointments to public positions by simple designation, without elections being required);

- the rights to freedom of expression, freedom of assembly and freedoms of association, petition and access to information in respect of political matters other than elections; and
- other political rights the exercise of which is reserved in some countries to citizens, but which do not involve making use of a ballot, such as defence of the homeland and its institutions.

In several countries, the means for the protection and defence of electoral rights are different from those for other political rights.

Figure 2.3. The principal electoral rights

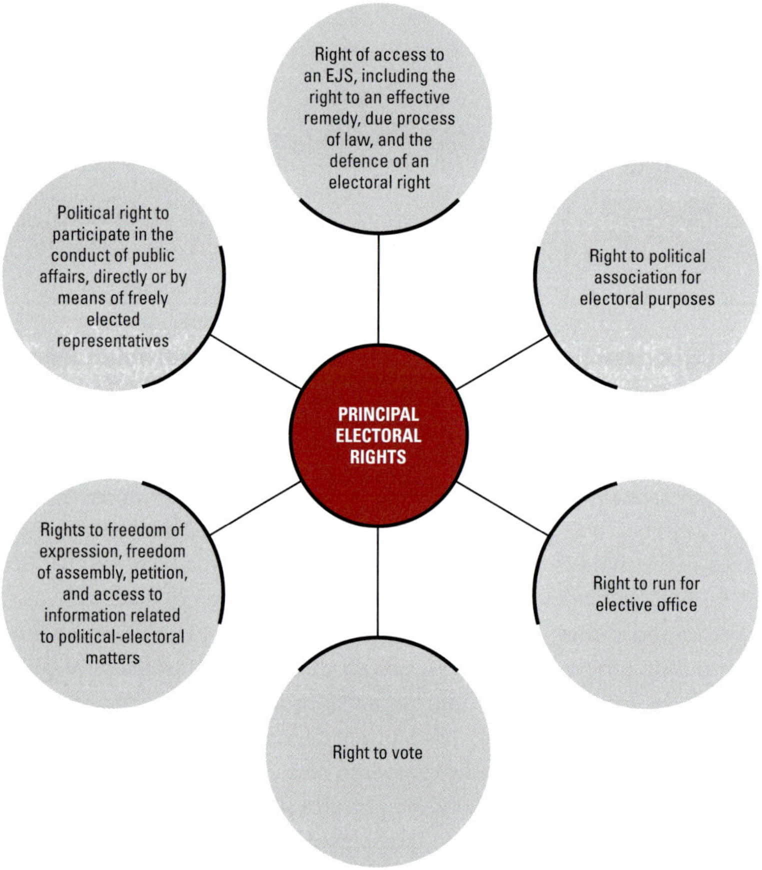

37. Several international human rights instruments have developed a series of principles related to the right of access to justice that should be observed in relation to the right of access to electoral justice and, in particular, to an EDRS that guarantees the protection and defence of electoral rights. These principles include, among others, the right to an effective remedy before an impartial,

previously established court, to the due process of law and to a public hearing in which the defence of an electoral right is guaranteed to all equally (see box 2.1).

Box 2.1. International obligations for electoral dispute resolution

Avery Davis-Roberts

The International Covenant on Civil and Political Rights as well as regional treaties such as the African Charter on Human and Peoples' Rights, the American Convention on Human Rights or the European Convention for the Protection of Human Rights and Fundamental Freedoms provide the foundation for an understanding of the principles for EDR mechanisms based on public international law. In addition, General Comments 31 and 32 of the United Nations Human Rights Committee, the Venice Commission's Code of Good Practice in Electoral Matters, and other sources can help to add detail and definition to these principles. Although they do not explicitly address issues related to EDR mechanisms, but instead focus on broader, more general rights such as the right to an effective remedy and the right to a fair and public hearing, they can inform our understanding of dispute resolution processes.

Underpinning all aspects of the electoral process must be respect for the rule of law, and the commitment of the state to take all steps necessary to ensure human rights. Of particular importance in the context of EDR are the rights to an effective remedy, to a fair and impartial hearing and to equality before the law.

Everyone is entitled to an effective remedy for acts that violate their Covenant rights, including their Article 25 rights to political participation. Once granted, a remedy must be enforced. An effective remedy need not be judicial, but if it is it must provide adequate redress for the alleged violation. States must investigate alleged violations of Covenant rights and should consider administrative mechanisms, such as national human rights institutions, that can give effect to this obligation. The state must also regulate human rights violations by third parties and non-state actors.

Similarly, everyone has the right to a fair and public hearing in the determination of his or her rights. In the determination of rights in a suit at law, everyone should be guaranteed access to a competent, impartial and independent tribunal in at least one stage of the proceedings. A tribunal must be independent of the executive and legislative branches of the government or enjoy judicial independence in deciding legal matters that are judicial in nature. Impartiality requires that decisions of tribunal judges do not harbour preconceptions about the particular case before them or act in ways that improperly promote the interests of one of the parties to the detriment of the other. Importantly, the tribunal must also appear to the reasonable observer to be impartial. A fair hearing is one that is expeditious, free from influence and open to the public. Public hearings ensure transparency and safeguard the public interest.

All are equal before the law and before courts and tribunals, and are entitled, without discrimination, to the equal protection of the law. In addition, everyone shall have equal access to the courts free from unreasonable restrictions or discrimination, and everyone is entitled to equality of means for defending their rights.

(cont.)

In addition, everyone has the right to seek and receive information, including information on procedures for filing complaints and on the essential findings, evidence presented and the legal reasoning of a tribunal, even if the hearing is not open to the public.

b) The means for defending electoral rights

38. The distinction between electoral rights and other political rights is relevant because of the different means established for protecting these rights in some legal systems. While electoral rights may be protected or restored through the electoral justice system or an electoral dispute resolution system, in some countries different legal instruments and procedures exist for the protection of other political rights. For example, in South Africa, the body of last resort for the defence of electoral rights is the Electoral Court, whereas the body with jurisdiction over all other fundamental political rights is the Supreme Court of Justice. In some other countries, the same body may cover both. In several European countries, including Germany and Spain, the lower organs for protecting rights vary, depending on whether they are electoral rights or other political rights: however, the Constitutional Court (Tribunal Constitucional) is the final arbiter in both cases.

39. The means used by different EDR systems to defend electoral rights are described in detail in chapter 7. These may be entrusted to *administrative bodies*, *judicial bodies*, *legislative bodies*, *international bodies* or, exceptionally, as a provisional or transitional arrangement, to *ad hoc bodies* in order to overcome a serious conflict situation in a country.

- Administrative bodies could generally be the EMB or EMBs in charge of organizing the election.
- Judicial bodies could be regular courts that are part of the judicial branch, or autonomous courts, such as constitutional courts or councils, administrative law courts or specialized electoral courts that are separate from any of the traditional legislative, executive or judicial powers. Even though, strictly speaking, judicial bodies are courts that are part of the judicial branch, for the purposes of this Handbook a broader view is taken which encompasses other autonomous tribunals such as those mentioned above.
- Legislative bodies could be the whole legislature or part of the legislature, for example one of its committees.
- International bodies could be those with jurisdiction in countries that have recognized an international or regional court, such as the European Court of Human Rights or the Inter-American Court of Human Rights, whose rulings are binding and must be adhered to by the competent national bodies.

Box 2.2. Types of bodies in charge of protecting electoral rights

- administrative bodies
- judicial bodies
- legislative bodies
- international bodies
- ad hoc bodies

40. Electoral rights are generally vested in the citizen. In some countries there is also a residence requirement, or people must prove that they have a tie to the political-legal community concerned as a condition for exercising electoral rights. Some countries grant electoral rights to resident foreigners. New Zealand does so for all elections. Other countries, for example, Argentina, Canada and Uruguay, do so for local elections, as do the countries of the European Union under the terms of the European Convention on the Participation of Foreigners in Public Life at Local Level of 1992.

41. Several countries have established specific provisions in their constitutions or statute law to promote the right to gender equality in the electoral realm, or even to uphold the electoral rights of women for the purpose of guaranteeing them access to elective office on an equal basis. Several international instruments also protect the electoral rights of women, such as the Convention on the Political Rights of Women of 1952 and the Convention on the Elimination of All Forms of Discrimination against Women of 1979 (see figure 2.2).

42. Generally, all stakeholders who consider that a given electoral action or decision has a detrimental impact on them (e.g. a citizen or political party considers that he, she or it has suffered prejudice) are entitled to lodge a complaint (see chapter 7). Several EDRSs give political parties a predominant role when it comes to defending electoral rights, and in some they are the only legal entities entitled to challenge certain actions or decisions (e.g. election results), in which case the candidate involved does not have the same right to challenge. In some countries candidates are accorded the status of third-party plaintiffs at best, and are therefore subject to the decisions of their political party.

43. A good practice for any EJS or EDRS is to establish the right of any natural or legal person to bring a challenge before an administrative or judicial body against any electoral act or decision that it considers prejudicial. This requires an effective remedy before a previously established impartial tribunal, which protects or restores in timely fashion the exercise or enjoyment of the electoral right violated (see for example the 1966 International Covenant on Civil and Political Rights, the 1969 American Convention on Human Rights and the 1950 European Convention on Human Rights). In any event, if an EDRS

grants both a candidate and his or her political party the right to challenge an act or decision that they consider harmful to their rights, it should also provide mechanisms for resolving the possible contradictions that could arise between the two proceedings which would take place.

3. Electoral justice systems and the electoral cycle

44. An integrated, comprehensive and effective approach to designing and implementing an electoral justice system is only possible if the three periods of the electoral cycle are taken into account: pre-electoral, electoral and post-electoral.

Figure 2.4. The electoral cycle

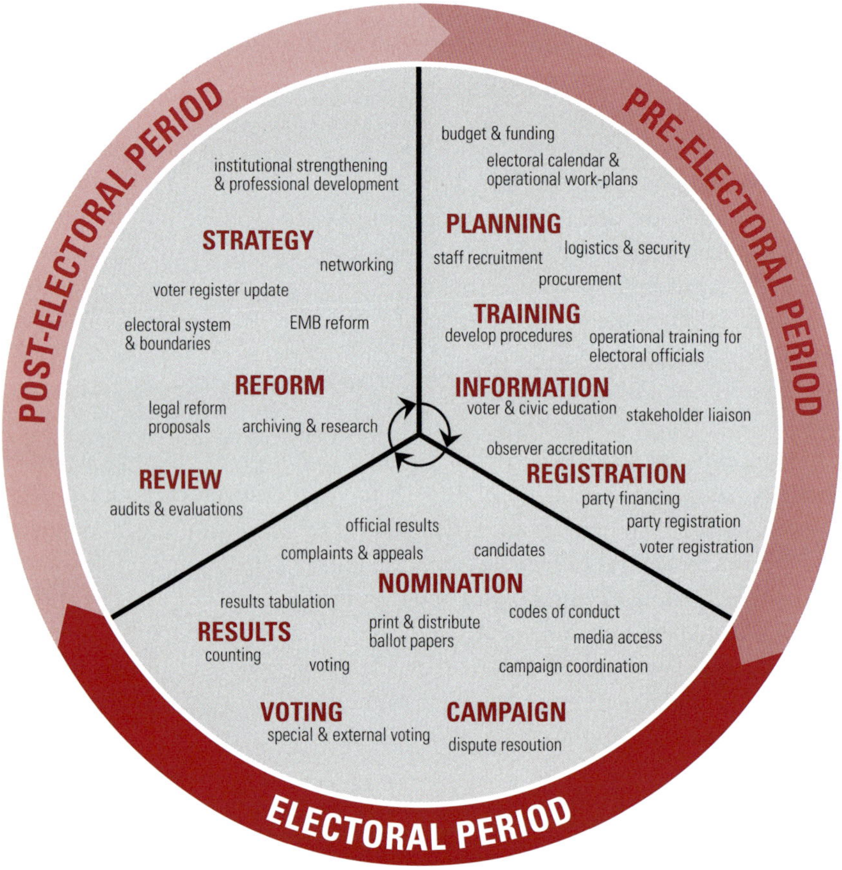

45. An EJS that is focused only on the most active part of the electoral cycle – that surrounding polling day – is not the best way to ensure that electoral processes and their outcomes comply with the legal framework.

The pre-electoral and post-electoral periods can offer better opportunities for improper efforts to place obstacles in the way of free, fair and genuine elections, or to manipulate or divert procedures for partisan interests through illegal and illegitimate practices (for example, with respect to the electoral register or political party revenues).

46. A number of activities are carried out during the pre-electoral period, such as designing and drafting election laws, employing and training electoral personnel, and planning by the authorities entrusted with organizing the electoral process and resolving electoral disputes. Some of these activities may be subject to challenge as part of the EDRS, such as decisions related to the delimitation of electoral district boundaries; determinations on whether to grant, reject or cancel the registration of political parties; the updating of voter registers; and information on the electoral process and civic education. Also, some actions of political parties related to their internal democracy – such as approval of their constitutions and internal procedures, selection of party leaders and candidates for office or the expulsion of members and other sanctions – may be subject to regulation and challenge.

47. Practically all activities during the electoral period can give rise to challenges, including the nomination or registration of lists of candidates, the conduct of the campaign, the distribution and placement of polling stations, the appointment of polling officers, the accreditation of election observers, the process of voting, the vote count, and the announcement and publication of the results.

48. During the post-electoral period certain election-related activities may also give rise to challenges that could influence the development and sustainability of the next election. Examples are the procedures for overseeing where political parties' funds come from and how they are used; reviews of the declarations of candidates' campaign expenses; and reviewing the boundaries of electoral districts. In some countries, challenges with respect to types of election other than for nationwide elective office or matters related to direct democracy events such as referendums and recall votes may also arise. Reforming the relevant legislation and procedures based on lessons learned is also an important activity that is carried out during the post-electoral period.

49. Unless there is an efficient and effective EJS with sufficient powers, resources and tools to be capable of responding adequately to these demands throughout the electoral cycle, and issuing without delay decisions that can be enforced, the electoral process may be derailed and its results may be rejected.

50. A healthy and good practice for any EDRS is to envisage the possibility of any electoral action or decision being challenged before the EMB that issued it or before any other competent body by any person who considers

himself or herself to be prejudiced by it. This is part of the fundamental human right of access to justice provided for in several international human rights instruments. The objective is to ensure that no electoral action or decision escapes review regardless of whether it occurs in the pre-electoral, electoral or post-electoral period. Chapter 7 of this Handbook examines this in more detail.

51. An EDRS needs to provide mechanisms to ensure that all electoral actions and decisions carried out in the different periods of the electoral cycle are in keeping with the law. This is especially important where the electoral laws provide the entities in charge of the EDRS with mandates that do not authorize them to continue operating beyond the electoral period. In such cases, other organs must be entrusted with resolving the possible challenges raised during the pre-electoral and post-electoral periods. It might also be considered good practice to entrust EDR to permanent and independent bodies (see chapter 6).

52. There is a strong public interest in the certainty of electoral proceedings and results. In this regard, every EDRS should adopt the principle that all acts and decisions of the electoral authority that have not been challenged in a timely fashion within a period specified in the electoral law become irrevocable. This procedural feature makes it possible to wrap up each successive stage of the election as a clear and firm basis for the next, and to decide the outcome of the election in a consolidated manner. It would make it impossible to call into question the validity of a particular electoral action or decision at a later stage. For example, in several countries it is not legally permissible for an irregularity committed during the election campaign to be raised during the stage of announcing the results as grounds for annulling the election, if it has not already been challenged by the person or party affected during the pre-election stage. It is important to note that this principle only operates when the alleged irregularity committed at an earlier stage was susceptible to challenge at that moment. If no means of challenge is provided for at the earlier stage, there would be grounds for considering it proper to challenge it later.

53. Once started, an electoral process cannot, in general, be halted, because timely renewal of the representative organs of government depends on it. As a result, another common principle of an electoral dispute resolution system is that the filing of a challenge does not suspend the validity of the action challenged. Thus, until the challenge is resolved the action or decision will continue to have effect. In addition, in order to avoid abuse it is a healthy practice to provide for short timescales for resolving any challenges that have been filed (see chapter 7).

CHAPTER 3

CHAPTER 3

Prevention of electoral disputes

1. Introduction

54. It is important that every EJS establish means or measures to prevent or avoid electoral disputes. The more respect for the rule of law becomes the norm, the fewer will be the electoral disputes that need to be resolved by the organs entrusted with the EDRS.

55. There are several means or measures by which electoral disputes can be prevented. Some of them come from sources outside the EJS, while others are generated from within it:

From external sources:

- designing and implementing an appropriate constitutional and statutory framework for democratic and representative government, human rights and electoral processes;
- participation by the main political parties and key sectors of society in designing or reforming the electoral legal framework;
- the development of political culture and civic education, including democratic principles and values and respect for the rule of law and human rights;
- the development of a pluralistic political party system and of internal democracy in political parties;
- gender and minority inclusiveness in government and the political arena;
- the establishment of equitable conditions for elections, particularly with regard to financing and media access;
- development of the role of civil society, including its ability to monitor all stages of the electoral process;

- the adoption of codes of conduct by the media, civil society, election observers and political parties;
- establishing a professional, inclusive and, preferably, permanent, independent and autonomous EMB;
- the adoption of appropriate election procedures by the EMB, which are made available to the public and consistently followed;
- and so on.

From internal sources:

- designing and implementing an appropriate constitutional and statutory framework for an accessible and effective EJS;
- appointment of members of the EMB and EDRB at the highest level by consensus among the various political forces active in society, especially those represented in the legislative body;
- an EMB and an EDRB committed to democratic principles and values, especially those of independence and impartiality;
- the ability of the EMB and the EDRB to make transparent decisions and to explain and disseminate them;
- appropriate electoral training for EMB and EDRB staff;
- the adoption of codes of conduct by the staff of the EMB and the EDRB;
- gender and minority inclusiveness in the EMB and the EDRB;
- the adoption of security measures for receiving, counting and tallying the vote;
- and so on.

56. In addition, it should be noted that a committed, sensitive and effective EMB plays an important role, on an ongoing basis, in preventing electoral disputes. Indeed, it is common in EMBs – particularly those which include representatives of political parties – for there to be extensive debate before any decisions related to an election are made, and an effort made to harmonize the conflicting interests of the political parties.

2. An appropriate legal framework

57. Electoral disputes may be prevented through the adoption of provisions and mechanisms that are in line with the democratic principles and values generally shared in a society, and that stem from that society's traditions and context.

58. If an electoral reform achieves the effective participation of the principal parties and political forces as well as key sectors of society, it is likely that fewer disputes will arise – especially if consensus-based approaches, and not just majority rule, are used in adopting the reform. This implies a commitment

on the part of the political protagonists to respect the resulting rules and to use institutional channels to resolve possible disputes in the reform process. While majority rule is the basis of the democratic principle, in the case of electoral rules in particular it is fundamental that the rights of minorities are respected, that the majority is not given undue advantage, and that conditions and assurances are put in place to enable any minority to become the majority on a future occasion.

59. For a legal framework to be appropriate, the EJS needs to be designed in simple, clear and consistent terms that make it easy to understand and ensure complete and effective access to electoral justice. It should guarantee to any person who believes her/his electoral rights have been infringed the opportunity to go before an independent and impartial EDRB which will provide an effective and timely remedy to protect or restore the enjoyment of those rights. The awareness of this possibility helps to build trust in the EDRS and helps to prevent disputes from arising.

3. Development of a political culture and civic education

60. The external element that contributes most to preventing electoral disputes is the development of political culture and civic education, with an emphasis on the importance of effective adherence to democratic principles and values. These principles include strict respect for the rule of law and human rights and the peaceful settlement of disputes using institutional channels. The values include participation, pluralism, tolerance, cooperation, stability, social peace and strengthening the public institutional framework.

61. In societies where cultural attitudes facilitate the installation or maintenance of authoritarian regimes, electoral conflicts arise more frequently. In between a democratic and an authoritarian society it is possible to identify a range of types, such as a democracy with authoritarian elements or an authoritarian regime with democratic elements. Where the law is not ordinarily observed without the need of proactive enforcement and breaches of the law are not always subject to social disapproval, it is more difficult to establish an effective and efficient EJS. In this sense, electoral justice systems that are similar in their legal framework and institutional design may function quite differently in practice given their different political cultures and historical contexts.

62. What is important to take into account is the need to promote a political culture and strict respect for the democratic rule of law and electoral human rights, as well as the different democratic values, in order to prevent electoral disputes. The development of a political culture based on democratic principles and values is the responsibility not only of political leaders but of every citizen as well. Certainly, government institutions and the mass media play a crucial role.

Box 3.1. Familiarization with electoral processes in Bhutan

Deki Pema

The parliamentary elections in Bhutan in 2008 were the first in the country's history. For this reason, just prior to the announcement of the official campaign period, a 'familiarization period' ensued during which the political parties and candidates engaged in activities similar to those of a genuine election campaign.

Even though there were only two registered political parties, this trial period was an intense part of the electoral process and it became necessary to regulate it to ensure that voters were not confused or disillusioned and that party politics were not misinterpreted or misunderstood from the outset. As the familiarization period was not technically part of the official period of the election campaign, the party Code of Conduct was not officially in effect. To address the situation, the Election Commission of Bhutan issued a public communication on 'Permissible and Non-Permissible Activities' based on the Code of Conduct. This was sent to all the administrative units in the country (i.e. the 20 districts, 15 sub-districts and 205 counties). Furthermore, the heads of the counties, the *Gup*, were required to disseminate the contents of the communiqué at public meetings held specifically for this purpose.

As polling day approached, competition intensified and a number of baseless and damaging rumours, for example, about hidden cameras in voting booths compromising the secrecy of the ballot, circulated in the small and closely knit society. In response, the Commission developed a brochure, written in simple and conversational local language, to address all such allegations and baseless rumours. The brochure also sought to reassure voters of their rights, including the right to a secret ballot, and the measures put in place to uphold these rights. The brochures were widely distributed to the *Gup* of all 205 counties, who were required to read them out at public gatherings. Even schoolchildren were encouraged to read the brochure to illiterate parents and family members.

By using a variety of techniques and including all stakeholders in the civic education process, the familiarization process not only ensured that action was taken to educate the population and put rumours to rest, but also served as an important step in the prevention of possible election-related violence or mal-practice.

4. Political consensus on the composition of the EMB and of the EDRB

63. Consensus among political parties and forces in defining the structure and composition of the EMB and the EDRB – especially when these parties and forces participate in and oversee decision making – helps to prevent electoral disputes. Such consensus contributes to the legitimacy and credibility of the electoral process, and its trustworthiness in the eyes of voters translates into greater participation.

64. Balancing or offsetting partial or conflicting interests is not the same thing as ensuring impartiality. This is the case even if there is a general consensus among the political forces that select the members of the highest-level organs of the EMB and the EDRB. It is more viable to achieve impartiality, which can only be shown by actual performance in the position, by ensuring that the person to whom decision making has been entrusted:

- is not a party activist (at least in the period immediately preceding their taking up the position);
- has a record of honesty and professionalism; and
- is committed to upholding the democratic rule of law.

Such a person is more likely to attract a significant consensus among all the political forces around his or her appointment. This bestows greater legitimacy and general trustworthiness on the electoral process. In addition, it would be advisable to provide the person chosen with guarantees, such as job security, independence, a level of remuneration that reflects the importance of the position, and immunity from criminal prosecution. Their position may be incompatible with other tasks and there may be a need for a temporary disqualification from holding certain political positions at the end of the appointment (see chapter 6).

5. The performance of the EMB and the EDRB: professionalism, functional independence and commitment to democratic principles

65. The EMB entrusted with organizing or administering the electoral processes may be independent, governmental or a mix of both. Whichever model is used, professionalism in the actions of an EMB should be understood as the appropriate performance in a timely manner of the functions of organizing the electoral process, in keeping with legal and ethical principles.

66. Professionalism as a guiding principle of the functioning of the organization and holding of electoral processes is based primarily on creating a career civil service (if possible or necessary, one that is specialized in electoral matters) and the establishment of clear rules on the relevant legal instruments for the selection or recruitment, promotion and mobility of the EMB personnel. This ensures that the security of such jobs is not at the mercy of electoral cycles or related to the renewal of government authorities or political interests.

67. In addition, professionalism should be understood as the formation of a corps of fully trained electoral officials and staff, and gradual reductions in the levels of improvisation that can lead to serious deviations from the rules. Professionalization, in addition to increasing the levels of preparation

and knowledge in the performance of electoral functions, assigns individual responsibilities and helps to make it possible to hold officials accountable.

68. The performance of the electoral function is synonymous with continuous and assiduous activity throughout the electoral cycle, rather than work undertaken in a sporadic, casual or haphazard manner. Permanent engagement contributes to specialization and specialization to professionalism. A professional approach leads to the optimal performance of the service to which someone dedicates him or herself.

69. Legality, certainty, objectivity, independence and impartiality are guiding principles in the day-to-day performance of the EMB that constitute a reliable and credible electoral authority and contribute to the prevention of electoral disputes. The independence or autonomy of the function of organizing and administering electoral processes means that the actions of the members of the EMB will be exclusively within the mandate of the law, and without any interference from the organs of the government or the political parties.

70. The members of the EMB and the EDRB should carry out their work with functional independence and in a manner that is strictly impartial and politically neutral. To this end, they should implement a set of 'good practices' to help generate trust in their actions and increase their credibility. For an electoral process to be successful, participants need to be able to trust that those in charge of managing and judging it will carry out their functions in a manner that is independent of the government and political parties, and in a politically neutral and strictly impartial way. If it is thought that the people who administer electoral processes and resolve disputes show allegiance to one or other electoral force, the credibility of the electoral process in the eyes of the public will be seriously damaged, to a point where it will be difficult to restore confidence in the process.

71. At times a country may opt to appoint as members of the EMB and/or EDRB persons who represent political parties or tendencies. In such a case, even though the members are chosen for their political affiliation, they must perform their electoral management tasks with functional independence and in a manner that is strictly impartial and politically neutral.

Box 3.2. Burkina Faso: party control over the electoral process and its supervision

Augustin Loada

The EMB in Burkina Faso, the National Independent Electoral Commission (Commission Electorale Nationale Indépendante, CENI), has 15 members, made up of representatives of the majority party, opposition parties and civil society. It is in charge of monitoring and supervising the electoral process.

(cont.)

The constitution provides for free, fair and secret universal suffrage but leaves all other necessary details for the conduct of elections to be regulated through the electoral law, which is highly unstable. Electoral laws often change depending on the political situation, and are passed or modified unilaterally by the ruling party.

Two different institutions are responsible for the settlement of electoral disputes: the Constitutional Council (Conseil Constitutionnel) and the administrative tribunals that deal with internal disputes in local elections. The Constitutional Council is composed of a presiding judge whose term of office is unlimited, three judges appointed by the President of Burkina Faso on the recommendation of the Minister of Justice, three people appointed by the President of Burkina Faso and three other members appointed by the Speaker of the Parliament. The members serve for a single term of nine years.

The independence of the Constitutional Council has been questioned since nine of its members are appointed by either the President (six members) or the Speaker (three members), who both belong to the ruling party. However, the members of the Constitutional Council can only be dismissed in exceptional circumstances. Moreover, the presiding member can be dismissed at any time by the President of the Republic – and cannot hold other positions simultaneously.

The administrative tribunals are responsible for the settlement of local election disputes. As magistrates, the judges of the tribunals enjoy a high level of guarantees, including the principles of irrevocability and independence enshrined in the legal instruments. In reality, interference by the political powers, corruption, bribery and difficulties related to funding, professionalism and transparency are all obstacles to the independence of these tribunals, just as is the case with other types of jurisdiction in Burkina Faso.

It should be noted that there are usually very few electoral disputes. This is due to the politicians' poor mastery of the available mechanisms and the prevailing lack of trust in the institutions responsible for settling electoral disputes. Many parties or candidates prefer to expose cases of fraud, irregularities or corruption they claim to know about in the media instead of referring them to the competent institution responsible for settling electoral disputes.

Moreover, there is a problem of access to the courts, which are both geographically and socio-culturally far from the people. Such distance can prevent a citizen from appealing against a decision made by an electoral authority, even though the procedure is theoretically free of charge.

72. Similarly, it is a positive factor if EMB and EDRB members can demonstrate a permanent commitment to absolute respect for democratic principles and values and the postulates of the international human rights instruments, without favouring political parties, candidates, voters or representatives of the press and other media outlets.

73. It is important that the EMB or EDRB reach their decisions transparently, and undertake to explain them to both the parties involved and society at large. This prevents information being manipulated by those who are negatively affected and may seek to delegitimize the electoral process or weaken the electoral authority.

6. Electoral codes of conduct

74. Codes of ethics or codes of conduct that supplement a country's legal framework have emerged for both EMBs and EDRBs. Similar codes exist for political parties and, sometimes, the media in relation to election campaigns, and for election observers, in order to ensure that they adopt ethical and professional criteria.

75. Internationally, several efforts have been made by international organizations and professional associations with global aspirations to implement professional ethical codes of conduct, such as those aimed at avoiding the perversion of the legal profession and promoting the full and faithful performance of both the judicial function and the electoral function. In addition, there are other efforts aimed at political parties during electoral campaigns, and at the national and international observation of elections. In this respect, special mention should be made of the *Code of Conduct for the Ethical and Professional Administration of Elections* and the *Code of Conduct for Political Parties Campaigning in Democratic Elections*, both of which are published by the International Institute for Democracy and Electoral Assistance (International IDEA).

76. The fact that an EMB or an EDRB does not have an applicable written code of ethics or similar document does not mean that its members and staff have no body of professional ethics. Often, several such principles and values are enshrined and protected in various provisions of the constitutional and statutory framework. Nonetheless, the direct recognition of such provisions by the body responsible for the electoral process helps to underscore its commitment to their proper observance.

77. Principles and values in the context of electoral processes are often established in the codes of ethics and codes of conduct of certain professions or of certain public servants, including judges and electoral officials (see, e.g., box 3.3), as well as political parties, media organizations and journalists. Among those applied to the legal profession and public servants are:

- a commitment to human rights and the dignity of the person;
- diligence and professionalism;
- honesty;
- honour;
- impartiality;

- independence;
- institutional loyalty;
- respect; and
- responsibility.

78. In judicial codes of ethics the principles and values that stand out are:

- commitment to justice;
- excellence (including training);
- efficiency;
- integrity;
- independence;
- probity;
- restraint;
- confidentiality;
- diligence;
- respect for the human being, especially one's colleagues;
- not intervening improperly in matters that are before a lower court; and
- equal treatment by the media.

Box 3.3. The Code of Ethics of the Judicial Branch of the Federation of Mexico

Among the codes of ethics that are expressly directed at judges and the members of an EDRB, it is worth mentioning the Code of Ethics of the Judicial Branch of the Federation of Mexico (Poder Judicial de la Federación). It contains the principles, rules and judicial virtues considered suitable as a professional-ethical standard to guide the conduct of federal judges and their auxiliaries, while also facilitating the ethical function of the various aspects of the role they play. The five guiding principles of the code, which by constitutional mandate derive from the judicial career service, are:

a. independence, in terms of the prohibition on influences from outside the law that come from the social system;
b. impartiality, rejecting any influence from outside the law or which stems from the parties to the proceedings before the courts;
c. objectivity, in terms of the need to distance oneself from the influences from outside the law that may come from the judge himself or herself;
d. professionalism, understood as the responsible and serious exercise of the judicial function; and
e. excellence, as an archetype to which judges should aspire by cultivating the judicial virtues set out in the code of ethics.

Box 3.4. The Code of Conduct for commissioners and staff of the Islamic Republic of Afghanistan Electoral Complaints Commission (ECC)

This Code of Conduct is developed and adopted pursuant to Article 2 of the ECC Rules of Procedure. The legal and ethical standards described within are intended to guide the activities of ECC members and the ECC Secretariat during the electoral process. This Code of Conduct must be implemented with common sense, sound judgement, and good faith. Breaches of the present Code shall constitute an electoral offence and will be addressed pursuant to the Electoral Law. ECC Commissioners and staff members shall:

- Comply with the Constitution, the Electoral Law, and applicable Decrees, Regulations and Procedures, and implement them in an impartial, non-partisan and politically neutral manner;
- Uphold the highest standards of efficiency, competence and integrity;
- To the best of their ability, ensure everyone's fundamental rights of freedom of opinion and expression, association, assembly, and movement are protected at all stages of the electoral process;
- Treat voters, candidates, agents, members of the press or media, and all other entities or individuals participating in the electoral process in a respectful, impartial, and politically neutral manner;
- Not communicate to any person or other source any information or documents known to them by reason of their functions that they know or ought to have known has not been made public, except as appropriate in the normal course of their duties or by authorization of the Commission.
- They shall not keep such documents in their possession any longer than required to fulfill their duties in their possession these obligations do not cease upon completion of their service with the ECC.
- Not indicate on clothing, possessions, or by action, attitude, or speech, support for any political party or candidate;
- Behave honestly and transparently with regard to their duties and decisions by cooperating to the extent allowed by law with Observers, Agents, Voters, Candidates, and members of the press or media;
- Not use or attempt to use their position for personal gain, and shall not seek or receive instructions from any government or non-government official or authority, except as permitted by law;
- Declare any private interests relating to and conflicting with their duties to the ECC and take all actions necessary to resolve those conflicts in a way compatible with their duties;
- Respect the secrecy of the ballot;
- Protect the privacy of any personal or otherwise confidential information;

(cont.)

- Familiarize themselves with all relevant electoral laws, regulations, rules, and ECC procedures; and Commissioners shall, whenever possible, attend all ECC sessions.

I have read, understand, and will abide by the above Code of Conduct:

Signed in ______________________ on ______________________ 2009 by

Name of ECC Commissioner/Staff Member   Signature of ECC Commissioner/Staff Member

Source: <http://www.ecc.org.af/en/images/stories/pdf/ECC2009CodeOfConduct20090506English.pdf>

79. The *Code of Conduct for the Ethical and Professional Administration of Elections* prepared by International IDEA merits special mention. It represents a set of universal minimum rules for the ethical and professional administration of elections. It is an effort to systematize the principles that should guide the action of election officials. This Code of Conduct is available at <http://www.idea.int/publications/conduct_admin/index.cfm>. The main body of the code sets out the ethical principles that form the basis for electoral management, as well as detailed explanations and guidelines for applying these principles. It argues that in order to ensure both the integrity of the electoral process and the appearance of integrity, electoral administration should be based on fundamental ethical principles: (a) respect for the law; (b) independence and neutrality; (c) transparency; (d) meticulousness; and (e) service-orientation.

80. The *Code of Conduct for Political Parties Campaigning in Democratic Elections*, which was also prepared by International IDEA, pulls together a set of minimum rules for political parties and their supporters for participating in an election campaign. Ideally, these rules should be agreed or voluntarily accepted by the parties themselves and in due course could become law. There may therefore be codes of conduct which have been agreed directly by the political parties as a result of negotiations among themselves, often with the moderation of a third party (e.g. the agreement reached in September 1989 leading up to the elections after Namibia gained independence); they may form part of an agreement among parties that is intended to become law (as occurred with the code of conduct agreed by the parties prior to the 1996 elections in Sierra Leone, even though it did not become law); or on occasion the conduct of the political parties during campaigns may be regulated by an electoral law, approved by the sovereign authority, even though it may not be called a code of conduct (as is the case with the annex to the 1992 United Nations Election Law for Cambodia).

81. Mention should also be made of the *Code of Conduct for International Election Observers*, which is attached to the *Declaration of Principles for International Election Observation* and was endorsed on 27 October 2005 by the United Nations, through the support of many regional and international organizations including International IDEA.

82. Other means and measures to prevent electoral disputes include the development of pluralistic political party systems as well as internal democracy in political parties; more inclusive electoral regimes in relation to gender and ethnicity in order to reduce discrimination; the establishment of fair and equitable conditions for the electoral contest, particularly in respect of financing and access to the media; appropriate electoral training for EMB and EDRB staff; and the adoption of security measures for receiving, counting and tallying the vote.

CHAPTER 4

CHAPTER 4

EDR mechanisms

1. Introduction

83. The term 'electoral dispute resolution system' (EDRS) refers to the whole set of institutional and technical-legal means or mechanisms for making a challenge or exercising oversight (through court proceedings, tribunals, claims or other remedies) of electoral actions, procedures and decisions by an administrative, judicial or legislative body or even an international body.

84. EDRSs aim to ensure the integrity of the electoral process. Through their operation, irregular electoral actions or decisions may be annulled or amended through challenges, or a sanction may be imposed on the perpetrator or person responsible for the irregularity or wrongful action. Depending on the applicable law, the same irregularity may trigger both types of oversight mechanism.

85. It is important to distinguish between the means for bringing an electoral *challenge* and the procedures for determining administrative or criminal *liability in electoral matters*. The processing and resolution of electoral challenges through institutional or formal means should in turn be distinguished from the informal means provided for in some countries, which are known as alternative EDR (AEDR) mechanisms. These are analysed in chapter 8 of this Handbook.

86. The purpose of providing for electoral challenges, which are corrective in nature, is to ensure that elections (and referendums) are held in compliance with the law (in keeping with constitutional and/or statutory principles), that possible errors or irregularities are acknowledged, modified, revoked or corrected, and that the enjoyment of an electoral right that has been violated is protected or restored. In this respect an EDRS is a means of direct oversight

of the electoral process, ensuring that elections are held in keeping with the principles of the constitution and/or statute law.

87. In addition, EDRSs ensure that the electoral process complies with the legal framework through a structure of electoral *responsibilities* or *liability*. The procedures for determining liability seek to impose a sanction, either criminal or administrative, on the perpetrator or person responsible for the criminal act or the infraction (that is, a violation or breach of the law which is not a crime) of the electoral provisions. This regime is therefore predominantly punitive. It does not correct or annul the effect of an electoral irregularity. It punishes either the person who committed the violation or the person responsible for ensuring that the violation does not happen, through either the electoral administrative law, which imposes the sanctions, or the electoral criminal law. It therefore involves the indirect oversight of elections (see table 4.1).

Table 4.1. The EDR system

EDRS distinctions	Type of function	Action	Result	Kind of oversight
Electoral challenges	Corrective	Annul, amend or acknowledge the irregularity	Protecting or restoring the enjoyment of the electoral right	Direct
Procedures for determining electoral liability or responsibility	Punitive	Punish the perpetrator or person responsible for the electoral crime or infraction		Indirect

88. In some cases, the same law establishes the definitions and procedures both for electoral challenges and for processes to establish criminal or administrative liability. Equally, the same EDRB also adjudicates on both simultaneously. If, for example, electoral officials were shown to have modified the results of the count, it could be possible both for the result of the election to be annulled (following a challenge by which it is shown that the wrongful conduct is so extensive that it may reasonably be supposed to have affected the result, but it is not possible to identify the correct result) and for a criminal penalty to be imposed on the election officials responsible. The possibility could also exist of an administrative penalty, financial in nature, being imposed on a political party by an EMB or an administrative law court if there was evidence that the political party was involved in influencing the officials.

89. In the United Kingdom (UK), two High Court judges sit without a jury to try, without recourse to appeal, the electoral petitions through which the result of a parliamentary election is challenged. The judges must determine:

a. whether there is reason to believe that extensive corruption or illegal practices have taken place; and
b. whether any corrupt or illegal practice has been proved to have been committed by or with the knowledge and consent of any candidate.

The judges then submit a certified report to the Speaker of the House of Commons, the lower chamber of Parliament, as to whether the election result should stand or whether the election is void. If the judges differ, they must certify their differences but the candidate is deemed to be duly elected. If a successful candidate is found personally guilty of a corrupt or illegal electoral practice, his or her election is declared void and he or she is subject to sanctions which include for example a ban on standing for election again.

2. The regime for bringing electoral challenges: annulling, modifying or acknowledging the irregularity

90. A direct mechanism to verify compliance with the election framework is one that offers a remedy, making it possible to reverse the effects of the unlawful or wrongful conduct, and also correcting or repairing the damage or harm caused by such conduct. As a general rule, this is achieved when the EDRB declares that the electoral action or decision subject to an electoral challenge should be invalidated, annulled, revoked or modified. Additionally, in some circumstances the mere formal recognition that an irregularity was committed implies a form of *redress*. For example, a citizen who has been wrongly denied the right to cast his or her vote could be entitled to a declaration that the electoral authorities had acted wrongly. However, unless the result of the election had been decided by a single vote, it would not be overturned.

91. Electoral challenges provide direct oversight to ensure that elections comply with the legal framework and they have the effect of preserving or restoring the correct electoral legal order. As such, they are the principal and most effective safeguard of an EJS, although this does not imply that it is not advisable to promote the other mechanisms for resolving electoral disputes as well. This Handbook thus places special emphasis on analysing the different systems for bringing electoral challenges in different countries around the world, their guiding principles, guarantees and basic elements.

92. Electoral challenges are not only for verifying that specific electoral actions and decisions comply with the legal framework. They may also allow judicial review of the constitutionality of election laws and statutes. Such challenges generally come under the jurisdiction of the organs in charge of constitutional justice. These may be constitutional courts or councils, or the highest court of justice in a country's judiciary, which usually have the jurisdiction to review statutes and general provisions in respect of all areas of the law, not only electoral matters. Their effect in some systems may be

to invalidate or revoke a statute or general provision that is found to be unconstitutional. However, reference is only made in this Handbook to those specifically electoral challenges that come under the jurisdiction of the organs entrusted with a country's EDRS.

93. However, some EDRSs provide that the court with jurisdiction to resolve challenges, and in specific instances to ensure that a particular electoral action or decision is compliant with the legal framework, is authorized to exercise oversight over not only its legality but also its constitutionality – or at least is authorized to put the question of unconstitutionality before the organ with jurisdiction over constitutional justice. In Spain, for example, the Administrative Court (Tribunal Contencioso Administrativo) can refer a matter to the Constitutional Court (Tribunal Constitucional), which hands down the ruling. This means that if the action or decision concerned is based on an unconstitutional law or general provision, it is overturned as a result. This happens in EDRSs which confer jurisdiction on the constitutional court or council, on a supreme court which is part of the judiciary, or on some of the specialized electoral courts – as in Ecuador and Mexico. In this way, the EJS provides a comprehensive defence of electoral constitutionality and legality.

94. Regardless of their effects, electoral challenges that can be brought against actions, procedures or decisions related to electoral processes can be classified as administrative, judicial (being a court which is either part of the judiciary or autonomous), legislative or international, depending on the legal nature of the organ in charge of resolving the matter. This is analysed in greater depth in chapter 7 of this Handbook.

Box 4.1. Types of electoral challenges

- Administrative
- Judicial (being a court which is either part of the judiciary or autonomous)
- Legislative
- International

3. The regime of electoral liabilities: imposing sanctions

95. The law governing electoral processes also encourages compliance with its provisions through a regime of criminal or administrative *liability* for election-related matters, constituted by the full set of sanctions applicable to those responsible for crimes or administrative infractions related to electoral processes. This regime is predominantly punitive, as it does not correct or annul the effects of an electoral irregularity or wrongful conduct but merely punishes the person responsible for the criminal offence or administrative infraction. It therefore constitutes an indirect mechanism for ensuring that

elections comply with the legal framework. In some EDRSs, cases involving an alleged punishable criminal offence or administrative liability are heard and adjudicated together with electoral challenges, with potential corrective effects or remedies.

96. A penalty in the case of electoral offences is always imposed by a court, generally a criminal court but in some countries – as in Panama – the specialized electoral court itself. In some electoral justice systems, however, an administrative sanction may be imposed by the EMB after a proceeding in the form of a hearing or trial, the result of which can be challenged before an EDRB. In other EJSs, only a court may impose an administrative sanction – a criminal court, as generally occurs in those common law countries which make no distinction between administrative and criminal liability; a civil or administrative court; or even on occasion the EDRB itself.

97. In some EDRSs, for example that of the UK, if the winning candidate is found guilty of corruption or illegal practices, regardless of whether he or she has been convicted and punished for the offence, the election is annulled as a consequence. In others (e.g. Kyrgyzstan's) it is up to the EMB or EDRB to decide whether the offences determined by the criminal court affected the outcome of the election and to declare an annulment as appropriate.

98. Electoral criminal offences and electoral administrative infractions are both examples of 'unlawful or wrongful conduct'. In other words, they are conduct that entails engaging in prohibited acts, such as vote-buying or having campaign expenditure in excess of the ceiling allowed by electoral statute, or the omission of actions ordered by the legal framework, such as failing to file a report on campaign revenue and expenditure. The perpetrator or person responsible is subject to a criminal and/or administrative sanction.

99. Electoral crimes or offences and electoral administrative breaches or infractions are usually classified on the basis of:

- *The values or legal interests protected*: (e.g. freedom of the ballot or fair conditions in the electoral contest). It is often the more fundamental values that are protected by criminal statutes.
- *The types of sanction that can be imposed*: imprisonment is commonly used for a criminal offence as a way of punishing a person convicted of a serious criminal offence. The penalty for administrative electoral infractions does not entail any loss of liberty, but may for example take the form of a financial sanction, the suspension or loss of a political party's registration or the cancellation of a candidacy.
- *The nature of the active subjects or persons responsible:* legal entities, such as political parties, are not usually subject to criminal liability, although this is no impediment to the imposition of an administrative sanction.

- *The procedures used to inquire into whether certain conduct constitutes an administrative infraction or a crime:* the procedures on administrative infractions are generally the responsibility of EMBs, while criminal offences are prosecuted by the public prosecutor or an equivalent authority.
- *The organs with the authority to adjudicate on whether an electoral crime or infraction has been committed and to impose the appropriate sanction*: in non-common law countries, administrative sanctions are generally imposed by the EMB or a civil or administrative law court; criminal penalties are however imposed by the criminal courts.

100. Despite these basic differences, regimes for administrative liability and criminal liability have some common characteristics. According to the principle of legality implicit in all punitive or sanction-imposing powers of the state (*ius puniendi*), there can be no crime or infraction without a punishment or sanction having been provided for in the applicable written law. In this respect, the following principles or guarantees should be applied in every case of criminal or administrative responsibility:

- The definition of a criminal offence or administrative infraction and the sanction or penalty to be applied for committing it must be determined by law before the crime or infraction is committed. Retrospective legislation should not be permitted. The EMBs and judicial bodies (criminal courts, civil or administrative law courts or EDRBs) entrusted with the proceedings or trials to determine the facts and rule on them do not have the power to create new classes of administrative infraction or crime, since this falls within the exclusive power of the legislative body.
- The legal provision that establishes an administrative infraction or criminal offence and the corresponding sanction or penalty should embody the principles of certainty and objectivity. This means it should be stated in writing in an abstract, general and impersonal manner, so that it is clear what conduct is regulated or prohibited and what the legal consequences of a breach are.
- The provisions setting out the sanction or punishment need to be interpreted and applied strictly. The principle of legality requires that no argument by analogy should be applied, nor should the argument of 'common sense' be applicable. The use of such arguments would lead to uncertainty as to what conduct or omission is punishable and what is not.

101. The 'argument of a stronger case' would provide for example that if a 14-year-old child cannot sign a binding contract, then a 13-year-old cannot do so either. However, this kind of reasoning should be avoided in criminal and administrative law.

102. Some differences persist between the electoral process-related criminal framework and the framework for electoral administrative sanctions, as is shown below.

a) Electoral criminal law

103. Criminal conduct may be positive or negative: actions or omissions may both be condemned by society. A crime is an action that the law has made punishable. Criminal conduct is any act or omission defined as unlawful and any culpable conduct to which one or several criminal sanctions have been attached. The state defines these in legal provisions prohibiting such conduct and establishes a sanction in cases where such conduct takes place, often a penalty that entails deprivation of liberty. The essential purpose of defining and imposing sanctions for electoral crimes or offences is to protect the values and legal interests that are intended to be attained or realized through the exercise of electoral rights, that is, the individual's right to participate in the conduct of public affairs through elections.

104. Electoral crime is not a new problem. In ancient times it was necessary to punish conduct that represented an attack on public functions or on the free expression of the vote. For example, the ancient Greeks applied the death penalty to a citizen who voted twice or who bought or sold a vote; the Romans issued the Lex Julia de Ambitu, which punished the use of unlawful means for obtaining access to public office. Later *broglio* appeared in Rome, which nowadays could be translated as electoral fraud or vote-buying.

b) Criteria for codifying electoral crimes or offences

105. There are two schools of thought on the law governing electoral crimes or offences with regard to where such provisions should be situated in the national legal system. The first favours such offences being included in the penal or criminal code, whereas the second argues that they should be included in the electoral law. Those who defend the first position argue that it is best for electoral crimes or offences to be regulated in criminal codes in order to protect them from constant changes in electoral law. Others argue that electoral crimes or offences are not and should not be outside the evolving dynamics of elections, and that the definition of such crimes should be revisited whenever the general legal framework governing elections is subject to change in order to maintain consistency between the substantive electoral law and the punitive electoral law.

106. Such a review may be particularly desirable where participants in electoral processes actively seek ways in which to subvert the intent of the law while keeping within its letter. In some cases, this could demonstrate a general wish to undermine good law, and such conduct should be kept

under continuing review. In others, it could be evidence that aspects of the law are outdated and may need reconsideration. The expenditure limits for a campaign provided by UK electoral law have been considered too low by major political parties, especially in elections to fill single casual vacancies in the Parliament. Political parties have therefore become adept in finding ways to spend more on campaigns while technically keeping within the law – for example, instead of the candidate's campaign buying equipment and declaring the full cost in the return of expenditure required by law, the party buys equipment and rents it to the campaign, and the campaign declares only the much lower cost of the rental.

Box 4.2. The regulation of electoral offences

- Include them in the penal or criminal code
- Include them in the electoral law

107. The bases for codifying electoral offences also vary from country to country. Several focus on the perpetrator of the criminal conduct, such as citizens, election officers, party leaders, and so on. Others focus on the legal interest they are protecting, such as the freedom of the vote or equal conditions for all candidates. The body of law in which an offence is included or the criterion used to regulate it are less important than the existence of a proper legal framework on electoral crimes or offences that helps to ensure that elections are free, fair and genuine.

108. The historical and socio-political context of each country will be influential when defining electoral crimes and offences. A country's political culture and electoral practices may influence whether conduct is deemed unacceptable because it is at odds with principles such as liberty or equality, and thus should be prohibited, or whether it is considered to be in accordance with such principles and therefore permitted. Such notions may also vary in the same country over time.

109. Thus, for example, in some countries criminal sanctions apply to the conveyance of electors to or from the polling station by candidates or political parties. Such sanctions are found for example in countries that are emerging from a time when there were no truly competitive elections. Under a system where the previous established governing party was well resourced, freedom to transport voters to the polls could be judged to have a detrimental impact on the freedom with which votes are cast, and thus likely to be associated with vote-buying and coercion to affect results. In the United Kingdom, however, the history of transporting voters to the polling stations is different: it was the response of the party whose strength lay more with relatively poorer people to the ability of their richer opponents – at the time the owners of most transport –

to take their supporters to vote. It could thus be regarded as a provision to promote a level electoral playing field. Further, in many countries where elections are more open, transporting voters is allowed because the capacity for electoral mobilization is considered a legitimate part of political competition.

c) Examples of electoral crimes and offences

110. Possible perpetrators of electoral offences include electoral officials, party officials, candidates, non-electoral public employees, and citizens. The role of religious or community leaders in seeking to influence the electoral will of their followers is also an area in which there can be considerable discussion as to what is considered acceptable and what amounts to undue pressure.

111. Table 4.2 lists some examples of the forms of conduct that different legal systems define as electoral offences.

Table 4.2. Forms of conduct that different legal systems define as electoral offences

Electoral offence	Actors					
	Electorate	Electoral official	Party official	Party leader or candidate	Public servant	Anyone
Electoral fraud	Voting without complying with legal requirements	Knowingly allowing fraudulent behaviour on the part of the electorate				Committing personation or using documents that are not an elector's own to vote
	Voting more than once in a single election					
Voter coercion		Propagating false news regarding election day or results	Propagating false news regarding election day or results		Requiring subordinates to vote in a certain way	Bribery through gifts or money to voters, or promises of such
						Placing undue pressure on citizens to vote a certain way or not vote at all
					Making provision of a public service conditional on citizens' voting in a certain way	Exercising pressure or engaging in campaigning inside the polling station
						Violating the secrecy of the vote or the right to cast a vote freely
						Disseminating results of opinion polls outside the period allowed by law

(cont.)

Electoral offence	Actors					
	Electorate	Electoral official	Party official	Party leader or candidate	Public servant	Anyone
Obstructing the electoral process		Depriving someone of right to vote	Taking possession of electoral documents or materials			Depriving someone of right to vote
		Interfering with the normal conduct of the voting; unduly collecting voters' credentials; altering electoral documents or impeding the installation of a polling station				Interfering with the normal conduct of the voting; unduly collecting voters' credentials; altering electoral documents or impeding the installation of a polling station
		Impeding the lawful exercise of rights by political party representatives at the polling station	Obstructing the normal course of the voting			Impeding the lawful exercise of rights by political party representatives at the polling station
		Unlawfully taking ballot papers from the ballot boxes				Unlawfully taking ballot papers from the ballot boxes
		Altering election results or documents, impeding their timely delivery, or opening or closing a polling station outside the legal time frames	Impeding the opening or closing of a polling station			Altering election results or documents, impeding their timely delivery, or opening or closing a polling station outside the legal time frames
		Failing to carry out obligations particular to their post				
Crimes or offences against voter registration		Improperly replacing or altering voter registration documents				Providing false documents to or inputting false data into the electoral register in order to obtain a voter registration card
						Destroying or altering voter registration documents or voter registration cards

(cont.)

Electoral offence	Actors					
	Electorate	**Electoral official**	**Party official**	**Party leader or candidate**	**Public servant**	**Anyone**
Unlawful or wrongful campaign financing				Making a false declaration on election expenses incurred	Illegally supporting a political party or its candidates through directing subordinates to campaign during working hours, or illegally earmarking property or funds to provide such support	
				Using funds raised through unlawful activities for political campaigns	Illegally earmarking property or funds to provide support	
				Making use of funds unlawfully given by a public servant		

d) Authorities in charge of handling electoral crimes and offences

112. In the vast majority of countries, the criminal procedure for electoral offences is the same as that for any other crime. It is up to the public prosecutor or equivalent authority to investigate the possibility that a crime has been committed, to identify the person most likely to be responsible and, once this has been is done, to prosecute criminal charges before a judge with jurisdiction over criminal matters. The criminal law judge, after a trial with due process of law, imposes a punishment of imprisonment or a fine on the person convicted of an offence, in some systems after a jury verdict.

113. Some countries have public prosecutors specialized in electoral matters as part of the institution in charge of prosecuting crimes. In some cases, a specific office is established in that institution. In Mexico, for example, the Office of the Special Prosecutor for Electoral Crimes (Fiscalía Especializada Para la Atención de Delitos Electorales) is part of the Office of the Attorney General (Procuraduría General de la República). In Panama, the Office of the General Prosecutor for Electoral Crimes (Físcalia General Electoral) is an independent and autonomous public office in charge of prosecuting and investigating electoral crimes or offences.

114. Although the criminal courts usually have jurisdiction over electoral crimes and offences, in some countries EDRBs competent to resolve electoral challenges also have jurisdiction over electoral offences. Examples include the specialized electoral courts found in certain Latin American countries, for example Brazil and Panama.

e) Administrative sanctions for electoral infractions

115. An electoral process-related administrative infraction is wrongful, but not criminal, conduct by which a person breaches or violates the electoral regime, defined by the electoral law or included in a law on some other administrative function. It gives rise to the imposition of a sanction that does not entail the deprivation of liberty. Such infractions are usually investigated by the EMB. This approach is more commonly found in civil law countries.

116. In some EJSs administrative sanctions are also imposed by the EMB, after a proceeding that takes the form of a fact-finding process, the result of which may be challenged before an EDRB. In other EJSs administrative sanctions can only be imposed by a court. This can be a criminal court, as usually happens in common law countries, a civil or administrative law court or even, on occasion, the EDRB.

117. Electoral infractions are usually defined in the electoral law.

f) Categories of entity or person that commit infractions, and electoral administrative sanctions

118. All citizens and entities – be they voters, candidates, pre-candidates or election observers; general public employees or public employees of the electoral system; leaders of political parties; entities such as political parties or political groupings; organizations of election observers; religious or community leaders; or media organizations, among others – may be defined as capable of committing an electoral infraction.

119. The purpose of defining and therefore regulating the legal conditions for the application of the electoral law, and the sanctions applicable to electoral administrative infractions, is essentially to protect the values and legal interests to be attained or realized by the exercise of electoral rights.

120. Some examples of administrative sanctions for the indirect protection of electoral law are:

a. reprimand, suspension, removal or disqualification of a public employee or electoral official;

b. reprimand, suspension or cancellation of a political party's or political grouping's registration;
c. reductions in public financing for a political party;
d. suspension of a political party's officially allotted radio and television time for political advertising or political messages;
e. suspension of air time for radio and television broadcasts;
f. loss or cancellation of the right to register as a candidate;
g. cancellation of accreditation as an election observer; or
h. fines or other financial penalties.

g) Electoral infractions regulated in various countries

121. The election laws in several countries establish election-related administrative infractions such as:

- a breach by a political party, political grouping or candidate of its legal obligations and of the decisions of the electoral authority; wrongful actions by their supporters; failure to report where funds come from and how they are used; accepting gifts and financial contributions of unlawful origin; accepting gifts or contributions that exceed the legal limits; and spending more than the amounts authorized for campaigns;
- a breach by citizens or other individuals of the rules for electoral observation;
- failure by the media to transmit the messages of the political parties at the official time or to comply with legal provisions regarding the volume and content of coverage related to the electoral process;
- a breach by electoral officials of their obligations provided for by law; or
- an electoral official, public employee or religious or community leader offering inducement to vote for or against a particular candidate or political party, or to refrain from voting.

122. In order to increase the likelihood of compliance, it is advisable for the electoral law to provide for the sanctions imposed on political parties to be independent of the liability that may attach to their leaders, members, candidates or supporters.

123. Financial sanctions should be proportionate and therefore severe enough to fulfil their purpose of inhibiting prohibited conduct. If they are merely symbolic, this may be read as an invitation to break the law, as the person committing the infraction may calculate that the benefits of violating a prohibition may be greater than the cost of the sanction. In this regard, the timing of the sanction is also important. Extremely long administrative procedures which determine liability and impose the

sanction only after the election has been held and the person committing the infraction has obtained the improper benefits may also be an invitation to break the law. It is vital that the provisions that regulate the administrative procedures for imposing sanctions ensure adherence to the essential formalities of due process and respect, among other things, the right of the accused to a fair hearing.

Box 4.3. The effectiveness of financial sanctions may differ depending on the context

A provision for gender quotas was included in electoral law in France in the French 'Parity Law' of 2000. Under this provision, political parties that did not nominate a stated percentage of women would be fined by a reduction in the funding that their party received from the state. Some parties in France itself were not keen to comply, and regarded the fine as small: they did not nominate enough women, and they were fined. The same legislation applied in the overseas departments of France, including New Caledonia. The parties in New Caledonia, which is poorer than France, regarded exactly the same level of fines as high and as a deterrent, and ensured that they complied with the legislation. The election in New Caledonia produced a legislative body composed almost equally of women and men (in 2006, the level of women's representation in New Caledonia's Parliament is 44.4 per cent, while in France it is 18.9 per cent as of February 2010). What is proportionate and effective in one place is not necessarily so in another.

124. It is important that the imposition of an electoral sanction can be challenged before a judicial body that is either part of the judiciary or autonomous. This body conducts a review in order to ensure that there has been due process and respect for the rights of the person alleged to have committed the infraction, in line with the human right to justice and to an effective remedy before a pre-established impartial court.

h) Other legal instruments

125. In addition to criminal or administrative liability for the violation of the provisions of the electoral law, there are other forms of liability and penalty which could be characterized as political. These include those liabilities imposed by the legislative organ, or any other political assembly, on high ranking public servants such as cabinet ministers, governors, legislators, judges or members of EMBs for having committed a serious irregularity in connection with a particular electoral process. This includes, for example, an impeachment procedure provided for in some countries with a common law tradition. Another example is what is known as *juicio político* (political trial) provided for in several Latin American countries, the consequence of which is the removal by the legislature of the high-ranking public official found liable

and possibly also his or her disqualification from holding any other public office for a specified period of time.

126. There can also be civil liability for damages. This might stem, for example, from an inappropriate legal decision, a mistake by the EMB or a judicial error on the part of the EDRB, or an inadequate EJS design. An example occurred in 2008, when the Inter-American Court of Human Rights ordered Mexico to pay compensation (litigation costs) to a citizen who had brought a complaint. The complaint concerned Mexico's failure to provide in its domestic law by 2006 for an effective remedy before a court to challenge the constitutionality of an electoral statute which in the opinion of the complainant violated his electoral rights. The same Court, however, also decided that there had not been any violation of the citizen's electoral rights. By the time the Court decided the case, the Mexican Constitution had already been amended to provide for such a challenge (*Castañeda Gutman vs Mexico*, ruled on by the Inter-American Court of Human Rights on 6 August 2008).

Box 4.4. Learning from experience: evolution of the EDR system in Bhutan

Deki Pema

Lessons learned in Bhutan

A self-assessment of the first ever parliamentary elections, held in 2008, was undertaken using the comprehensive Learning from Experience Programme. In terms of election disputes, the following lessons were learned:

1. All sorts of complaints were generally lodged with the Commission during the elections. The lesson learnt was the need for coming up with rules or procedures specifying clearly how, on what grounds and to whom complaints should be lodged.
2. The electronic voting machines, which were used in all the polling stations, forestalled disputes relating to polling and counting.
3. An accurate voters' list that contained photographs of voters alongside voter photo identity cards proved useful in preventing complaints.
4. Public education and awareness-raising, using all means of communication, must continue to receive priority and attention as they can both prevent and resolve disputes, thereby ensuring confidence in the system (see box 3.1).
5. Elections must be credible and genuine both in practice and in perception. In this regard, the role of the media cannot be overemphasized as it promotes transparency in the system and ensures both that voters are informed and that they are not misinformed.
6. Depending on the degree of severity of the violation, some cases may be better resolved at the district level. This enhances the speed with which cases can be resolved while allowing the central body to focus on the more serious cases.

(cont.)

Improving the EDR system

Based on these experiences, the dispute resolution rules and regulations were revised to provide for an even more effective and transparent system. The revisions, which are discussed in more detail below, focus on the gradation of cases and the appropriate levels at which cases are to be settled. They also include precise provisions for a more systematic manner of registering and screening complaints, investigating cases and conducting hearings, reaching decisions and dealing with appeals.

[1] **A two-level EDRB**

The rules have been revised to provide for the establishment of two levels of dispute resolution body during the election period. The Central Election Dispute Resolution Body is at the national level. An Election Commissioner acts as Chairperson and its members include the Secretary of the Commission, the relevant Head of Department or Division of the Commission and a lawyer. The District Election Dispute Resolution Body has the Chief Election Coordinator of the district as Chairperson and includes the district or sub-district Administrative Head, the District Council Secretary, the Head of the county concerned and the District Electoral Officer as members.

[2] **Clearer rules for complaint adjudication**

The process of lodging complaints specifies that complaints may be lodged with the:

1. Chief Election Commissioner;
2. Chief Election Coordinator;
3. National observers; or
4. Returning officers.

This is intended to make the process more convenient and more accessible.

The Chief Election Commissioner or a Chief Election Coordinator is required to act immediately on receipt of a complaint. If a case is dismissed, a decision has to be given within two days. If a case is not dismissed, it must be registered and referred to either the central or the district dispute resolution body.

[3] **Proper presentation of a complaint**

In order to screen out baseless complaints, all complaints lodged must be signed and include the nature of the complaint, a proper address and contact details.

(cont.)

[4] **Establishment of investigation committees**

At the central level, a separate investigation committee shall be appointed to investigate a case and the central dispute resolution body shall give the ruling after the hearing process. At the district level, the district dispute resolution body may investigate cases and give a ruling on the matter by itself or give the ruling after investigations by a separate investigation committee appointed by it.

[5] **More regulation on hearings**

The regulations governing the hearings have been improved. They include three days advance notice of hearings, and the right of concerned parties to be represented and to present evidence, as well as rules for the dismissal of a case if a representative does not attend the hearing. There may only be a maximum of two hearings before a decision must be made.

[6] **Better guidance for decision-making**

The rules have been revised to provide for penalties, such as fines, public reprimands, cancellation of candidacies, nullification of results, detention of offenders and deregistration of political parties, which guide the decision making of both the central and the district EDRBs and in particular ensure a certain level of uniformity in the decisions of the different district bodies.

[7] **Summary decisions enabled**

If no real legal dispute exists a case may be summarily decided without further investigation. This may only be done after a hearing when either there is no dispute about the material facts of the case or there is a dispute about the facts but there is enough evidence to decide the case.

[8] **Better provision for final and binding decisions**

Processes for appeals and submission deadlines are more clearly defined. For instance, an appeal to the central EDRB must be launched within five days. If no appeal has been submitted within this time frame the original decision by the district EDRB shall be final and binding.

[9] **Time limits for considering cases**

The central EDRB must take a final decision on an election complaint received by it no later than seven days before the polling day. The district EDRB must take a final decision on an election complaint received by it or referred to it no later than ten days before the polling day. This is designed to allow for adequate time for an appeal to be lodged. The Election Commission is responsible for adjudicating any complaints received after these deadlines.

(cont.)

[10] **Mandatory referral**

Cases that the EDRBs find to be offences that clearly fall under the jurisdiction of other law enforcement agencies, such as the police, the Anti-Corruption Commission, and so on, are required to be referred to the relevant agency regardless of any action taken against a political party, candidate or individual by the bodies.

[11] **Complaints during the non-election period**

Any complaints received during the non-election period shall be addressed to the Chief Election Commissioner. On receipt of the complaints, the Commission may appoint an Investigation Committee to take action as per the Election Act.

CHAPTER 5

CHAPTER 5

A general classification of EDR systems

1. Introduction

127. There is no magic or single formula for ensuring that the electoral process complies with the legal framework or for upholding electoral rights. This leads to a diversity of EDR systems.

128. Each country's EDR system is generally the result of its own historical and socio-political context and of its own legal tradition. Thus it is not always possible to extract lessons from the experience of one country and export it to different contexts. Nonetheless, a comparative approach does make it possible to identify certain trends, which offer additional elements of analysis for those interested as well as lessons from successful experience or good practice and the strengths and weaknesses of respective systems.

129. Several international human rights instruments establish the fundamental right of all persons whose rights have been infringed to an effective remedy before a pre-established independent tribunal (see, e.g., box 5.1).

Box 5.1. Declaration on Criteria for Free and Fair Elections, adopted by the Inter-Parliamentary Council in 1994

Paragraph 4.9

'States should ensure that violations of human rights and complaints relating to the electoral process are determined promptly within the time frame of the electoral process and effectively by an independent and impartial authority, such as an electoral commission or the courts.'

130. To get a global perspective, it is helpful to classify the EDR systems found in the contemporary world. There are several criteria for such a classification.

2. Criteria for classifying EDR systems

131. One method would be to examine the various elements that constitute a given EDR system and attempt to identify those which offer the best ways of ensuring that electoral processes comply with the legal framework and respect electoral rights. Leaving aside the possible argument over the definition of 'best' in this context, the data that would be needed in order to undertake this task are not systematically collected and are therefore either scarce or non-existent.

132. Nor is it possible to find any significant correlation from a summary analysis between the type of EDRSs and democratic consolidation. Some emerging democracies have placed great emphasis on designing suitable preventive measures, satisfactory mechanisms for electoral challenges and a strict regime of electoral liabilities but, even so, have faced serious electoral disputes, triggering institutional crises. Some stable and mature democracies with fewer preventive measures and a simple and straightforward regime for bringing challenges and assigning liabilities have seen practically no electoral disputes, for example, the Scandinavian countries where the political culture abhors excessive regulation. Others have faced disputes arising from very close election results but, despite the tensions and difficulties at a particular point in time, have been able to overcome the crisis – the most notable recent case being the 2000 presidential election in the United States. It would appear that overcoming an electoral crisis is dependent not only on the framework for dispute prevention and resolution but also on the willingness of the political actors involved to find a compromise.

133. A country's legal tradition – for example, common law systems, those that follow Roman-Germanic tradition or the civil law, and those that follow a philosophical-religious tradition – is relevant to the functioning of its EDRS. However, it is not the only factor. The United Kingdom and the USA are both common law countries and there are important similarities between their EDRSs, but there are also essential differences between them. The same can be said of Spain, Italy and Uruguay, all of which belong to the civil law tradition. Meanwhile, there are many similarities in practice in the design and operation of EDRSs in countries that belong to different legal traditions, such as those of the USA and Italy; of Ethiopia, the UK, Pakistan and Taiwan; of Spain, Indonesia and Niger; and of the Palestinian Authority and Uruguay. This suggests that the most significant element for distinguishing between EDR systems is to be found elsewhere.

134. In addition, some democracies place greater emphasis on preventive measures, others on corrective measures or electoral challenges, and still others on punitive measures or mechanisms for adjudicating liability. There is no clear correlation between the emphasis chosen and the number of electoral disputes (which could also be argued as measuring stability and social cohesion in a society). It can be argued that if a dispute does arise, the electoral challenge is the mechanism with the most potential to produce satisfaction its corrective function revokes, annuls, modifies or acknowledges irregular or wrongful conduct and thus protects or restores the enjoyment electoral rights. By contrast, the liability regime is limited to penalizing the entity or person responsible for the irregularity and setting an example by doing so.

135. This Handbook therefore prioritizes the regime for bringing electoral challenges as the basis for classifying EDR systems. This regime provides a direct oversight mechanism for verifying that the electoral process complies with the legal framework, and has the effect of preserving or restoring this framework and the electoral rights involved. It therefore constitutes the principal and most effective guarantee of electoral justice.

136. However, there are several criteria by which electoral challenges can be classified. In many cases a single EDR system encompasses several types of electoral challenge (administrative, judicial and possibly legislative and international), and therefore various EDRBs. One criterion for classification could therefore be the nature of the organ that hears an electoral challenge *in the first instance*. This criterion is not very useful, however, as the vast majority of EDR systems provide that electoral challenges must be brought before the EMB in the first instance. The organs at the higher level may be more relevant to classifying the operation of the EDR system. For more information on bodies that handle challenges at first instance see the International IDEA online Unified Database at <http://www.idea.int>.

137. Another criterion is to look at the nature of the organ that hears and resolves *most electoral challenges*, at whatever level. Unfortunately, little if any statistical information on this exists on the various EDR systems. There is also a risk that the conclusions would vary from one election to the next. For example, there might be a large number of challenges to the result of one election in contrast to what happened in previous elections, but the EDRB with jurisdiction to resolve challenges to results might be different from the one entrusted with addressing those brought against actions prior to the election. It is often the case that most challenges are related to the electoral register, and the organ in charge of resolving these challenges – even though it is an essential and important aspect of any election – is not always the one that contributes most to the soundness of elections or to the credibility and legitimacy of the EDR system.

138. Whatever the criterion chosen for classifying EDR systems, it is important to consider the important function played by an EMB that enjoys functional independence, and therefore autonomy, when resolving disputes in the first instance and at the most basic levels of electoral administration. Examples include the EMBs of India (the largest democracy in the world), Mexico and South Africa (see *Electoral Management Design: The International IDEA Handbook*). EMBs, especially in less mature, independent or autonomous democracies, make an essential contribution to processes of democratic transition and consolidation. They also play a significant and positive role in the operation of EDR systems even when they do not make the final decision in the chain of electoral challenges.

139. This Handbook thus uses the nature of the body that is vested with the *final decision* or the *challenge of last resort* for ensuring that electoral results comply with the legal framework as the criterion for the global classification of EDR systems. This body will be vested with such powers in respect of national legislative elections, which are held in each and every democratic country, regardless of the form of government. Using this classification, it is possible to classify the EDR systems of the world into four major types or models (see box 5.2).

Box 5.2. General classification of EDR systems

- Legislative body (the legislature or other political assembly)
- Judicial body
  - Regular courts of the judicial branch
  - Constitutional courts or councils
  - Administrative courts
  - Specialized electoral courts
- EMB with judicial powers
- Ad hoc bodies created with international involvement or as an internal national institutional solution to a specific electoral process.

140. Of course, this is not the only classification possible. It is used here, but five points need to be recognized.

141. First, international human rights instruments include provisions for the exercise of electoral rights. As a result, there is a possibility that complaints will be lodged before international bodies with respect to the final actions and decisions of a particular state. However, it appears that no international body has ever made a decision on election results.

142. Second, in some EDR systems jurisdiction over challenges to election results is different from jurisdiction over other electoral challenges.

143. Third, the final resolution of electoral challenges on some matters (for example, oversight of where the resources of political parties come from and how they are used) may be entrusted to a body which is not the one with jurisdiction to issue the final decision on the validity of an election and the declaration that a certain person has been elected. In Italy, the final decision on the validity of an election and the assignment of seats in the legislature lies with the national Chamber of Deputies (Camera dei Deputati) or the Senate (Senato), as the case may be, after any challenge to the election results has been resolved by the National Central Electoral Office (Direzione Centrale dei servizi elettorali), which is part of the Court of Cassation (Corte Suprema di Cassazione). However, the final decision on challenges related to overseeing the political parties' resources lies with the Court of Audit (Corte dei Conti). In this Handbook, Italy is classified as having an EDRS entrusted to legislative organs rather than to autonomous administrative courts.

144. Fourth, electoral challenges regarding voter registration, the registration and accountability of political parties, the registration and announcement of candidacies, and election campaigns are common. Some countries entrust the final decision on all types of electoral challenge to the same body; for example, many assign such authority to constitutional courts or specialized electoral courts. In other countries, however, these challenges are dealt with by an administrative body, the EMB, or a judicial body, the identity of which can provide a good idea of the operation of the EDRS concerned.

145. Fifth, an EDRS is generally made up of various types of challenge mechanism, which could be administrative, judicial or, in some cases, legislative. Accordingly, EDRBs may be administrative, judicial or legislative in type even though, for the purposes of this Handbook, in classifying them attention is paid only to the *legal nature of the body* that issues the final decision on legislative elections.

146. The classification is based on the *legal nature* of the body competent to make the final ruling on the last challenge provided for against the election results, even if it is almost never used. The competent organ to make the final ruling on national legislative elections in the United States is the House of Representatives or the Senate for the election of their own members, or the whole of Congress for presidential elections; a concurrent majority vote of both the House of Representatives and the Senate is required in order to overturn a decision on this matter reached by a state. This has not happened since the 1876 presidential election. The most that has happened is that a challenge has been brought before the Supreme Court. In the case of national legislative elections, there have been very few cases brought before the House of Representatives or the Senate. Nonetheless, in the light of the criterion adopted, the US EDRS falls into the category of those conferred on a legislative organ, and not among those entrusted to a judicial body.

147. Similarly, it is common for constitutions to provide that one of the powers of the legislature or one of its chambers is to review the credentials or certifications of those elected to it so that they can take their seats, or to declare who is the president-elect and publish that declaration. At the same time these constitutions establish that a judicial body has jurisdiction or the authority to issue a final and definitive ruling on challenges to election results. Taking into account the practice and constitutional experience of these countries, in this Handbook it is considered that the power of the legislature is a mere formality and that, strictly speaking, the final decision of the EDRS is with the respective judicial organ.

3. The evolution of EDR systems

148. The rise of the first representative democratic regimes was characterized by the adoption of an EDR system that entrusted the final decision on electoral outcomes to legislative assemblies. In the last third of the 19th century, however, a judicial EDR system was established for elections in the UK and the regular courts were given jurisdiction over challenges to legislative elections. Although some countries still give such powers to the legislature, in most this authority was gradually transferred, in the course of the 20th century, to judicial organs in the various democratic regimes – either regular courts as part of the judiciary, constitutional courts, administrative courts or specialized electoral courts.

149. In general terms, there has been an evolution away from EDRSs entrusted to a legislative organ, to mixed EDRSs that combine a legislative body with administrative and/or judicial challenges, to exclusively judicial EDRSs – be they regular, constitutional, administrative or specialized electoral courts or a combination of these.

150. Obviously, the different EDRSs are the result of the legal tradition and evolution of each country, and of the specific social claims of and possible agreements among the various political forces involved. It is difficult to draw any general lessons that can be exported to different historical and political contexts. Nonetheless, a comparative approach makes it possible to identify trends and offers elements of analysis for those interested in electoral matters and for those who are endeavouring to improve all aspects of the electoral process, in addition to identifying successful experience and good practices and the strengths and weaknesses of the respective systems.

151. In general, there has been a marked trend towards the 'judicialization' of electoral procedures. Judicial organs are increasingly entrusted with the resolution of electoral conflicts and ensuring that any dispute is resolved lawfully and in keeping with principles of constitutionality, that is, in keeping with the law. This can avoid the broadly discretional criteria and opportunist

political negotiation that are often found when an EDRS is entrusted to legislative organs or political assemblies. This trend even holds in the EDR systems that still confer the power of final decision on the legislature or one of its chambers (as in the United States or Italy), so long as they provide for prior challenges before judicial organs: this probably makes it difficult for the legislative body, which is political in nature, to overturn a judicial decision. Another indicator of this trend is that some of the members of EMBs are often required to come from the judicial branch, or are appointed in a similar fashion to judges with the same requirements demanded of them, or are given conditions of employment that are equivalent to those of the highest-ranking members of the judiciary.

152. The role played by political parties in oversight of electoral procedures has also evolved. In the early days of representative democracy it was often the political parties who participated in organizing elections (in the EMB) and resolving electoral disputes (in the EDRBs). Their representatives served as polling officials at the polling stations and in the entities that administered the various phases of the election and resolved disputes, making the relevant decisions. This active decision-making function with respect to the electoral process has gradually been transformed into one of oversight and supervision of the work entrusted to the electoral authorities, which in general they no longer serve on – at least not with a right to vote, although several systems still confer decision-making powers on them at various stages or provide that they can have a seat on the relevant bodies.

a) EDR systems entrusted to a legislative body or another political assembly

153. Some EDRSs vest the power of final decision on the validity of elections, including any challenges brought, in the legislature, one of its committees or some other political assembly. In the French tradition this has been called 'verification of powers' and in the US tradition 'qualification or certification of elections'.

154. This is the oldest type of EDR system. It is associated with the origin of parliaments in the UK, even though by 1868 the British EDRS had been entrusted to a regular court. Even though in their origins the legislature or presumptive legislators may have certified or judged the election of their respective members, the advent of presidential elections in several countries meant that final jurisdiction for certifying an election result was also entrusted to political assemblies (in bicameral systems, this was often done in a joint session of the two chambers). An EDRS entrusted to a political assembly was adopted in France from the Estates General (États-Généraux) in the 18th century until the 1958 constitution. In the United States it was established by the 1787 constitution. Entrusting the EDRS to legislative

organs or political assemblies became the general practice in the democratic regimes that emerged during the 19th century and a good part of the 20th.

155. The historical justification for entrusting the EDR system to a legislative organ is based on the principle of the separation of powers, according to which each branch of government is independent of the other and should not therefore become involved in decisions that affect the composition of the others. In particular, it was considered a defensive weapon in the hands of the legislature against the executive in order to ensure its autonomy and independence. It seeks to avoid tarnishing the judicial branch, which would be dragged into partisan political struggle to the detriment of its essential function – that of resolving cases on a technical-legal basis. Moreover, those who tend to favour entrusting the EDRS to the legislative organ use the non-democratic nature of most judicial bodies to argue that the decisions of such bodies should not prevail over the decisions of the legislature.

156. A fundamental characteristic of EDRSs that are entrusted to legislative organs or political assemblies is that, although they are governed by the constitutional and statutory framework applicable to a particular election, given their composition and their inclination to act politically – as no legal mechanisms are provided to verify that their decisions are lawful – it is common for political criteria such as opportunism or the negotiation of conflicting interests to prevail over legal considerations in the decision making. Such decisions have tended to favour the political forces that have come to constitute the legislative majority. It was the abuses committed by the respective legislatures in certifying the election of their own members that were among the most influential reasons for transferring jurisdiction in the UK in 1868 and in France in 1958 to *judicial bodies*, in the final instance, over the question of the validity of legislative elections.

Box 5.3. An EDR system: legislative abuses in France before 1958

From 1958, the system for verifying the powers entrusted to the political assembly in France was modified and jurisdiction was vested in the Constitutional Council (Conseil Constitutionnel). The powers entrusted to the political assembly dated back to the Estates General. Although abolished by the Consulate and during the Empire, they were re-established in 1814–15 as a sign of independence of the Chamber and they acquired constitutional status under the Third Republic. However, abuses led to the system being discredited from around 1940. Nonetheless, the Constitution of the Fourth Republic of 27 October 1946 retained Article 8, establishing that 'Each of the two Chambers is judge of the eligibility of its members and of the regularity of their election'. This led to a breakdown of the system of verification of powers by the chambers. The assemblies that existed from 1946 to 1958 often acted without respect for legality, and there were obvious contradictions in the decisions they reached as

(cont.)

well as deliberate violations of the law. In 1946 they validated persons who were ineligible for the National Assembly (Assemblée Nationale) and the system led to unjustifiable validations in the overseas elections of 1946 and 1951 and to the majority parties recovering seats in the National Assembly in 1951 and 1956. Debates on issue of verification became notorious and were one of the factors which contributed to the loss of credibility of the National Assembly of the Fourth Republic.

157. To curb possible abuses by the legislative bodies and political assemblies, several EDR systems aimed to combine the means for prior electoral challenges, put in the hands of judicial bodies, with still entrusting the final decision as to the validity and results of an election to the legislative bodies. This was an effort to reconcile the rule of law with entrusting the final decision on an election to an organ whose members were selected democratically, although it should be noted that its democratic nature would be called into question in some challenges. In practice it is now exceptional for a legislative or political organ to fail to recognize, or to overturn or modify, a judicial decision, given the political cost that this would entail. Those EDR systems that still provide for this possibility are characterized by the traditional restraint of legislative organs in this regard.

158. There is now practically no system of government remaining in which an EDR system is entrusted exclusively to a legislative organ or political assembly. Those countries which still have such a system for legislative elections – and, for those that hold them, presidential elections – do so in a way that coexists with either: (a) prior judicial review, at least with respect to electoral actions and decisions other than electoral results (as in Argentina and Belgium), or including decisions on electoral results, as in the United States, Italy, Latvia and Lithuania but not Denmark, the Netherlands, Norway and Switzerland; or (b) subsequent judicial review of decisions by parliament on legislative electoral results (as in Germany through the Constitutional Court, Verfassungsgerichtshof). These are therefore mixed legislative-judicial, legislative-administrative or judicial-legislative EDR systems.

159. A mixed legislative-judicial EDR system exists in the United States. Challenges to federal elections regulated and organized by the authorities of each state generally combine a hearing of the challenges before a regular state court, which is usually part of the judicial branch (after the Supreme Court has reviewed the state court's ruling and by writ of certiorari by the Supreme Court) with provision for subsequent challenge before a legislative organ – the House of Representatives or the Senate – which hands down the final ruling. In addition, the US Congress has the constitutional authority to count the votes for presidential elections. A concurrent vote of the majority

of the House of Representatives and the Senate is required, according to the Electoral Count Act of 1887, for the decision of a state to be overturned regarding the results of the presidential election. In the case of local challenges, this takes place after decision by a state court.

160. The situation is similar in Italy. Article 66 of the 1948 Constitution provides that it is up to each chamber – the Chamber of Deputies or the Senate – to judge 'the titles of admission of their members and the grounds for incompatibility or disqualification' once claims and challenges have been resolved by the National Central Election Office, which is part of the Court of Cassation. The Court of Cassation is made up of a presiding judge and four other judges. There is no judicial remedy against the ruling of the relevant chamber.

161. Similarly, according to articles 105 and 107 of the Constitution of the Republic of Lithuania, the Constitutional Court (Lietuvos Respublikos Konstitucinis Teismas) can present its conclusions on whether there were violations of election laws during an election for the President of the Republic or elections for members of the Seimas (Parliament), and the Seimas takes the final decision on the basis of the conclusions of the Constitutional Court. In Latvia, the Law on Administrative Process establishes administrative courts to which the revision of election results are delegated. According to the constitution, it is the Saeima (Parliament) that reviews the qualification of its members.

162. In the Swiss Federation, the National Council (Nationalrat) and the Council of the States (Ständerat) have the authority to make the final ruling on the election of their respective members once appeals over the vote count and verification of the results have been decided by the political authorities in the cantons.

163. In addition to Argentina (see box 5.4) and Switzerland, this category should include the EDRSs of Belgium, Iceland, the Netherlands and Norway, as well as certain Central and East European countries which, during their transformation from socialist states to democratic states, preserved for some time the system of self-certification by the presumptive legislators even though they gradually established EDRSs entrusted to one or another judicial organ.

Box 5.4. A mixed legislative-administrative EDR system in Argentina

Argentina has a mixed legislative-administrative EDR system so far as challenges to the results of legislative and presidential elections are concerned. All other electoral actions and decisions can be challenged before the National Electoral Chamber (Cámara Nacional Electoral), which is part of the judicial branch. The final decision on the validity of elections is a power of a political organ or assembly, once the respective national election boards, which are strictly administrative even though they are composed of

(cont.)

judges, have ruled on any challenges brought against these results. The constitutional reform of 1994 provides that it is a power of the National Congress (Congreso de la Nación, both chambers) to resolve disputes regarding the direct election of the president and vice-president. As regards the elections of members of the two houses of the National Congress, the power of the Chamber of Deputies (Honorable Cámara de Diputados de la Nación) and the Senate (Honorable Senado de la Nación) to be 'the judge of the election, rights, and titles of its members in terms of their validity' is preserved without any express remedy against their decisions, although there are judicial precedents that argue that judicial review is called for with respect to arbitrary decisions of the Chamber of Deputies, or by the National Electoral Chamber, as occurred in the Patti case (Case no. 4207/06 CNE, judgement of 14 September 2006 – see box 5.5).

164. Despite the political nature of the ultimate decision-making body that determines the validity of the elections in these countries, the authorities in charge of EDR systems must carry out their responsibilities and ensure the conduct of free, fair and genuine elections, and not use their position to obtain advantage or engage in political revenge or horse-trading. The incorporation of various means of judicial and/or administrative challenge into these systems, as is mentioned above, has contributed to this end and to making them mixed EDRSs.

Box 5.5. The Luis Patti case: Argentina

Luis Patti had been a winner in the federal deputy election of 2005, according to the Electoral Board (Junta Electoral Nacional). However, on 23 May 2006 the Chamber of Deputies disqualified him as a deputy and raised obstacles to his joining the legislature, alleging his lack of moral integrity. Patti challenged that decision but his petition was dismissed by a judge. On the appeal, the National Electoral Chamber (Justicia Electoral Nacional) of the Federal Judiciary overruled the judge's decision and favoured Patti, establishing that the will of the people expressed in the election should be respected and that the Congress was not able to modify it by an arbitrary decision (since this could lead to an elected candidate not being admitted on the grounds that he/she was anarchist or a socialist, or just for religious or gender reasons). In 2008, the Supreme Court (Corte Suprema de Justicia de la Nación) confirmed the National Electoral Chamber's decision after an extraordinary appeal. Notwithstanding, the Chamber of Deputies insisted on its own power to judge the election of its members and defended its 2006 decision. It is important to mention that by the time the Supreme Court ruled on this case, Luis Patti had been prosecuted for crimes against humanity, his case had been concluded, and there was no decision about his being freed from prison, so that the Supreme Court's ruling could not be enforced.

b) EDR systems entrusted to a judicial body

165. In response to certain abuses committed by legislative bodies or political assemblies in charge of an EDRS, or simply because the adoption of a different system would better guarantee that electoral disputes are resolved based on the provisions of the constitution and the law, various countries have opted to establish an EDRS that entrusts the authority to make the final decision on a challenge to a particular election to a judicial body. Since its adoption in the UK in the late 19th century, this type of EDRS has proliferated and, whether entrusted to a regular court as part of the judiciary, a constitutional court, an administrative court or an electoral court, it is now the most widespread in democracies worldwide.

166. Advocates of a judicial EDR system argue that the action of judging and certifying elections is essentially judicial in nature. Consequently, the exercise of these powers should be vested in a judicial body in order to seek to ensure that elections are free, fair, genuine and valid. This avoids a situation in which, as happens in some EDR systems located exclusively in a legislative body or a political assembly, members judge and certify their own election. In particular, there is a risk that the predetermined legislative majority could act in accordance with its political and party interests, ignoring considerations of law and justice. Vesting the power to resolve electoral disputes and challenges in judicial organs emphasizes that this power should be exercised in keeping with the principles of constitutionality and/or legality – the rule of law – and not on the basis of discretional considerations of political expediency.

167. This has meant a change in the attitudes and strategies of political parties, election officials and third parties interested in a particular electoral challenge. Institutional means have been accorded priority for resolving electoral disputes. The facts, lines of argument and evidence that may be put before a competent judicial body have been brought into line with the technical-legal requirements to ensure that they are admissible and well-founded. It is increasingly accepted that mere political mobilization and political delegitimization do not provide sufficient means or grounds for resolving electoral litigation objectively, impartially and lawfully. A much more consistent and scientifically founded body of electoral case law has emerged that makes the resolution of electoral disputes more predictable, which is beneficial for legal certainty.

168. Even after recognizing the advisability of conferring the resolution of disputes on a judicial organ, it can be argued that a war of attrition may ensue if the judicial branch becomes involved in political disputes. Some EDRSs have opted to confer the function on non-regular courts, such as constitutional courts, autonomous administrative courts or specialized electoral courts.

169. Judicial EDRSs can be subdivided into four categories, depending on the nature of the organ to which the ultimate or final resolution of a given electoral challenge is entrusted:

- regular courts of the judicial branch;
- constitutional courts or councils;
- autonomous administrative courts; and
- specialized electoral courts.

(See also box 5.2).

i) Regular courts of the judicial branch

170. The first type of strictly judicial EDR system is that which entrusts the final decision on challenges to election results to regular judges or courts which are not specialized in electoral matters but are part of the judicial branch. Often this power is conferred on the Supreme Court of the country, either by its assuming direct jurisdiction or through jurisdiction on appeal if there is a decision by a lower judicial body.

171. This type of EDR system began in the UK in 1868 (reformed in 1983) for the purpose of eradicating the abuses committed by majorities in the House of Commons. By a legislative act, the resolution of challenges to elections was entrusted to two regular judges of the Queen's Bench Division of the High Court of Justice (membership of which rotates among the members of the judicial branch). It was also established that decisions on which these judges agreed would be adopted by a resolution of the House of Commons, in order to safeguard the sovereignty of Parliament. The judges report their decision to the Speaker of the House, who submits it to the plenary House. If the judges decide that a candidate other than the member who occupies the seat concerned should have been elected, the House orders that steps be taken as necessary to give effect to that decision. Although jurisdiction over electoral challenges has been moved to the judicial branch, the House of Commons retains its jurisdiction over its membership if this is raised for other reasons.

172. A slightly different system was adopted in other Commonwealth countries, such as Australia, Pakistan and English-speaking Caribbean countries such as Jamaica. Here, a final ruling is made by the High Court on appeal against a ruling by the electoral court, which is constituted by a judge chosen in rotation who hears the challenge in first instance. The same holds in Canada and India through their respective supreme courts, which hear on appeal challenges to the election of legislators. In addition, challenges to the election of the President and Vice-president in India are heard directly by the Supreme Court. Especially in Australia, Canada and India, independent and autonomous EMBs have played a fundamental role in the EDRS.

173. Some Central and East European countries have this type of EDRS. Examples are Bosnia and Herzegovina, Estonia, Hungary, Poland, Russia and Serbia, where the final decision on challenges to election results is entrusted to the country's Supreme Court, after administrative challenges before an independent and autonomous EMB during the stage of preparing for the election have been exhausted. Some of the EMB's decisions, in some of these countries, such as Hungary and Russia, can also be challenged before lower courts.

174. In Ethiopia, Kenya, Lesotho, Taiwan and Uganda the final resolution of challenges to the results of legislative elections is entrusted to the judicial branch. It vests in a superior court, usually on appeal after a decision from a district court, which is at a lower level than the Supreme Court. Challenges to the results of presidential elections in Taiwan and Uganda are entrusted, on appeal, to the Supreme Court. In Taiwan, all other challenges to electoral actions and decisions come under the jurisdiction of an autonomous administrative court, the rulings of which are final.

175. Challenges to the results of legislative elections in Japan, Kyrgyzstan, South Korea, Uzbekistan and Vanuatu are entrusted to the Supreme Court – in Japan and Kyrgyzstan on appeal but in South Korea, Uzbekistan and Vanuatu directly.

176. The most common EDR system around the world is one that entrusts the final resolution of challenges to election results to the regular courts of the judicial branch. Anyone designing such a system must take account of the independence and credibility of the judicial system. This is very important in emerging or consolidating democracies. Any lack of credibility of the judicial system and any perception, however unjustified, that it lacks independence or is under the control of the executive or the political party in government will seriously harm the credibility of the EDR system.

ii) Constitutional courts or councils

177. Many European constitutions that date from the period immediately after the First World War (1914–18) follow, to varying extents, the model of the Austrian Constitution of 1920, which entrusted the task of ruling on the validity of elections to bodies with an expressly constitutional jurisdiction, some of which are part of the judicial branch while others are not.

178. In Austria, the verification of parliamentary elections has, since 1920, been assigned to the Federal Constitutional Court (Verfassungsgerichtshof), the jurisdiction of which, through successive reforms, has been expanded to include the validation of other democratic exercises (referendums since 1929, presidential elections since 1931, and elections to local authorities and the organizations that represent professionals as provided for in law). The decisions

or judgements of this court can mandate the partial or total repeat of an election for members of the National Congress or a provincial Parliament.

179. Germany may also be included in this type of EDRS (see box 5.6). The certification of elections is entrusted to the Bundestag (usually considered as the lower house of the Parliament). Appeals can be made to the Federal Constitutional Court. This is a mixed judicial-legislative EDRS, in which the judicial component is predominant because the final decision is in the hands of the Federal Constitutional Court.

Box 5.6. A mixed judicial-legislative EDR system in Germany: executive and legislative control of elections

Ralf Lindner

The conduct of federal elections in Germany is overseen by the Federal Election Supervisor (Bundeswahlleiter) in cooperation with the 16 *länder* election supervisors (Landeswahlleiter) and the constituency supervisors (Kreiswahlleiter). The Bundeswahlleiter, who is traditionally the President of the Federal Statistical Office (Statistisches Bundesamt), is appointed by the federal Ministry of the Interior and the other election supervisors are designated by the *länder* governments. The supervisors chair the respective election commissions (Bundeswahlausschuss, Landeswahlausschuss and Kreiswahlausschuss).

The federal EDR system is run by a parliamentary committee (Wahlprüfungsausschuss) that is composed of nine members of the Parliament (Bundestag) and nine deputies. Any parliamentary caucus not represented among the regular members is granted an advisory representative. The members of the committee are chosen by the Parliament as a whole and deal with all formal complaints. By convention, the committee is representative of the party composition of the current Parliament. All the decisions made by the committee are subject to appeal to the Constitutional Court, but for an appeal to be originated by citizens requires 100 supporting signatures.

Even though the court of final appeal is the Constitutional Court, the electoral process can be seen to be under executive control (through the EMB) and its supervision is led by Parliament (the EDRB). The dispute resolution process can take two years (one year in committee and another at the Constitutional Court), and in some instances considerably longer. Complaints can only be filed after the elections are over and the Parliament has formed itself; thus even disputes over pre-electoral issues are decided after the elections. Although reform proposals have been made a major reform currently seems unlikely.

180. The French Constitutional Council (Conseil Constitutionnel) is also an example of this type of EDRS. Since 1958, it has had jurisdiction over verifying that the election of the President of the Republic and any referendums comply with the legal framework, as well as examining claims, announcing the results of the vote and ruling on challenges to the election of deputies and senators.

The French EDRS is a combination of constitutional and administrative jurisdictions. The administrative jurisdiction is autonomous, belonging to the Council of State (Conseil d'État), and hearings may proceed during the preparatory phase of an election. Under the constitutional jurisdiction, certain decisions of the Council of State may be reviewed and challenges to electoral results heard. In certain cases connected with the electoral register, challenges may be brought before a court of original jurisdiction (Tribunal d'instance) and eventually before the Court of Cassation (Cour de Cassation), both of which are part of the judicial branch, and whose rulings are final.

181. Examples of EDRSs that combine constitutional and administrative jurisdictions include Spain, where the final decision on a challenge to an election is made by the autonomous Constitutional Court, which can be resorted to after exhausting the possibilities of an administrative remedy before the Administrative Court, which is part of the judiciary. Another example is Portugal, where the final decision on a challenge to election results is directly entrusted to the Constitutional Court (Tribunal Constitucional), which is part of the judicial branch.

182. A significant number of the Central and East European countries that have recently undergone democratic transitions have given their Constitutional Court the last word in the EDRS when it comes to challenges to election results. These include Bulgaria, Croatia, Moldova, Montenegro, Romania and Slovenia, as well as Armenia, the Czech Republic, Georgia and Slovakia for which the corresponding court is part of the judicial branch. In Indonesia and Niger the final resolution of electoral disputes is also entrusted to a constitutional court, which in Indonesia is part of the judicial branch.

183. It is also possible to classify under this model the cases of Burkina Faso, Cambodia, Cameroon, Kazakhstan and Mozambique, which give a Constitutional Council which is not part of the judiciary the power to make the final decision on challenges to election results.

iii) Administrative courts

184. A third type of EDRS, which is not widely used, gives jurisdiction over the final resolution of electoral challenges to an administrative court that can be either autonomous or part of the judicial branch.

185. Mindful that electoral challenges are generally brought against the actions, procedures and decisions of the EMB, some countries have vested jurisdiction over contentious electoral cases in an administrative court, either making it autonomous in keeping with the French tradition of administrative justice (entrusting it to the Council of State and even calling it that) or situating it within the judicial branch.

186. The countries with an EDRS entrusted to an administrative court include Colombia, where it is autonomous since it is not part of the judiciary and is called the Council of State (Consejo de Estado). Another example is Finland, through the Supreme Administrative Court (Korkein Hallinto-Oikeus) on appeal from provincial administrative courts – all of which are part of the judiciary – adjudicating on complaints in respect of the decisions of electoral district commissions on election results.

Box 5.7. Citizen challenge in Colombia

In Colombia, any citizen has the standing to bring a challenge, or *acción popular*, before the Council of State (Consejo de Estado) against the actions and decisions of the independent EMB – the National Electoral Council (Consejo Nacional Electoral). Such challenges can be related to the general vote count in any national election, the declaration of the outcome, and the issuance of credentials. The Council of State is an independent administrative law court with full jurisdiction to annul, rectify, or modify decisions made by the EMB.

iv) Specialized electoral courts with functional independence

187. This type of EDR system confers the power of final resolution of electoral disputes on courts that are specialized in electoral matters and enjoy functional independence, either as part of the judicial branch or independent of the three branches of government.

188. The first such EDR system, under the Electoral Court (Corte Electoral) of Uruguay, was provided for in statute in 1924. In 1925 the Electoral Certifications Tribunal (Tribunal Calificador de Elecciones) of Chile was provided for in the Chilean Constitution. Over the course of the 20th century, this type of electoral court was gradually established in the vast majority of Latin American countries. It can be said that such electoral courts are a Latin American contribution to political science and to election law, and have contributed significantly to the processes of democratization and democratic consolidation in the countries of the region, especially since the 'third wave of democratization' of the late 1980s and 1990s.

189. The creation of specialized electoral courts was a response by various countries to the need to safeguard the judicial nature of the function of passing judgement on elections, and take it away from the political assemblies which had previously had the responsibility, without exposing the judicial branch (where the specialized court is autonomous) or at least the Supreme Court (where it belongs to the judicial branch) to recurrent questioning and pressure by political party interests.

190. On the basis of the classification criteria adopted above, the only courts that should be included in this category are those specialized electoral courts (whether part of the judicial branch or autonomous) that are authorized to issue the *final ruling* relating to challenges brought against election results, against which no judicial or constitutional remedy or appeal may be invoked – as in Chile, the Dominican Republic, Ecuador, Mexico, and Peru, as well as Albania, Greece, the Palestinian Authority, South Africa and Sweden. While the electoral courts in Albania, Greece, and Mexico are part of their respective judicial branches, those in the other countries mentioned are autonomous. All, however, enjoy functional independence.

191. Specialized electoral courts whose decisions can be challenged on constitutional grounds before the Supreme Court (as in Brazil, El Salvador, Honduras, Panama and Paraguay), or a Constitutional Court (as in Bolivia and Ecuador) or both in succession (as in Guatemala) should therefore be classified with those EDR systems in which the final decision on electoral challenges vests with the regular courts of the judicial branch or in constitutional courts or councils. All the electoral courts mentioned in this paragraph, apart from those of Brazil and Paraguay which are part of the judiciary, are autonomous or independent.

192. Not included in this category are the specialized electoral courts which, although the final resolution of all types of election is entrusted to them, simultaneously have the functions of organizing and administering the electoral process, meaning that they also act as the EMB. This is the case in Costa Rica, Nicaragua and Uruguay. Regardless of whether they are designated electoral tribunals or courts, because these three perform electoral management functions as well being autonomous or independent, they are placed with those EDR systems in which the final resolution of election disputes is entrusted to the EMB.

193. Many EDRSs in Latin America confer on specialized electoral courts the final resolution of challenges to elections. Most of the region's autonomous and independent electoral organs have administrative, judicial and even regulatory functions. However, some countries have two autonomous and independent specialized electoral authorities, one of which is entrusted with administrative aspects, organizing, directing and overseeing elections (the EMB), while the other makes judgements on challenges to the EMB's decisions (the EDRB). Systems that combine the possibility of bringing a challenge before an independent EMB with an appeal to an autonomous and independent electoral judicial body (as in Chile, Dominican Republic, Ecuador, and Peru) should be distinguished from those where the appellate body is part of the judiciary (as in Mexico and Venezuela). Outside Latin America, Albania, Greece, the Palestinian Authority, South Africa and Sweden also fall into the latter category.

194. Challenges to the election results issued by the independent EMB are resolved in the last instance in Albania by the Electoral College (Kolegji Zgjedhor), which is a specific tribunal made up of eight judges from the courts of appeal who are selected and appointed by the Superior Judicial Council. In Greece they are resolved by the Special Supreme Court (Anωtato Eidiko Dikasthrio), which is made up of presiding and regular judges from other courts of the judicial branch. In the Palestinian Authority they are resolved by the Electoral Cases Court (Intikhabat mahkamet al iste'naf), which is composed of nine judges appointed by the President of the Palestinian Authority, based on the recommendations of the Supreme Judicial Council (Majles al qada' al a'la). In South Africa, they are resolved by the Electoral Court, which was established in 1999, and in Sweden by the Elections Review Council (Valprövningsnämnden), made up of seven members appointed by the Parliament (Riksdag). The electoral courts in South Africa, Sweden and the Palestinian Authority are autonomous and independent from any other branch of government.

195. Several of these specialized electoral tribunals operate on a permanent basis, at least as regards the members of the highest-ranking organs; this the case in most Latin American countries. However, others are temporary and are only constituted when elections are to be held. Examples are to be found in Albania, Chile and Greece, although the members of these tribunals also enjoy security of tenure, and therefore judicial independence, since they belong to other courts when they are not performing the electoral jurisdictional function. Exclusive and full-time specialization in electoral jurisdictional matters can lead to more professional performance and makes it possible to keep up with the latest developments in the field and to address any challenges filed throughout the electoral cycle, including its pre- and post-electoral stages. This, however, may entail greater costs. In societies that do not have a high level of electoral litigation certain sectors of society may not appreciate that their existence during the pre- and post-electoral periods is justifiable.

c) EDR systems entrusted to an electoral management body with judicial powers

196. Under this type of EDR system, responsibility is entrusted to an independent EMB which, in addition to taking charge of organizing and administering electoral processes, has judicial powers to resolve challenges and issue a final ruling as to the validity of the electoral process.

197. This model has been developed mainly in Latin America. An EDR system in this category not only has jurisdiction to resolve challenges, which is common, but also takes decisions that are final, including on the validity of electoral processes, and not open to review by any judicial, administrative or legislative body.

198. Among the EDR systems entrusted to independent EMBs with ultimate judicial power are the Supreme Electoral Council (Consejo Supremo Electoral) of Nicaragua, the Supreme Elections Tribunal (Tribunal Supremo de Elecciones) of Costa Rica and the Electoral Court of Uruguay as well as the Supreme Election Council (Yüksek Seçim Kurulu Başkanliği) of Turkey. The Nicaraguan Constitution defines the Supreme Electoral Council as the 'Poder Electoral' (electoral branch of government). The constitutional powers conferred on the Supreme Elections Tribunal of Costa Rica and the Electoral Court of Uruguay, as well as the structural safeguards with which they are endowed, make these three bodies tantamount to a fourth branch of government.

199. Some of the EDR systems whose bodies are included in this section are called electoral tribunals or electoral courts and their respective members enjoy conditions of security of employment equivalent to those enjoyed by members of the judicial branch. They are vested with the authority to organize and administer electoral processes, and are therefore independent EMBs, but have significant judicial powers and thus from a technical standpoint they should be considered judicial bodies in their own right.

200. In contrast to the specialized electoral courts discussed in the previous section, EMBs with judicial powers are not in charge of resolving challenges brought against the actions, procedures and decisions of all other bodies, but only challenges to the actions of a lower ranking body. In addition, unlike other specialized electoral courts, the decisions of which may be reviewed by a Supreme Court or Constitutional Court, the decisions of the EMBs with judicial powers considered here are final and not subject to review.

201. In general, EMBs with judicial powers have a pyramidal structure, at the top of which is a central, high ranking entity at the national level, to which other intermediate bodies are subordinated. For the most part, they reflect the territorial, political, administrative and electoral divisions of the country (often called regional, state, provincial, departmental, municipal or district councils or boards) right down to the polling station where citizens cast their ballots.

202. Special mention should be made of Uruguay where, since the 1997 reform, the Electoral Court also hears all matters related to electoral actions, procedures and decisions of the political parties' internal elections to choose their candidates for the national presidency and the legislature (presidential and legislative elections are held simultaneously on the same day nationwide), and also for elections for members of a party's internal national decision-making bodies. The Electoral Court organizes those internal party elections in addition to its jurisdiction over national elections, issues the regulations needed to hold them, and judges all claims and appeals brought against electoral and party actions and decisions. No appeal is possible against its rulings.

203. In Latin America there is a growing interest in safeguarding elections from the influence of any external authority, especially from the three branches of government. Many consider that the best guarantee of free, fair and genuine elections is to keep all electoral matters, including the EDR system, under the responsibility of an independent and autonomous electoral authority – an independent EMB with judicial powers which directs the electoral process from beginning to end and resolves any challenges with rulings that are final.

204. Article 79 of the Turkish Constitution establishes that the Supreme Election Council (Yüksek Seçim Kurulu Başkanliği) shall execute all the functions for ensuring the fair and orderly conduct of elections from the beginning to the end of the electoral process, as well as carrying out any investigations and taking the final decision on all irregularities, complaints and objections concerning the elections during and after the polling, and verifying the election returns for the members of the Turkish Grand National Assembly (Büyük Millet Meclisi). It also sets out that no appeal shall be made to any authority against the decisions of the Supreme Election Council.

205. There are cases of EDR systems entrusted to an independent EMB that are highly successful and credible, as in Costa Rica and Uruguay. These have become paradigms in their region by virtue of their respective normative frameworks and, above all, the performance and quality of their members. Both are examples of EDRSs in democracies that are not large and have adopted good practices. One factor contributing to their success is undoubtedly the deeply ingrained political culture in their societies, which are considered to be among those most committed to democratic principles and values in Latin America. The electoral courts in both countries have probably contributed to the development of that political culture during their many years of service.

206. Even so, the possible adoption of an EDR system entrusted to the EMB, with absolute judicial powers, should be considered very carefully in view of the potential for the abuse of such powers by independent bodies – especially when their decisions are not subject to appeal or to review. There may be more likelihood of abuses of power when a single authority is responsible for both running elections and adjudicating on disputes which arise out of these elections, and the EMB acts both as judge and challenged party in the same matter. The same argument is used to support moving jurisdiction over EDR systems from legislative bodies to judicial organs, insofar as a great many electoral disputes stem from challenges to the actions, procedures and decisions of the EMBs.

207. Nonetheless, the Declaration on Criteria for Free and Fair Elections (see box 5.1) regards an independent and impartial electoral commission as an acceptable body to determine complaints relating to the electoral process.

208. Various factors affect the credibility of electoral commissions. Among these special mention should be made of the system for selecting and appointing their members, as well as the procedures for determining liability and ensuring accountability that must be addressed in line with the law. These are analysed in chapter 6 of this Handbook. One effective approach may be to combine an independent EMB with an EDRS entrusted to an independent judicial body, in which challenges begin at the administrative level but parties who are not satisfied with a ruling can challenge it before an independent judicial organ. Several recent electoral legal frameworks have adopted this type of EDRS in an effort to resolve a large number of challenges at the administrative level by binding and enforceable decisions, thereby reducing the need to involve a judicial body. Although it might be considered optimal for such a judicial organ to be a specialized electoral court, as is the case in several countries, such an alternative could hardly be considered viable in many democracies for financial reasons.

d) EDR systems entrusted to an ad hoc body

209. Finally, some EDR systems involve an ad hoc body derived from a provisional or transitional arrangement. This might be an institutional solution, often sponsored by international organizations, in order to guarantee the holding of a free, fair and genuine election according to the legal framework following serious conflict in a country, as in Cambodia in 1993, Bosnia and Herzegovina in 1996 or Nepal in 2008. The important feature of this type of EDR system is that the mechanism for resolving electoral disputes is provisional in nature: it may be used for a specific election or perhaps more than one, but it is a transitional measure until a permanent EDR system is established.

i) An ad hoc body created with international involvement

210. This type of EDR system derives from the creation of an ad hoc body for the resolution of challenges to the conduct and results of an election. This ad hoc body may be the same as the ad hoc body which organizes the election itself, but need not be so. It is a solution sponsored by the international community through one or more international organizations, such as the United Nations, the Organization for Security and Co-operation in Europe (OSCE) or the Organization of American States (OAS), as part of the process of post-conflict transition. The ad hoc body often includes members designated by an international organization. Its purpose is to ensure that a free, fair and genuine election is held from which no group or sector is excluded. Such bodies contributed to elections in Cambodia in 1993, Bosnia and Herzegovina in 1996, Timor-Leste in 2001, and Afghanistan in 2005.

ii) An ad hoc body created as an internal national institutional solution

211. On occasion, an ad hoc body is established in a country to be in charge of the EDR system for one or more specific elections as a transitional, internal solution. This is usually the result of agreement and negotiation among the main political forces in order to get round a serious conflict, possibly as a result of a constitution not having entered into force or the non-functionality of the electoral institutions originally provided for. This type of EDR system is usually established by a body of national law – with transitional, constitutional or statutory provisions – or even a peace agreement between belligerent forces. It is made up exclusively of nationals from the country involved, with the purpose of holding free, fair and genuine elections in line with the law.

212. This happened in Nepal, where the Constituent Assembly Court (Sambidhan Shabha Adalat) was provided for in Nepal's Interim Constitution of 2006 to resolve challenges to the election of members of the Constituent Assembly (Sambidhan Shabha) which took place as a result of the 2006 Comprehensive Peace Agreement. The Constituent Assembly was installed in May 2008 and was given two years to approve a new constitution for Nepal. To this end, the Constituent Assembly Court was made up of three members selected from among the members of the Supreme Court of Nepal (Sarbochcha Adalat), on the understanding that there would also be an EMB (the Election Commission of Nepal, Nirbachan Aayog) entrusted with organizing elections.

213. The key characteristic of this type of EDRS is its provisional or transitional nature. The ad hoc body is tasked with resolving the challenges arising from a specific election or series of elections held in a given period. This ad hoc body may be legislative, judicial or administrative in nature, but it contrasts with the EDRSs analysed in the sections above.

214. This type of EDRS is also different from cases in which a serious conflict arises in the context of an election related to the process or the results, and the resolution of the conflict or of the respective challenge involves the creation after the event on an extraordinary and exceptional basis by the political actors of an ad hoc body other than the one originally provided for in the electoral legal framework. Examples of the latter occurred during the elections in the United States in 1876 and Kenya in 2007. It is always important to support the observance of the laws and institutions of an EDR system by all involved as an essential characteristic of the rule of law; however, occasionally severe differences arise among the political forces with respect to the development or outcome of an election process and the institutions in place are not robust enough to resolve them in a way that is

accepted as legitimate. It is then possible, and even advisable – in order to avoid, for example, the outbreak of violence – to adopt on an extraordinary and exceptional basis an alternative and institutional mechanism for settling such disputes (on AEDR mechanisms see chapter 8).

CHAPTER 6

CHAPTER 6

Principles and guarantees of EDR systems

1. Introduction

215. Whichever type of electoral dispute resolution system is adopted, certain principles and guarantees should be provided for and applied to ensure the holding of free, fair and genuine elections. These principles should be observed and applied not only by the EDRB, which is the instance of last resort for deciding an election, but also at every level or instance of the EDRS, starting from the first decision on an electoral dispute.

216. 'Principles' here mean the supreme and paramount ethical/political values of a legal order, a sector of it or an institution. They set a standard or inspire those to whom they are directed – either the voters in general or the EDRBs in particular. Their observance or enforcement not only bestows legitimacy or moral or political authority, but also increases the likelihood, based on experience, that they will serve their purpose. 'Principles of the EDR system' thus refers to the fundamental values that help to guarantee the holding of free, fair and genuine elections, strictly in keeping with the law.

217. An EDR system needs to adhere both to fundamental principles on elections, such as holding free, fair and genuine elections or universal suffrage, and to general principles that apply in the various areas of the law such as constitutionality, legality, judicial independence, due process of law and the right to a competent defence. Further principles exist that are specific to EDRSs, such as the principle of irrevocability, which establishes that the successive stages of the electoral process must be definitive, that is, once any particular stage is concluded (e.g. the preparatory stage of the election), there can after a specific deadline be no further challenge during a later stage (e.g. on election day or at the post-election stage) to actions or decisions made about that stage. However, there could be exceptions to such a principle in some

EDR systems. For example, although the EMB reviews candidates who are registered or nominated to verify that they meet the qualifying requirements to become a legislator during the stage of preparation of the election, some systems allow or even require this to be reviewed again at the post-election stage before the proclamation of the winner, and both decisions could be challenged before an EDRB.

218. 'Guarantees' are any legal means or instruments by which values, rights or institutions that are protected or established by the legal order on behalf of the voter are assured, protected, supported, defended or safeguarded. The guarantees, both structural and procedural, of the EDR system seek to ensure that elections are held in line with the law and are free, fair and genuine, and also to protect or restore the enjoyment of electoral rights. In this sense, the EDR system constitutes the overarching guarantee of the observance of democracy and the rule of law.

219. The main guarantee of an effective EDR system is the availability of a remedy that can correct an irregularity by annulling, revoking, modifying or even just acknowledging it. Other mechanisms can either deter or punish a transgressor through a regime of criminal or administrative liability (see figure 2.1). Proper institutional design can safeguard or foster certain values; for example, it is more likely that impartiality will be observed if the EDRB has more than one member.

220. It is common for the body of first instance for the hearing of an electoral complaint to be an organ of the EMB, the action of which – for example, a refusal to register a candidate – is challenged by that candidate or by a political party. Several EDR systems provide for the possibility of an administrative challenge before a higher-level official or a complaints organ of the EMB. Once that higher-level person or organ issues its decision, the possibility of a challenge is often provided for – if the refusal is confirmed, by the political party or candidate that brought the original challenge; if it is overturned, by some other political party or candidate. This challenge is heard by a judicial body – a regular court of the judicial branch, a constitutional court, an administrative court or an electoral court – which generally issues the final judgement. In some cases, however, two successive judicial challenges are provided for – for example first before a regular court and then before a constitutional court. It is most common, however, for the challenge mechanism to include first a hearing before the highest decision-making level of the EMB and then a hearing before a judicial body.

221. Similarly, in the case of election results, it is common in various EDR systems that, faced with an irregularity at a polling station on election day, the political parties or candidates affected may question or challenge the result set out in the official vote count from that polling station before an organ

of the EMB at a higher level. This organ generally has the power to correct the alleged irregularity. Once the official result with respect to an election is issued, several EDR systems provide for the right of political parties or candidates that are not satisfied to challenge it before a judicial body (regular, constitutional, administrative or electoral court). On occasion this judicial stage provides for a challenge first before a regular court of the judicial branch or an electoral court, and then before a constitutional court, which issues the final ruling. Some EDR systems still provide for the possibility of a subsequent challenge before the legislative body, which in such systems has the final decision on the validity of the election and its results.

222. It is thus common for an EDRS to provide for several types of challenge and several mechanisms for resolving them – the EMB, one or more judicial bodies and, on occasion, a legislative body. While EDR systems generally provide for different types of mechanism, all of them should be consistent with the principles and guarantees of EDR systems in order to ensure that all electoral actions, procedures and decisions are in line with the principles of constitutionality and legality.

223. In identifying the principles and guarantees of EDR systems, the intention is to establish parameters in keeping with international commitments and standards, 'good practices', and 'minimum conditions' required for considering an EDR system to be in line with the principles characteristic of constitutional democracy under the rule of law. It should be noted that identifying such principles and guarantees is not intended to inhibit other experiments or practices, as long as their purpose is to consolidate the holding of elections that are free, fair and genuine, and in keeping with the law. Commitments and standards are constantly evolving in both theory and practice.

224. Citizens, candidates, political parties, the media, the authorities and all those who play a role in electoral processes are expected to comply with electoral law voluntarily, of their own accord. However, an EDR system is needed to ensure the observance of the entire electoral law and to address those cases in which the law is violated. The EDR system is an essential form of support to ensure that electoral actions, procedures and decisions are in keeping with electoral and other law.

225. Among the measures aimed at ensuring that electoral challenges are resolved lawfully, there exist both structural guarantees and procedural guarantees. Structural guarantees are those legal instruments for ensuring that EDRBs act with autonomy, independence and impartiality (for example the procedure for selecting and appointing their members). Procedural guarantees are those legal measures that help to ensure that the mechanisms for bringing and resolving electoral challenges have attributes which promote electoral justice and ensure that the EDR system is both effective and efficient

(for example by guaranteeing effective and inclusive access to the electoral justice system).

2. The tendency towards establishing judicial EDR systems

226. Even though the first democratic regimes to adopt an EDR system entrusted the final decision on the certification of electoral processes to the legislative bodies themselves, by the last third of the 19th century a judicial EDR system had been established in the UK, when the regular courts were given jurisdiction over resolving challenges to parliamentary elections (see paragraph 171). Gradually, in the course of the 20th century, authority was transferred to judicial bodies (regular, constitutional, administrative or specialized electoral courts), an EMB with judicial powers or, exceptionally, an ad hoc body as a provisional or transitional arrangement. In general, there has been a marked trend towards establishing judicial bodies to handle EDR, or to including EDR within the remit of existing judicial bodies.

227. Judicial bodies entrusted with EDR may have the formal power to make the final decision on a challenge. However, even where the final decision remains in the hands of a legislative body or political assembly, there is generally provision for prior challenges before judicial bodies. This applies not only to challenges to election results but also to disputes during the preparatory phase of the election cycle. In addition, it increasingly applies to political parties' internal procedures for selecting their leaders and candidates for office and for disciplining their members, as is provided for in a growing number of countries. Examples can be found in Argentina, Bolivia, Costa Rica, Germany, Mexico, Puerto Rico, Spain and the United States. Another indicator of this judicial trend is that several of the members of the body in charge of organizing, administering and overseeing elections (the EMB) either come from the judicial branch or are appointed in a similar way to that of judges, and must meet the same requirements as judges or be accorded guarantees equivalent to those given to high-ranking judicial officers. The trend in the judicial EDRSs that were established in the early 20th century was to give jurisdiction to regular courts that are part of the judiciary – particularly in those countries with a common law tradition, although it has spread to others and continues to be the most widespread system. After the First and Second world wars it became more common to assign responsibility to constitutional courts, particularly in several continental European countries but also in Africa and Asia. Since the third wave of democratization in the late 20th century it has been common to attribute such jurisdiction to specialized electoral courts, especially in Latin America but also in some countries in Africa, Asia and Europe.

228. The judicial approach to EDR systems is also consistent with the right to an effective public remedy before a judge or court with jurisdiction that is

independent and impartial, and previously established by law with the proper guarantees, as prescribed by several international human rights instruments (specifically, articles 2(3)(a) and 14(1) of the 1966 International Covenant on Civil and Political Rights).

229. The rationale for establishing judicial bodies in EDRSs is that electoral disputes and challenges must be resolved on the basis of the principles of constitutionality and legality, that is, in keeping with the law. They must not be resolved based on political expediency, which often happened with EDR systems that were entrusted to legislative bodies or political assemblies. This has also implied – as experience in comparative law shows – a change in attitude on the part of political parties, election officials and all the other third parties or persons with an interest in a given electoral challenge. Such a system accords priority to institutional means for resolving electoral disputes, and the facts, arguments and evidence that may be produced before a judicial body have had to be brought into line with the technical-legal requirements for their admissibility and consideration.

230. Jurisdiction over a political matter is not the same thing as political jurisdiction, that is, jurisdiction based on political criteria. (One example of political jurisdiction is the jurisdiction that some EDR systems confer on political assemblies or legislative chambers to certify or sit in judgement on the election of their respective members.) A clear-cut distinction needs to be drawn between the two. The fact that a dispute (such as an electoral dispute) is political does not imply that a judicial decision that puts an end to it should be made on the basis of political considerations, convenience or expediency. It must be based on the law. In this way, power is subjugated to reason, not reason to power. Hence the fundamental importance of legal argument in recent times, in both theory and practice, such as that developed by judicial EDRBs. Their importance means that EDRBs and their decisions generally undergo strict scrutiny by the public. The credibility of an EDRS depends on the solid foundation and reasoning of its electoral judgements.

231. The legal oversight undertaken by EDR systems, particularly judicial review, has a number of characteristics which distinguish it from political review.

- It has an objective basis, since the standard of review is a pre-existing normative framework, not one determined or chosen by the body that carries out the review.
- It is based on legal reasoning and not on political considerations.
- It is mandatory; a judicial EDRB must necessarily undertake such a review whenever a matter that falls under its jurisdiction is brought before it.
- It is entrusted to an independent and impartial body, which needs to be endowed with the specific technical capacity to resolve legal issues.

232. In adopting the judicial approach to EDR systems, it is desirable that the judicial bodies entrusted with resolving electoral challenges (both the body with the authority to issue the final decision of judgement, and any other body which forms at least one of the prior mechanisms involved in considering challenges) should have at least three members. This is particularly important for the highest level body of the EDRS, as it helps to ensure the guarantees of independence and impartiality inherent to that body and its members individually, in addition to providing other personal guarantees, such as responsibility and accountability.

3. Guiding principles for EDRBs and the design of structural guarantees to entrench them

233. One fundamental aspect of electoral justice is thus the design of what are called 'structural guarantees' or 'judicial guarantees', which are those legal instruments for ensuring that the bodies entrusted with EDR systems can act independently in relation to all other government bodies, political parties and other electoral stakeholders. This is essential if the EDRBs are to be able to resolve the cases put to them objectively and impartially on the basis of the merits of the case.

234. These structural or judicial guarantees are designed especially for *judicial* EDRBs (whether these are regular, constitutional, administrative or specialized electoral courts). It is also advisable, to the extent possible, to provide for such guarantees in other types of EDRB, whether it is an EMB or an international, ad hoc or even legislative body (when the corresponding EDRS combines final decision by the legislative body with a prior challenge before a judicial body). This is intended to ensure that such bodies will resolve the challenges under their jurisdiction with functional independence and impartiality and in keeping with the law. This is more difficult in principle in the case of *legislative bodies* or *governmental EMBs*, but if they are entrusted with part of the EDRS they should still demonstrate their functional independence and impartiality for the sake of the legitimacy and credibility of the system even though in general they do not embody all the guarantees analysed below. EDR systems entrusted to specialized electoral courts incorporate more of these guarantees.

235. Structural or judicial guarantees embody the guiding principles of EDR. These include, among others, legal recognition of the independence of the EDRB, and of the independence and impartiality of its members; a regime for accountability and liability of the EDRB; the integrity and professionalism of EDRB members; and the financial autonomy and sustainability of the EDRB (see box 6.1). In this respect, chapters 4, 6 and 7 of *Electoral Management Design: The International IDEA Handbook* are a useful reference point: many of the principles and guarantees relating to EMBs that are analysed there are also applicable to the design of EDRBs.

Box 6.1. Guiding principles of EDRB design from which structural guarantees are developed

- The independence of the EDRB
- The independence and impartiality of EDRB members
- A regime for the accountability and liability of the EDRB and its members
- The integrity and professionalism of the members of the EDRB
- The financial independence and sustainability of the EDRB

a) Independence of the EDRB

236. The independence of the EDRB is, like that of any court of law, a cornerstone of the rule of law. It is also a cornerstone of respect for electoral and human rights. The functional independence of the EDRB, including the office of the competent body to investigate and prosecute electoral crimes and offences, is a precondition for the fair, effective and impartial resolution of electoral challenges. The same is true of the EMB in its role of hearing and deciding some electoral challenges.

237. While those EDRBs that are part of a country's judicial branch embody the guarantees inherent to that judiciary, the constitutional arrangements in most countries that entrust the EDR system to other bodies (a constitutional court or council, administrative court, specialized electoral court, independent EMB or an ad hoc body) generally grant them broad functional independence in relation to the traditional branches of government (legislative, executive and judicial).

238. Constitutional courts or councils generally have a constitutional rank and status equivalent to that of the other branches of government. The other EDRBs that are judicial in nature are often considered independent constitutional organs, and there are even specialized electoral courts and independent EMBs that are designated either implicitly or explicitly in the constitution as a branch of government. This is the case, for example, with the Supreme Electoral Council of Nicaragua, which, as is noted above, is explicitly considered the Poder Electoral (electoral branch), tantamount to a fourth branch of government (see paragraph 198), and is also the case in Venezuela.

239. According to contemporary constitutional theory, it is possible to have constitutionally created bodies (e.g. constitutional courts or councils, autonomous administrative or electoral courts and/or independent EMBs) that are not situated in any of the three classic branches of government. Although constitutions generally provide that sovereignty is exercised indirectly through the legislative, executive and judicial branches of government, none prohibits

the existence of autonomous constitutionally created bodies that are not part of any of these three branches of government.

240. Although the discussion below deals with the structural guarantees that are generally conferred by the constitutional order in most of the judicial EDR systems, it often focuses on guarantees with respect to the specialized electoral courts that are found mainly in Latin America.

Box 6.2. Guarantees of the independence of EDRBs

- Independence is provided for in the constitution
- Functional independence
- Administrative and, in some cases, financial independence

i) Constitutional and statutory provisions for the independence of EDR systems

241. Constitutional or statutory provisions often expressly establish that EDRBs enjoy autonomy or independence in the performance of their functions. Given the importance of the work of EDRBs, their functional independence is essential.

242. EDR systems entrusted to regular courts which are part of the judiciary (see paragraphs 170–176) frequently have their independence established in the constitution. Examples include: 'The courts and tribunals shall constitute a separate power and shall be independent of other branches of power' (Poland); 'Courts are independent and subject only to the Constitution and the law' (Timor-Leste); 'No law shall be passed reorganizing the Judiciary when it undermines the security of tenure of its Members' (the Philippines); 'Judiciary power shall be independent. ... Courts shall be separated and independent in their work and they shall perform their duties in accordance with the constitution, Law and other general acts, when stipulated by the Law, generally accepted rules of international law and ratified international contracts' (Serbia). This independence may also be established in a specific act or statute, such as the Federal Constitutional Law on the Judicial System of the Russian Federation, which provides that the 'judicial power shall be separate and shall act independently of the legislative and executive powers'.

243. Constitutional provisions on the independence of the judicial branch also apply to an EDR system entrusted to constitutional courts which are part of the judiciary (see paragraphs 181–182). For example, 'The independence of courts shall be guaranteed by the Constitution and laws' (Armenia); 'The courts shall be independent and subject only to the law' (Portugal); or 'the

judicial powers shall be independent with the authority to conduct judicial affairs in order to uphold law and justice … implemented by … a constitutional court' (Indonesia). Sometimes, however, there are special provisions: 'The Constitutional Court… is an independent judicial body charged with the protection of constitutionality' (Slovakia).

244. Although constitutional provisions about the independence of constitutional courts or councils which are not part of the judiciary are unusual, such bodies have a constitutional rank and status equivalent to that of the highest judicial body and their members enjoy similar structural guarantees, as is discussed in paragraph 298.

245. As for EDRSs entrusted to administrative courts, Article 5 of the Regulatory Statute on the Administration of Justice of Colombia expressly establishes that 'The Judicial Branch is independent and autonomous in the performance of its constitutional and statutory function of administering justice'. Similarly, Article 1 of the Constitution of Finland provides that 'Judicial powers are exercised by independent courts of law, with the Supreme Court and the Supreme Administrative Court as the highest instances'.

246. In an example of an EDR system entrusted to specialized electoral courts, Article 99 of the Mexican Constitution provides that the EDRB – the Electoral Court of the Judicial Branch of the Federation (Tribunal Electoral del Poder Judicial de la Federación) – will, except for an action challenging the constitutionality of general election laws and statutes which comes under the jurisdiction of the Supreme Court, be the highest-level judicial authority in relation to electoral matters. Also, Article 17 of the Constitution provides that the statutes shall establish the means necessary for guaranteeing the independence of the courts and the full enforcement of their rulings provided for in the Organic Law on the Judicial Branch of the Federation.

247. An example of an EDRS entrusted to the EMB is found in Article 99 of the Costa Rican Constitution, which states that 'The organization, direction, and supervision of acts pertaining to suffrage are the exclusive function of the Supreme Electoral Tribunal, which does enjoy independence in the performance of its duties'.

ii) Functional independence of the EDRB

248. An EDRB enjoys functional independence when it is separate from any other body and acts without institutional subordination to any other body. It cannot be under any legal obligation in the performance of its functions to any other body, either superior to it or belonging to any other type of authority. It is bound only by the provisions of the constitution, statute law and any other applicable provisions. In several EDRSs, greater functional independence

derives from the fact that the decisions of the EDRB are specified to be not subject to subsequent review or modification by any other body.

249. The fact that an EDRB belongs to the judicial branch, in which there are higher-ranking bodies such as the Supreme Court, does not mean that it has to answer to a higher-ranking court. Nor does the possibility of its decisions being subject to review, overturned or amended mean that its functional independence is lost or limited. The relevant consideration is that the EDRB should be subject only to its mandate as set out in the constitution and the law when ruling on the merits of the challenges filed.

250. In general, it may be considered good practice to entrust an EDR system to permanent and independent bodies. When electoral laws provide EDRBs with mandates that do not authorize them to continue to operate beyond the electoral period, other bodies must be entrusted with resolving any possible challenges that arise during the pre-electoral and post-electoral periods. While arguments about the overall priorities for use of scarce human and financial resources are important, they need to be set against the potential costs arising from lower credibility in resolving electoral disputes which arise outside the electoral period itself.

251. Several countries vest an important power to develop and adopt regulations under a country's electoral law in the supreme body of an EDRS which takes the form of special electoral courts. Some electoral courts are authorized to issue by-laws, as for example in Mexico. This power can also be given to an EMB with the authority to resolve electoral disputes, which is the case in the Dominican Republic, El Salvador, Gambia, Uruguay and Yemen.

252. In addition, some countries give EDRBs the power to initiate electoral legislation, for example, Ecuador and Peru. Others establish an obligation to consider the opinion of the EDRB in the legislative process relating to electoral issues, as in Costa Rica where a two-thirds majority of the legislature is required before it can go against the opinion of the Supreme Elections Tribunal.

253. Some EDR systems also empower the highest-level court in the EDR system to establish binding judicial precedent through case law. The Superior Chamber of the Electoral Court of the Judicial Branch of the Federation in Mexico does so when it reiterates the same view in three consecutive cases, or when it resolves the conflicting views of two regional chambers, or of one regional chamber and the Superior Chamber, and determines the criteria that should prevail. This case law is binding in future cases, not only on the lower EDRBs but also on the EMB. This is common practice in judicial systems, particularly in common law countries that have the *stare decisis* doctrine. However, some countries with a civil law tradition, such as El Salvador, do not allow binding case law.

iii) Administrative and financial independence

254. Another important aspect to consider in evaluating the degree of functional independence of specialized electoral courts or EMBs with judicial powers is their authority in budgetary and administrative issues. In some cases a preliminary proposed budget is drawn up by the president of the EDRB; in others, the EDRB itself draws up a proposed budget while in plenary session.

255. Special legal provisions in electoral laws for EMB financing are commonplace (see chapter 7 of *Electoral Management Design: The International IDEA Handbook*). However, such provisions for EDRBs are much less common, and it is rarely possible to speak of the financial self-sufficiency of EDRBs. However, there is a spectrum of financial independence which ranges from the annual allocation of a given percentage of the state budget provided for by constitutional law, as in Guatemala (see box 6.3), to those cases where there is no specific financial provision for the EDRB, as in Chile and Panama where the general common provisions on budgetary matters apply. These consist of a negotiation with the appropriate office of the executive branch in charge of drawing up a proposed budget to be submitted to the legislative branch for its consideration and approval. In Uruguay, although the executive branch can introduce changes to the proposed budget of the electoral body, both the amended and unamended budgets have to be submitted to the legislative branch for debate and approval.

Box 6.3. Guatemala

In Guatemala, 0.5 per cent of the General Budget of Regular Outlays is allocated to the EDRB, and in an election year this allocation is increased by the amount necessary as estimated by the Supreme Electoral Tribunal (Tribunal Supremo Electoral). If it does not receive the funds it needs, the Tribunal is authorized to take out bank loans or request any external assistance that does not compromise government finances or its own independence.

256. Between these two extremes are EDRBs which are allowed to submit their proposed expenditure budget directly to the legislative branch, as in Bolivia and Peru, and those in which no office of the executive branch is able to modify such proposals, as in Costa Rica and, as part of the budget for the judicial branch, Mexico and Venezuela.

257. Lack of financial autonomy can hinder effective dispute resolution. The Election Supervisory Committee for the Indonesian General Elections in 2004 (Panitia Pengawas Pemilihan Umum, PANWASLU), a body that was tasked by law with supervising the electoral process and had authority

over dispute resolution, relied on the EMB for funding. Despite public calls for it to be made independent of the EMB and other institutions of the state, the General Election Law stipulated that it should be established by the EMB and be administratively accountable to the EMB. This legislation resulted in a bottleneck when the EMB failed to forward the Committee's draft budget to the legislature in due time, resulting in severe budget cuts. One notable request that was cut by the EMB was the appointment of election supervisors at the village level (one per village). This weakened the Committee's dispute resolution capacity. This scheme was later reinstated by lawmakers and included in a subsequent law that governed the 2009 general elections.

258. Following the trend that courts should not be involved in administrative issues, which are entrusted to judicial councils (on which usually only some of the members are judges), administration, oversight and discipline of Mexico's federal Electoral Court (Tribunal Electoral del Poder Judicial de la Federación) is entrusted to an Administrative Committee made up of the President of the Electoral Court, who chairs it, a judge from its upper chamber, chosen randomly, and three members of the Federal Judicial Council (Consejo de la Judicatura Federal).

b) Independence and impartiality of the members of the EDRB

259. In order to impart justice in a manner that is absolutely faithful to the mandate of the constitution and the law, it is not enough for EDRBs to enjoy structural autonomy and functional independence. It is also necessary that *those who judge* electoral matters act with absolute independence, impartiality and professionalism in their individual capacity, without recognizing any subordination to any interest or will other than those stated by law. The mechanisms for guaranteeing the independence and impartiality of the members of the EDRB are shown in box 6.4.

Box 6.4. Guarantees for the independence and impartiality of the members of the EDRB

- Establishing their independence and impartiality in the constitution
- Procedure for selection and appointment
- Requirements for suitability and professionalism
- Stability and career service
- Appropriate remuneration
- Incompatibility with holding other positions
- Provisions for standing aside from a case where impartiality may be questioned

i) Establishing the independence and impartiality of EDRB members

260. The independence, impartiality and professionalism of the members who make up EDRBs (whether judicial, administrative, international, ad hoc or legislative bodies) may be guaranteed, among other general principles, by entrenching them in the constitution or in statutes. Judicial independence means not only resolving disputes lawfully, independently of any political pressures that may be brought to bear, and in timely fashion, but also that no other government bodies or political forces impose sanctions or reprisals on honest judges who decide cases against them, or reward judges who resolve them in a manner that is favourable to their political interests.

261. Constitutional or legal provisions to entrench the independence of EDRB members may for example:

- establish requirements of suitability for appointment as an EDRB member;
- regulate the procedure for the selection and designation of EDRB members in a way that ensures that they will not be bound by debts of gratitude, fidelity or animosity to any individual or group;
- determine that EDRB members will be barred from deciding specific cases in which there is a basis for considering that they have or may be perceived to have a personal interest which may jeopardize the objectivity and impartiality with which the court treats a litigant;
- ensure the long-term stability, predetermined by law, of the mandate of those who sit in judgement, the amount of their salary, and the time frames and terms and conditions of their appointment. These would not be subject to change by a political or administrative decision of any person or group, but only by a change in the law; and
- regulate the regime of accountability and liability by virtue of which those EDRB members who abuse the public authority they hold may be sanctioned.

Box 6.5. Constitutional provisions for the independence of EDRB members

Regular court as EDRB

Article 35 of the Constitution of the Republic of Ireland:
'All judges shall be independent in the exercise of their judicial functions and subject only to this Constitution and the law.'

Article III Section 1 of the Constitution of the United States of America:
'The Judges, both of the supreme and inferior Courts, shall hold their Offices during good Behavior, and shall, at stated Times, receive for their Services a Compensation which shall not be diminished during their Continuance in Office.'

(cont.)

Article 131 of the Constitution of the Republic of Guyana:
'Judges shall have full security of office…'

Constitutional court which is part of the judicial branch as EDRB

Article 82 of the Constitution of the Czech Republic:
'Judges shall be independent in the performance of their duties. Nobody may threaten their impartiality.'

Box 6.6. Oath of Office of a Justice of the Constitutional Court

Indonesia

'In the name of Allah I swear (or I solemnly promise) that I will do my best in fulfilling all obligations as a Constitutional Court Justice, and I will be as good and fair as possible, abide by the 1945 Constitution of the Republic of Indonesia, and apply all legislations and laws as strict as possible in accordance with the 1945 Constitution of the Republic of Indonesia, and serve the country and the nation.'

Czech Republic

'I pledge upon my honour and conscience that I will protect the inviolability of natural human rights and of the rights of citizens, adhere to constitutional acts, and make decisions according to my best convictions, independently and impartially.'

Slovakia

'I promise on my honour and conscience that I will protect the inviolability of the natural rights of man and civic rights, protect the principles of the state governed by the rule of law, abide by the Constitution, constitutional laws and international treaties that the Slovak Republic ratified and were promulgated in a manner laid down by law, and decide independently and impartially, according to my best conscience.'

ii) Selection and appointment of EDRB members

262. The substantive composition of an EDRB reflects the historical, normative and institutional evolution of a country and the competing claims and agreements of the various political forces at the time when new legislation was adopted. This can make it difficult to identify lessons that can be exported to different historical and political contexts. It is however possible and important to establish parameters for the way in which EDRB members are selected and appointed.

263. The public's trust in an EDRB is strengthened when the constitution or statute that established it contains:

- transparent mechanisms for selecting and appointing its members, or at least those of its highest-level organ, based on the merits of the candidates and according to gender- or ethnic-based inclusiveness criteria, and ensuring that they will not be bound by debts of gratitude, fidelity, or animosity with respect to any individual or group;
- the technical and professional requirements necessary to be nominated to be a member of an EDRB in order to be able to undertake the important and complex responsibility of delivering electoral justice in an impartial way;
- a reflection of necessary consensus among political parties on the importance of criteria for the selection and/or appointment of EDRB members; and
- a stipulation that the composition of EDRBs should take account of gender as well as, where applicable, being inclusive with respect to ethnic diversity (see box 6.7).

Box 6.7. Ethnic representation in the EDRB in a post-conflict setting in Bosnia and Herzegovina

Zoran Dokovic

In 1995 the representatives of three conflicting parties signed a peace agreement in Dayton, USA, defining Bosnia and Herzegovina as the state of three constitutive nations: Bosniacs, Serbs and Croats, composed of two entities: the Federation of Bosnia and Herzegovina (FBiH) and the Republika Srpska (RS) with Brcko District. The political landscape is divided along these ethnic lines and few political parties manage to secure votes on other grounds. The rotating presidency is divided between the three ethnicities: voters in the FBiH vote for the Bosniac and Croat President and those in the RS vote for the Serb President. These peculiarities remain in the constitution regardless of the diminishing control of the international community over the post-conflict process.

The EMB, which is also responsible for some first- and second-instance EDR, is the Central Election Commission (CEC, Centralna Izborna Komisija Središnje Izborno Povjerenstvo), which is appointed by the Parliament (Parlamentarna skupština Bosne i Hercegovine) for a five-year term. Its composition also ensures ethnic representation, including two Bosniacs, two Serbs, two Croats and one member who represents other ethnic minorities. The final-instance EDRB is the Appellate Division of the Court of Bosnia and Herzegovina. Until 2001, the OSCE mission in Bosnia and Herzegovina was fully empowered to conduct elections and work on the design of the permanent electoral legislation. The 2006 general elections in Bosnia and Herzegovina were the first elections since the Dayton Agreement to be fully administered by the Bosnia and Herzegovina authorities. However, the international community retained an advisory role within the CEC for these elections.

264. For every type of EDRS, the selection and appointment of members of the highest-level organ of the various EDRBs can be categorized by the nature of the body with authority to make the appointment. This may be:

a. the judiciary, whether persons are appointed from outside the judicial branch, or someone is chosen, designated or selected by lot from among the members of a judicial body;
b. the legislature, whether someone is chosen or appointed at the suggestion of the judiciary, the head of state, political parties or different social sectors;
c. the head of state, whether at the proposal of or with prior consultation with the judiciary, the legislature or some other area of government; or
d. a combination of these options, perhaps also involving another international or national body.

It is possible for the process of selection to be opened up through invitations to submit names, followed by a competitive process. It is usual for candidates to be sounded out as to their willingness to undertake the job. Whether or not there is a competitive process, it is commonly desirable for the qualities and qualifications of the candidates to be probed and assessed openly and transparently.

Box 6.8. Systems for the selection or appointment of members of the EDR system*

Appointed by:

a. The judiciary:
   - Free nomination or shortlisting of candidates
   - Among specific court members (free nomination or by lot)
b. The legislature:
   - Free nomination or shortlisting of candidates
   - Nominated by the judiciary
   - Nominated by the head of state
   - Nominated by political parties
   - Nominated by other social actors
c. The head of state:
   - Nominated by or after consulting the judiciary
   - Nominated by or after consulting the legislature
   - Nominated by another area of government
d. Combination of the previous three:
   - Nominated by judiciary and/or legislature and/or head of state, and may also involve an international or other national body

* Often after public nomination and/or a competitive selection process

265. Many analysts believe that the presence of representatives of political parties on EDRBs helps to achieve consensus among the contenders in the election process and can help to strengthen transparency. In practice, three approaches to political party nominations to EDRBs can be found: (a) none (the most common approach), (b) party nominees forming the minority (Uruguay), and (c) party nominees forming the majority (Colombia and Ecuador). It is however possible that a multiparty EDRB may obstruct or endanger decision-making processes or the enforcement of the law and the delivery of electoral justice, particularly when matters arise related to party political interests. EDRB members nominated by political parties need to be aware that their task is not to try to ensure that the EDRB's rulings always benefit their political party, but to guarantee that the rulings are consistent with the law. EDRB members should never attempt to rule in favour of one party or against another by failing to observe what is prescribed in constitutional law or the statutes. In this regard, once a person becomes a member of an EDRB, even if he or she is an activist or has been nominated by a political party, he or she must cease to act as such in the performance of the body's functions and focus on resolving the cases that come up strictly in accordance with the law.

266. In general, EDRSs entrusted to regular courts which are part of the judiciary or to constitutional courts or councils and administrative law courts do not provide for any formal or direct representation of political parties.

267. EDRBs entrusted to specialized electoral courts or EMBs with judicial powers whose members are designated by the judicial branch also do not provide for political party representation. This is the case:

- in Costa Rica, where the members of the Supreme Elections Tribunal (Tribunal Supremo de Elecciones) are appointed by a two-thirds majority of the Supreme Court of Justice (Corte Suprema de Justicia de Costa Rica);
- in Chile, where the Supreme Court of Justice (Corte Suprema) freely chooses four members of the Electoral Certifications Tribunal – three from among its members or former members, and one from other lawyers – while a fifth member is chosen by lot among the former presidents of the legislative chambers;
- in Turkey, where six of the EMB members are elected by the Plenary Assembly of the Supreme Court of Appeals (Yargıtay) and the other five by the Plenary Assembly of the Council of State (Daniştay) from among its own members; and
- in Albania, where the Electoral College is composed of eight judges for appeals selected by lot and nominated by the High Council of Justice (Këshilli i Lartë i Drejtësisë).

268. In Colombia, the Council of State (Consejo de Estado) is the highest court of administrative jurisdiction. It is made up of 27 magistrates, each chosen by the Council of State itself for individual terms of eight years from lists of more than five candidates who meet the constitutional requirements for each vacancy which are sent by the Administrative Chamber of the Superior Judicial Council (Sala Administrativa del Consejo Superior de la Judicatura).

269. In France, challenges relating to presidential elections, national legislative elections and referendums are heard by the Constitutional Council. This body has nine members, three nominated by the President of the Republic and three nominated by the presidents of each of the two chambers of the legislature, the National Assembly and the Senate. These nominations have recently become subject to legislative approval under the Constitution, although as of 2009 the implementing legislation for this change was not yet in place. In addition, former presidents of the Republic may serve on the Council if they so wish and if they are no longer involved in politics. The nominated members serve only one term of office, which lasts nine years. Three of the nine nominated members are replaced every three years.

270. Designation by the legislative branch, possibly with the participation of other public bodies, has several different modalities. It is the most common mechanism used by judicial EDRSs entrusted to regular, constitutional, administrative or specialized electoral courts as well as by EDRSs entrusted to EMBs and ad hoc bodies. The procedure for appointing magistrates to the Electoral Court of Mexico requires a two-thirds majority of the Senate, electing one from a three-person list proposed by the plenary of the Supreme Court (Suprema Corte de Justicia) after public advertisement and nomination hearings. In Guatemala and Peru, the process is entrusted to the Congress but some professional law associations and universities have participation rights. In Sweden, Elections Review Council (Valprövningsnämnden) members are elected by the Parliament, on the understanding that the President should be a tenured judge.

271. In some countries one or both chambers of the legislature elects or approves all the members, often acting on a proposal from the head of the state. This is one of the most common practices around the world. In Kyrgyzstan and Slovenia, Supreme Court and Constitutional Court members, respectively, are elected by the National Assembly, having been proposed by the President. In the Czech Republic, the justices of the Constitutional Court (Ústavní Soud) are appointed by the President of the Republic with the consent of the Senate (Senát Parlamentu). This is similar to the US system, in which the President, with the advice and consent of the Senate through confirmation hearings, appoints the judges of the Supreme Court. Some US states provide for the popular election of judges, many of whom serve in first instance courts for challenges to the results of federal legislative elections.

272. In Lithuania, the Parliament (Seimas) appoints justices of the Constitutional Court from nine candidates, three each submitted by the President of the Republic, the President of the Seimas and the President of the Supreme Court (Aukščiausiasis Teismas). In Croatia, the 13 judges of the Constitutional Court (Ústavní Soud) are elected by the Croatian Parliament (Hrvatski Sabor) from among notable jurists, especially judges, public prosecutors, lawyers and university law professors, after due notice has been given to civil society to propose candidates and public hearings.

273. An example of an EDR system entrusted to the head of the state is the Constitutional Court (Ústavný Súd) of Slovakia. Judges are appointed by the President acting on a proposal from the National Council (Národná rada) of the Slovak Republic. The National Council proposes twice the number of candidates that the President is to appoint. In Finland, tenured judges (including those of the Supreme Administrative Court) are appointed by the President according to procedures established by law.

274. In Vanuatu, the Supreme Court consists of the Chief Justice and three other judges. The Chief Justice is appointed by the President (who is the head of state) in consultation with the Prime Minister and the Leader of the Opposition. The other judges are appointed by the President on the advice of the Judicial Service Commission, which consists of the minister responsible for justice, as Chairman, the Chief Justice, the Chairman of the Public Service Commission and a representative of the National Council of Chiefs appointed by the Council.

275. In Jamaica, the provisions for electoral disputes are contained in the Election Petitions Act. They are pursued by the lodging of an election petition and are heard by a single judge of the Supreme Court, with the possibility of an appeal to the Court of Appeal. The Chief Justice is appointed by the Governor-General (who still acts as head of state as a representative of the British monarch) on receipt of a nomination from the Prime Minister made in consultation with the Leader of the Opposition. The remaining judges are appointed by the Governor-General on the advice of the Judicial Service Commission.

276. Some form of nomination from the executive to the legislative branch based on prior study by a judicial services commission is often considered a viable formula. The countries with a judicial service commission are mainly those which have inherited derivations of British colonial legal systems. Their EDRBs are therefore often located within the ordinary judicial system. In South Africa, the Judicial Service Commission publicly advertises Electoral Court vacancies and invites interested persons to apply. After interviewing shortlisted candidates, the Commission submits a final list of successful candidates to the President, who makes the final appointment. The Electoral

Court has five members: the Chairperson from the appellate division of the Supreme Court, two other judges from the Supreme Court and two further members, who must be South African citizens.

277. Mention should also be made of those situations where the appointment is made by the head of government based on the recommendation of the superior judicial council, as in the Palestinian Authority, or cases in which it is up to a specialized body or commission to select and appoint the members, such as a public service commission or judicial commission, or the Council for Citizen Participation and Social Oversight (Consejo de Participación Ciudadana y Control Social) in Ecuador.

278. Another variant is appointment by different public bodies. In Panama, for example, the executive branch, the legislative branch and the Supreme Court of Justice each appoint one member of the Electoral Court. As an example of the composition of an ad hoc body, in Afghanistan up to 2010, the Special Representative of the United Nations Secretary-General appointed the three international members of the Electoral Complaints Commission, and the two Afghan members were appointed by the Supreme Court (Stera Mahkama) and the Afghan Independent Human Rights Commission respectively. However, this composition ultimately proved unacceptable to President Hamid Karzai.

279. In France, three of the nine Constitutional Council members are appointed by the President of the Republic, three by the President of the National Assembly and three by the President of the Senate (Sénat). In addition to the nine members provided for above, former presidents of the Republic are ex officio life members of the Constitutional Council. Similarly, two members of the Constitutional Council (Konstïtwcıq Kengesí) of Kazakhstan are appointed by the President of the Republic, two by the Chairperson of the Senate, and two by the Chairperson of the Majilis (the lower house of the Parliament). The Chairperson is also appointed by the President of the Republic, and every ex-President of the Republic has the right to be a member of the Constitutional Council.

280. The Constitutional Court (Konstitucionen súd) of Bulgaria consists of 12 judges, one-third of whom are elected by the National Assembly (Narodno Sabranie), one-third appointed by the President and one-third elected by a joint meeting of the judges of the Supreme Court of Cassation (Vurhoven kasatsionen súd) and the Supreme Administrative Court (Vúrhovnija administrativen súd). Similarly, three of the nine members of the Constitutional Court of Georgia (saqarTvelos sakonstitucio sasamarTlo) are elected by the Georgian Parliament (saqarTvelos parlamenti), three are appointed by the President and three are appointed by the Supreme Court (uzenaesi sasamarTlo). Half the members of the German Federal Constitutional Court are elected by the

Bundestag (the lower chamber of the Parliament) and half by the Bundesrat (the upper chamber). The Constitutional Court of Portugal (Tribunal Constitucional) is composed of 13 judges, ten of whom are appointed by the Assembly of the Republic (Assembleia da República). These ten go on to elect the remaining three.

281. In contrast to these cases, the composition of other specialized electoral courts that are part of the judiciary does not provide for any involvement by political parties in determining their membership. For example, the three members of the National Electoral Chamber (Cámara Nacional Electoral) of Argentina are appointed according to the constitutional reform of 1994 by the President of the Republic with the consent of the Senate, from a binding three-person slate proposed by the Judicial Council (Escuela Judicial). The Superior Electoral Court (Tribunal Superior Eleitoral) of Brazil is made up of at least seven members – three from the members of the Federal Supreme Court (Supremo Tribunal Federal), two from the members of the Superior Court of Justice (Superior Tribunal de Justiça) and two designated by the President of the Republic from a list of six attorneys proposed by the Federal Supreme Tribunal.

282. In some EDRBs entrusted to specialized electoral courts, EMBs or ad hoc bodies where the majority or a minority of members are nominated by political parties, the remaining members are designated in a manner similar to the cases outlined above, either by the legislative branch (from its own free nomination or at the proposal of the executive or the Supreme Court), or directly by the Supreme Court. In some countries it is emphasized that the members who are not appointed by political parties must act as the guarantee of impartiality. In Uruguay, the appointment of such members requires the approval of a two-thirds majority in both chambers.

283. Among the systems that provide for some participation by political parties in the selection of EDRB members, this may entail (a) participation that only involves making nominations – among several that vie for consensus among the political forces or (b) participation that is tantamount to designating a member or members. The latter case may give the advantage that, because political party nominees are involved in decisions, they may be seen as more acceptable by party members – and may be particularly appropriate if there is nobody in society who is really perceived as independent. However, this needs to be balanced against the risk that the EDRB members may be seen as partial in favour of the political party that nominated them in the performance of their functions. The credibility of the EDRB may easily be affected, in that the sum of partial positions does not necessarily add up to impartiality. A tendency may also develop for technical decisions to have to undergo political negotiation, usually to the detriment of the technical aspects.

284. Where the organization of the election and the judicial resolution of electoral issues are assigned to separate bodies, the EMB and the EDRB, this debate may then be resolved by distinguishing the composition of the two bodies: the EMB having the input and views of the political parties, the makeup of the EDRB being independent of the political parties. In such a system, it may be easier to prevent electoral disputes and to correct violations by administrative means – thus helping to make recourse to judicial decisions exceptional – and at the same time afford greater legal certainty and help ensure that the actions and decisions of the administrative authorities are always subject to the principles of constitutionality and legality. However, the establishment of two separate independent bodies may raise financial and sustainability issues.

285. To minimize the risks involved in political parties nominating EDRB members, selection by competitive process can be used, as in Iraq. Another approach is to give the power to designate members to the Supreme Court. In countries in which distrust is routine, however, some voices warn of the risk that appointments by the Supreme Court may be called into question. They suggest that its members, in turn, will designate someone who is inclined to support the interests of the political party that appointed them, which merely shifts the problem, perhaps undercutting the prestige of the Supreme Court by the alleged 'politicization of the system of justice'.

286. A further alternative is to give the legislative organs the power to designate members, but require a special majority (perhaps two-thirds of the legislators, as in Honduras and Mexico, and, for the independent members, in El Salvador and Uruguay). This may help to achieve a consensus at least among some of the representatives who are members of opposition political parties (with the proviso that there shall be recourse to alternative mechanisms to overcome a possible impasse and prevent certain minorities from blocking decision making). Unfortunately, however, under this latter system cases have arisen in which the positions to be filled are distributed among the parties that are able to constitute the required majority, thereby excluding other political parties.

287. The need for consensus in appointing EDRB members by requiring a special majority in the legislative branch is a proven formula in, for example, the appointment of the members of Constitutional Courts in Germany, Lithuania and Portugal.

288. One problem related to requiring a special majority of the legislature is that the public exposure that can be associated with participating in the nomination process, and the risk of not ultimately being elected/appointed, may deter the best-qualified people from participation. It may also be difficult for minorities to secure representation under this system, which is especially important in some countries – bearing in mind that such representation

should not be formally required in a technical body but may be justified for the benefits of consensus and inclusiveness that should characterize every democratic regime. There have also been cases of the legislative branch taking a long time to fill a vacancy because it is unable to reach consensus.

289. In most cases the choice of the President of the EDRB is left to the members of the highest-ranking body in the EDR system. There are, however, some exceptions. One such is the choice of the President by the body that appoints the members – for example, the National Assembly (Asamblea Nacional) for Nicaragua's Consejo Supremo Electoral, the Riksdag for Sweden's Elections Review Council or the President of the Republic for Slovakia's Constitutional Court. In France, the President of the Republic, who nominates some of the members of the Constitutional Council, also selects its President. Another option is that the presidency is conferred ex officio on a particular member of the EDRB by constitutional or statutory provision (for example in Peru it is the member designated by the Supreme Court of Justice, Corte Suprema de Justicia, while in Chile it is the member who is a current member of the Supreme Court of Justice, Corte Suprema, or, if there is more than one, the one with greatest seniority).

290. Some systems have independent EMBs whose President or highest-ranking member is appointed in a different way from the other EMB members, accompanied by specialized electoral courts – whether autonomous or part of the judicial branch.

291. EDRBs whose organs are made up of non-partisan experts often include members who are not politically aligned or are appointed on the basis of their professional capacities, often public figures recognized for their neutrality or political impartiality. In many cases the legal framework requires that the members of an EDRB of this sort have not been involved in party political activity in the recent past, and that they are not members of any political party while performing the functions of their position.

iii) Requirements of suitability and professionalism

292. The role of EDRBs in hearing and resolving electoral challenges requires legal knowledge. Some systems thus require that EDRB members must be attorneys (often including minimum levels of experience, such as 15 years in Croatia, Kyrgyzstan, Mexico and Slovakia) or a member of some similar profession in order to hold the position. The EDR systems that are entrusted to the regular courts of the judicial branch inherently possess such provisions, as do several of those that are entrusted to constitutional courts or administrative courts, and some in countries that accord jurisdiction to specialized electoral courts. Some impose the same requirements as for serving as a member of the Supreme Court.

293. Practically all legal systems establish as a requirement that EDRB members must be a citizen in the full exercise of their rights, with a minimum age limit ranging from 30 to 45 years. Some provide a maximum age of 70 or 75 years. In any event, equal opportunity to access the position of a member of an EDRB should be guaranteed, avoiding any vestige of discrimination and taking account of the desirability of inclusion, particularly of gender and ethnic minorities.

294. Given the impartiality with which the various types of electoral challenge must be resolved, the requirements not to have recently held any position in a political party, not to hold one while a member of the EDRB and not to support any candidate are especially important. Other explicit requirements are honesty and probity or a good reputation, and a large number of EDRBs require that members should not have been convicted of any criminal offence, or of one that entailed imprisonment.

295. In addition, some legal systems establish as a requirement for membership of an EDRB that a person must not hold certain public positions, or that having held an electoral position is a temporary disqualification from holding certain public positions in the future. In the vast majority of cases, this is a 'good practice' for safeguarding impartiality. Similarly, some systems require that members must not be members of the military, whereas others require that they do not have family members in the EDRB or even family members in certain public offices or who sit as legislators. Along these lines, it is good practice for members not to have any business dealings with the executive and not to hold any government concession or contract.

iv) Security of position and career service

296. To ensure that those sitting in judgement on electoral matters remain independent while they perform their functions, legislation often provides for various measures aimed at insulating members from any pressures by means of sanctions, reprisals or even apparent rewards from those who obtain judicial judgements contrary to or coinciding with their interests. Such safeguards include security of tenure.

297. The law generally establishes a predetermined term of office for judicial positions which cannot be reduced or prolonged except by provision of law. This consolidates the independence of those who judge electoral matters: they cannot be dismissed or removed for having handed down decisions that do not please, or are considered inconvenient by certain political parties or individuals. They can only be removed on the basis of the specific grounds set out in the constitution and the law.

298. The security of judges in their posts is considered to be one of the most important structural guarantees. The strongest guarantees for EDRB members

take the form of tenure, which is the case in most of the systems that confer jurisdiction to the members of the judicial branch, often in keeping with the Anglo-American tradition. In such systems, EDRB members remain in their positions until retirement age unless they are removed for misconduct through an adversarial procedure, as in Argentina, Kyrgyzstan and the USA. Other systems have less strong provisions, for example in Brazil, where EDRB members have two-year terms of office with the possibility of reappointment only once.

299. When an EDRB is permanent, it is especially important that its members have job security. Even in a temporary EDRB it is desirable for its members, who are often seconded from other judicial bodies, at least to enjoy job security in the body on which they normally serve as a guarantee of their independence.

300. Constitutional Court and Council members can hold a non-renewable term of 12 (Slovakia), nine (Bulgaria, France, Lithuania and Portugal) or eight years (Croatia). Among the countries with specialized electoral courts the longest period of service is ten years, with no restrictions on reappointment (Panama); other examples are nine years, either with the possibility of reappointment (Venezuela) or without any extension (Mexico), and six years, allowing for unlimited reappointments (Costa Rica). Indonesia's Constitution restricts its Constitutional Court judges to a five-year term only renewable for one more term. In Colombia the term for magistrates of the Council of State is eight years.

301. It may be an advantage for the period of service of the members of EDRBs to be longer than that of the President of the Republic (where there is a President), and the maximum term of office of the legislature.

302. Partial and staggered renewal of the membership of the EDRB, so that all members do not retire at the same time, is also often considered as an advantage. This allows for institutional stability and liaison between new members and those who are remaining in post, who are able to pass on the institutional memory and their own experience. In this way, the entire EDRB is not exposed to the recurrent costs associated with learning and with mistakes that could have been avoided with more experience available. In addition, staggered renewal prevents a controlling group of political forces in the legislature at the particular time when EDRB members are appointed from influencing the composition of the complete EDRB. Examples of partial and staggered renewal are provided by the Constitutional Council of France, three of whose nine members are renewed every three years; the Supreme Court of India, where the term of each of the maximum of 31 judges lasts until the age of 65; and the Supreme Electoral Court of Costa Rica, since three (one full member and two substitutes) of its nine (three full member and six substitute) magistrates are replaced every two years.

303. The possibility of the reappointment of members of the EDRB is often considered healthy as it allows for periodic evaluation of performance. This can give the opportunity to retain members who are professionally apt and suitable while incorporating new members who bring new insights and perspectives. However, this approach also carries a danger – the more frequent the reappointment process, the more opportunities there may be for the nominating body to control the appointments.

304. The stability of the EDRB itself is also important. There has been an evolution away from temporary bodies, whose lifespan often coincided with each election and the time needed to resolve any associated challenges, towards the establishment of permanent bodies. This has been fundamental to professionalizing and refining election procedures, and the lesson has been learnt that both the financial and the political cost of improvisation often turn out to be much greater than the cost of a permanent body.

305. A 'career electoral judicial service' is provided for in several countries, which acts as another structural guarantee which may promote stability and professionalism. It is characterized, among other things, by competitive or objective procedures for the recruitment, promotion and retention of the electoral service personnel. It is often good practice for vacancies in the top-level organs of an EDRB to be filled by professional personnel from within the ranks of the EDRB. This acts as a significant stimulus to permanent professional development and good performance. It also helps to maintain institutional memory and prevent EDRBs from having to bear the costs of learning that would accrue if their members and support staff were renewed in full. For example, the Electoral Court of the Judicial Branch of the Federation of Mexico has often conducted the recruitment of law clerks through public competition. There is a permanent training programme. Ten out of 15 regional electoral magistrates in post in mid-2010 had been law clerks at the Electoral Court before their appointment by the Senate, a process which involves the nomination by the Supreme Court of three candidates for each vacancy following a public advertisement and nomination hearings.

v) Appropriate remuneration

306. As a structural guarantee for the members of the EDRB, several EDR systems provide as a matter of principle, drawing on the Anglo-American tradition, that the remuneration of the members may not be cut while they are performing their functions. This is particularly the case for those who are part of the judicial branch; it may also be true for members of constitutional courts or councils and of administrative courts.

307. Although it is not always set down in law, it is often a matter of public policy that the members of the EDRB receive remuneration appropriate

to the importance of their function and the high level of professionalism required. Such remuneration should enable members to live without pressure and with dignity without the need to take another job. Indeed, doing so is often prohibited: the function of EDRB membership at the highest level requires full-time dedication not only because of its complexity and potential workload, but also to ensure independence and impartiality. With these objectives in mind, on occasion the law provides that the remuneration for members of the EDRB should be equivalent to that of judges or members of a high-ranking court such as the Supreme Court – for example, in Mexico.

vi) Disqualification

308. To guarantee that those who judge electoral matters act impartially and are not swayed by any personal or private interest, either their own or that of someone else, the law often establishes grounds for disqualifying a member of an EDRB from hearing a challenge in relation to which some conflict of interest might arise. These differ from country to country, but include:

- having prejudice or a strong bias, that is, a preconceived judgement formed without a factual basis;
- having a family relationship or an obvious friendship with or animosity towards, or being the debtor or creditor of, any of the parties;
- having a personal interest in the matter, or that a member's spouse or any family member has a personal interest;
- having accepted gifts, services or invitations paid for by the interested persons or their representatives;
- making a disclosure, that is, revealing facts related to a case under judgement; and
- having made promises that imply partiality in favour of or against an interested person or party.

309. When an EDRB member is called to sit in judgement and is affected by any impediment or disqualification (even if not expressly provided for by law), electoral legal frameworks provide that they must take the initiative and declare themselves disqualified from taking cognizance of the matter concerned. Should they fail to do so, it may be desirable for the party affected to have the right to move for their recusal.

c) The framework for accountability and liability of the EDRB and its members

310. As an indirect guarantee that every action, procedure and decision related to the electoral process is in line with the law, EDR systems generally provide for a framework of accountability and liability for the EDRB and its members through which the performance of their public function is monitored, allowing

for the imposition of some sanction (criminal, administrative or civil) for wrongful conduct. Thus the election laws of several countries establish not only the powers and functions of the EDRB and its members, but also its obligations and responsibilities, including mechanisms of accountability.

Box 6.9. Framework of accountability and liability for the EDRB and its members

- Transparency in and publicity for work of the EDRB
- Accountability of the EDRB
- Liabilities and accountability of the members of the EDRB

i) Transparency and publicizing of the work of the EDRB

311. Transparency on the part of an EDRB in the performance of its adjudicating function and administering the public resources allocated to it is fundamental to the credibility of the EDR system. Even when it is not provided for legally, it is recommended as good practice.

312. Often the requirement to publish extends not only to electoral judicial rulings but also to the proceedings of the sessions in which they are made. Some examples of good practice include those in which EDRBs have agreed to broadcast their public sessions in real time through the Internet, or post their judgements on their website as soon as they are issued, along with the judicial criteria that establish binding precedent where this is applicable. In addition, regardless of whether this is provided for by law or incorporated as good practice, it is important to establish that once each matter is resolved any interested person can consult the record of the EDRB in the public archive. Transparency in the work of the EDRB provides a basis for demonstrating its impartiality and increasing its credibility.

ii) Accountability of the EDRB

313. It is also fundamental to the credibility of the EDR system for EDRBs to be accountable to society. Accountability means that an EDRB is responsible for its activities, and should periodically provide public reports on its performance and activities. These should demonstrate that it is acting in line with the constitutional and statutory framework. They should also demonstrate that it is abiding by ethical, administrative, financial and service commitments and standards, including international ones where they exist.

314. In addition, EDRBs should provide public information on their procedures, and on any resources they have used or are seeking, whether these come from public or other sources. Such practices not only encourage

the proper administration of electoral justice but also help to generate trust among the public and the parties that come before them, in particular the political parties and political and governmental entities that allocate and oversee the use of resources.

315. Some systems expressly oblige EDRBs to submit reports to the legislative or judicial branches on both the performance of their adjudicating function and the administration of the public resources allocated to them. These are subject to oversight through the competent government bodies. Even when this is not provided for by law, the timely provision of this information to the public is recommended as good practice.

iii) Liability and accountability of EDRB members

316. The liability framework normally has two aspects: (a) it is a guarantee for the members of the EDRB that they can be removed only after a procedure in which some improper or wrongful conduct on their part is demonstrated; and (b) it is an institutional guarantee, as it provides for mechanisms for imposing some penalty or disciplinary measure and even removing members when they engage in improper or wrongful conduct in the performance of their functions. In addition, although not very common, civil liability may attach stemming from the damage caused by a wrongful act or what is known as 'judicial error'.

317. Immunity from prosecution is commonly provided for the members of the top-level organ of the EDRB during their term of office. Thus, a criminal action against such a member must have been previously authorized by the legislature (generally the lower chamber, as in Argentina, Brazil, Costa Rica, Guatemala and Mexico) or a high-ranking judicial body (as in Chile, where such power is exercised by the Court of Appeal (Cortes de Apelaciones) in Santiago).

318. Almost all the systems provide for a disciplinary framework for the personnel of the respective EDRB, entrusting its application in the final instance to the highest-level organ of the EDR system. In addition, in Latin America it is common for the members of the supreme bodies of the EDR system to be subject to a *juicio político* (political trial), equivalent to the US institution of impeachment. This may take place before both chambers of the legislature, as in Argentina, Mexico and the Dominican Republic. An example of the process where the legislature is unicameral is that the legislature indicts and the Supreme Court of Justice sits in judgement, as in Costa Rica. A special majority is usually needed to convict. The accused may have to answer directly to the Supreme Court for any alleged crimes or misdemeanours committed in the performance of his or her functions, as is the case in Panama.

319. Some countries impose an obligation on the members of the EDRB to submit statements of their net worth at the beginning of and during their period of office and at its conclusion as an accountability mechanism. Internal oversight mechanisms should be established in the EDRBs to monitor the performance of personnel and the budget. However, this should not exempt the EDRB from external monitoring and control for accountability purposes, for example through a Supreme Audit Commission or court.

320. While the members of EDRBs are independent, as they are not bound by the orders of any superior authority or of any other authority, they are always bound by the general provisions of the constitution and the law. The guarantees of the independence of those who judge electoral matters do not protect their specific or personal interests, but only their adjudicating function, which must be carried out independently and impartially. The guarantees of independence of an EDRB do not authorize its members to act beyond the scope of their authority or give them impunity if they do. Those who judge elections, like any authority, are entrusted with public powers which they must exercise strictly within the limits established by law.

d) Integrity and professionalism of the members of the EDRB

321. The institutional integrity of an EDRB resides fundamentally in the explicit and public commitment that is genuinely assumed and observed by the members of its highest-level organ and by all its personnel to conduct themselves with integrity in providing the electoral justice service.

322. Integrity means that the EDRB acts ethically and is strictly subject to its constitutional and statutory mandates. The existence of strict policies and practices and of codes of conduct for handling conflicts of interest will encourage public trust in the integrity of the EDRB. Such codes of conduct are discussed further in the IDEA publication *Code of Conduct for the Ethical and Professional Administration of Elections.*

323. Strict and unwavering adherence to the principles of constitutionality and legality in each and every one of its acts and decisions needs to be the main commitment of every EDRB. This goes hand in hand with the independence and impartiality of its members in decision making – they must act in an absolutely ethical manner.

324. The legitimacy of an EDRB depends not only on its rulings and judgements being properly grounded in the law, but also on the legal reasons on which they are based being sufficiently explained to society. Legality, certainty and objectivity in its decisions make the action of an EDRB more predictable, which provides a wider degree of legal certainty and may promote the consequent trust of society in its institutions. Explanations

should not only be included in the judgement or decision: in particularly high-profile or sensitive cases it could be considered good practice for them to be disseminated in a communiqué or a press release. There is a difficult balance to be achieved here which requires technical skill in ensuring both that the position taken in the judgement is not distorted and that the technical content of the judgement is accessible to and comprehensible by broad sections of society.

325. It usually appears advisable for individual members of the EDRB to avoid interviews with the press. Any imprecision or apparent contradiction may give rise to problems that go beyond the need to explain the scope or meaning of a ruling. If it is essential to give interviews, it may be desirable to limit them to a single person or electoral staff member officially designated by the EDRB, whose remit is to limit any remarks to stating and explaining the legal reasons upheld by the majority.

326. Once a matter is resolved by an EDRB, the reasons that prevailed and matter in terms of being explained to society right away are those of the majority. This is entirely independent of the right of the members of the EDRB who are in the minority to formulate a dissenting view which is included in the judgement and may be disseminated later, for example, in a specialized or academic journal. Extensive debate over points of disagreement during the session of the EDRB is essential in order to clarify and refine the thinking of the members in reaching a judgement. However, once the EDRB reaches its decision it is preferable not to address the issue again publicly, unless another case is heard that makes this unavoidable. Few things weaken an EDRB more than publicly airing differences among its members without reference to a specific case. Moreover, the message sent to society, if this happens, is confusing, contradictory, and vulnerable to political manipulation.

327. The vocation of service, a commitment to professional excellence, and dedication to electoral justice and democratic values all contribute to the credibility and prestige of an EDRB. Its internal and external activities should reflect the pluralistic composition of society and gender balance, as well as promoting equality and equity on a non-partisan basis. Its operation should be inclusive, adopting a gender perspective and reflecting ethnic diversity.

328. Reporting in a timely fashion on the volume and quality of the work carried out, including the scrupulous and transparent administration of public resources, creates incentives for the members of the top-level organ and all its personnel to offer an electoral justice service of the highest quality. It also establishes standards for the other groups involved in elections, including national and international observers, the academic sector and the media, to follow in order to emulate its performance.

329. The precise and careful implementation of the procedures necessary for hearing and resolving challenges is a key requirement if the EDR system is to deliver electoral justice and credible electoral results. It is essential for the EDRB to ensure that all the legal personnel and support staff involved in the EDR system, whether permanent or temporary, have the training required and abilities needed for their technical work in keeping with the highest professional standards, including training to develop political sensitivity to electoral issues. Professional training encourages a public perception that the EDR system is 'in good hands'.

330. Efforts have been made in several countries to promote professionalism, which is fundamental to the optimal organization of the electoral processes and the proper hearing and resolution of electoral challenges. Mexico has established the Centre for Electoral Judicial Training (*Centro de Capacitacion Judicial*) in the Electoral Court of the Judicial Branch of the Federation. Mexico's electoral judicial career service is an example of good practice. It attracts professional staff and encourages constant professional improvement and sound performance on the part of the EDRB's legal support staff. A staff training school has also been established, with the support of International IDEA, at the EDRB in the Dominican Republic.

331. In some countries EDRB staff members must take an oath before assuming their position to underscore their commitment and dedication to carrying out their role (see box 6.6).

e) The cost and sustainability of EDRBs

332. The principle that democratic elections must be sustainable implies that EDRBs should be capable of carrying out their electoral responsibilities within any legally established deadlines, with ever greater effectiveness and efficiency and, if possible, at an ever reducing cost.

333. It is possible to identify a number of elements relevant to the medium- to long-term sustainability of an EDRB: (a) institutional sustainability, through an appropriate constitutional and statutory framework; (b) financial and economic sustainability, through an arrangement that ensures adequate financing; and (c) sustainability of human resources, by means of a sufficient structure of qualified support staff, with the aim of having the capacity to impart electoral justice effectively and efficiently.

334. To this end, the EDRB should establish procedures and practices that are realistic and cost-effective and that satisfy the needs of all the groups interested in electoral justice, both in the present and in the future. Accordingly, an assessment should be made of the real capacities of the EDRB and the human, financial and technological resources it has at its disposal.

335. The capacity to provide a complete, effective and timely electoral justice service at the lowest possible cost is the first standard of sustainability. However, financial considerations should not be allowed to compromise the basic requirements of the service. Under certain circumstances, considerations of political sustainability may be more important than considerations of financial sustainability.

336. Human resources, and the related knowledge and accumulated experience, constitute the principal asset of an EDRB. Investment in developing and retaining personnel, and in ensuring that the institutional memory survives the loss of experienced personnel, is vital for the sustainability of any EDRB. In this regard, training and other efforts to foster professionalism at all levels of the EDRB are essential (see paragraphs 329 and 330).

337. Particularly in emerging and recently established democracies, support from donors in the international community can have a great impact on the sustainability of an EDRB. The support of donors may help to improve the quality of a given election, but any dependence or influence – or public perception of dependence or influence – must be avoided. It is particularly desirable that donor financing does not cover the salaries of EDRB members. These should always be paid out of the public treasury.

338. In addition, the use of technology seduces EDRBs and is often attractive to donors. EDRBs should objectively assess the long-term usefulness of technology and its possible impacts on sustainability, including the maintenance requirements of new technical equipment and systems. While it may be desirable to promote or sponsor the use of new technologies by an EDRB (for example computer equipment for the system of recording complaints or drawing up decisions and judgements), it is important to take account of the availability of resources in the country as a whole and evaluate the benefits that are offered by the proposed new technology.

Box 6.10. Electoral justice and electronic justice: a logical match? The experiences of Brazil and Indonesia

Domenico Tuccinardi and Adhy Aman

The development of new technologies for exchanging electronic documents from remote locations as well the growth of video-conferencing instruments are having an impact on many sectors of democratic life. These developments are generally labelled 'e-democracy' because of the way they are establishing a new balance between citizens and institutions.

The administration of justice does not escape this trend, and the development of 'electronic justice' applications in court proceedings is already a reality. The digitalization of all types of information offers new technical solutions to traditional problems that

(cont.)

have long been viewed as obstacles to the effective and impartial administration of justice. It can be argued that technology has already changed the way courts operate in many places around the world. The most frequent applications of electronic justice concern aspects such as electronic filing systems, automated case management systems, public prosecution services, digital recording of interviews and courtroom technology. In particular, the enhanced ability to use video conferencing tools leads to more expeditious case processing, minimizing the need for the physical movement of judges, plaintiffs and offenders and reducing costs and bureaucracy. However, as in many other fields where technological applications have been introduced, the solution of old problems often opens up new ones, adding new possibilities for bypassing existing procedural legislation.

How will these developments in electronic justice affect the administration of electoral justice and in particular the resolution of election-related disputes? Are such developments a logical and welcome consequence? In the administration of electoral justice, the use of modern technologies can have a largely positive effect in terms of efficiency, access to information and evidence, transparency, time-effectiveness and resource optimization. Even more importantly, technological applications as a whole can play an extraordinary gap-bridging role by bringing electoral stakeholders closer to the institutions in charge of the administration of electoral processes and electoral justice, thereby promoting confidence in the institutions.

The disadvantages currently attributed to technological applications in electronic justice, such as the difficulties arising from the so-called digital divide, appear set to decrease as Internet facilities become available to a growing number of citizens. Among other positive features, Intranet-based systems with secure access already enable information and electoral case data to be posted electronically in virtual workspaces shared by different territorial offices and different institutions (in case more than one institution is involved at the various levels of government and/or regions), eliminating the need for paper-based systems and reducing costs and lengthy procedural deadlines.

The one aspect that apparently remains difficult to overcome with the use of technology is that related to trust in the institutions, and this affects electoral management bodies (EMBs) and courts alike. There is no doubt that technology has already provided electoral administrations and electoral stakeholders with the opportunity to deter electoral fraud at the local level at any stage of the electoral process. However, control of the technological applications is concentrated in the hands of the administering authority. This means that the theoretical possibility of abuse or manipulation at the centre remains. Fears on this count can only be overcome if there is trust in those who administer the process. Can technological applications enhance trust in the administration of electoral justice more than in other facets of the electoral process?

The cases of Brazil and Indonesia offer a number of interesting insights in this respect. Brazil's EMB, the Superior Electoral Tribunal (Tribunal Superior Eleitoral, TSE) is probably

(cont.)

the most technologically advanced electoral justice institution in the world. It pioneered applications that have since been introduced in other sectors of the judiciary. The use of information and communications technology (ICT) applications by the TSE is regarded not only as having improved the impartial, efficient and transparent administration of the electoral process, but also as having enhanced the ability of the TSE to provide effective remedies.

The introduction of ICT applications as a way to bring Brazilian electoral stakeholders closer to the electoral process is an approach that dates back to the mid-1990s. It was gradually introduced to all aspects of the administration of elections, starting with the digitalization of the electoral register and the measured introduction of an electronic voting system. In this context, the TSE further developed ICT applications (video conferencing, electronic service of documents, electronic filing options and electronic evidence taking, and virtual case management and hearings) for the processing and resolution of electoral complaints as a natural extension of its other already digitalized electoral system components. In a logical extension to this approach, it was felt that the acquired technical ability of the TSE to administer elections and deliver electoral results in a fast, transparent and reliable fashion through electronic voting and an automated count needs to be accompanied by the ability to seek redress through electronic means, offered to all electoral stakeholders, in an equally expeditious manner and at any given moment in the electoral process. This approach also provides a check on the extensive powers vested in the TSE. The functionality of the TSE website encourages Brazil's electoral stakeholders to monitor and scrutinize the administration of their electoral rights at every stage of the process and enables them to file a claim whenever they have a doubt about the process. This ability by itself enhances the confidence of citizens in the TSE.

In Indonesia, the Constitutional Court (Mahkamah Konstitusi) has a mandate to resolve any election result-related disputes and, like Brazil's TSE, it manages its own budget and has procedural independence. Following an extension of its mandate (from legislative and presidential elections in 2004 to include gubernatorial and mayoral elections in 2009), the Constitutional Court had to equip itself to handle new and continual case-filing requests from all over the country for mayoral elections (of which there are 524, held at different times in different parts of the country – an average of nine elections each month over a five-year period) while remaining able to review and adjudicate on complaints from more than 1800 constituencies over the limited time frame for the legislative elections of 30 calendar days. The introduction of ICT in such a geographically vast and politically heterogeneous country was a logical way to implement the Constitutional Court mandate to settle electoral results disputes within such a short time frame in a country where the need for certainty in the post-electoral period has always been crucial to its stability.

The electronic submission of cases and preliminary evidence introduced by the Constitutional Court through its website has enabled it to keep its deadlines short, while

(cont.)

video conferencing tools allow faster conduct of hearings. The same mechanism allows stakeholders to propose witnesses or withdraw their case. This system required the Constitutional Court to adopt new security measures to verify the identity of complainants and witnesses who interact online. Above all, the expeditiousness of these proceedings is accompanied by an unprecedented degree of transparency, which in the past proved difficult to achieve within short timelines in such a vast country.

The successful cases of Brazil and Indonesia raise the issue of whether the administration of electoral justice by electronic means could become a complete substitute for traditional proceedings across the world. Will the traditionally golden principles of oral evidence in public and the immediacy of proceedings soon be redundant? More than that, e-justice applications in electoral matters could shake one of the central axioms of ICT applied to elections: that technological investment cannot make up for a lack of trust in the institutions administering the process. While this dilemma deserves careful consideration and continued research in the other disciplines of law, the notion of electronic justice certainly has additional appeal in the administration of electoral disputes. Electoral law is arguably the most political of all the branches of law, and the administration of electoral justice often suffers from this underlying tenet. The balance between time-effectiveness and accuracy that electoral justice authorities must always strike is affected by political factors that often have very little to do with the principles of the rule of law or due process. In this respect, the vast possibilities offered by ICT applications in the administration of electoral justice, especially in terms of the transparency of actions, access to information, effectiveness and the timeliness of the possible remedy, should be viewed as powerful motivations for the digitalization of electoral justice.

4. Procedural guarantees of electoral dispute resolution systems

339. Procedural guarantees are those elements or attributes which foster and safeguard electoral justice and have as the basic aim the effective and efficient operation of an EDR system.

340. Procedural guarantees are normally put in place to ensure that the proceedings of an EDRS (trials or hearings, remedies and, in general, the handling of any challenges) are *accessible, effective and efficient.* Any proceeding must be accessible to those who seek the protection or defence of their electoral rights, that is, *free of charge* or with charges are not onerous; *simple* in its procedures; *expeditious* and *timely* in offering a safeguard or restoring an electoral right or, in a general sense, restoring the electoral legal framework before it becomes irreparable; and respects the *essential formalities* that should be found in any judicial proceeding – corresponding to the nature of the electoral right that a challenge seeks to protect.

Box 6.11. Procedural guarantees or principles of efficiency and effectiveness of EDR systems

- Transparency, clarity and simplicity of the provisions that regulate the EDR system, as well as ensuring that they are duly published and consistently followed
- Access in terms of time, space and cost to complete and effective electoral justice, including the ability to complain at the lowest level (at the polling station)
- Availability of an electoral justice system either free of charge or at a reasonable cost
- Timeliness
- Right to a defence or hearing and due process of law for litigants
- Full enforcement of judgements and decisions
- Consistency in the interpretation and application of the electoral laws

a) Transparency, clarity and simplicity in the provisions that regulate the EDR system

341. An optimal design for an EDR system demands *clarity and simplicity*. The constitutional, statutory and regulatory provisions for challenges that guarantee compliance with the electoral legal framework and the defence of electoral rights must be drafted in simple and clear language in order to meet the requirements of access to justice and legal certainty. Their content must be broadly disseminated in the language of the community where the election is to be held to ensure that they are transparent and easily understood by all interested persons and consistently followed – especially by the EDRBs.

342. Professional development of the legal personnel at the EDRBs should be encouraged in order for them to be able to deal with any inadequacies, inefficiencies or gaps in the legal framework through technically sustainable interpretations. It is important to have good laws, but it is perhaps even more important to have good judges.

343. Ambiguous, vague, evasive or incomplete legal provisions can give rise to confusion about the challenges that may be brought against a particular electoral action and the organ with jurisdiction to rule on it. Such confusion can be detrimental to electoral justice, and could eventually be manipulated and exploited. It can obstruct the electoral process and the imparting of justice, as well as causing delays in elected candidates taking up their office and casting a shadow over their legitimacy.

344. Accordingly, the electoral and procedural laws should clearly lay down – preferably in a particular law on electoral procedures or in a particular chapter of the electoral legislation – the various electoral challenges that are available and the body authorized to resolve them. These should contain clear

rules in terms of the challenge that should be brought against a given action or electoral decision, avoiding having two different challenges available to the same action or decision before different EDRBs. Such duplication of jurisdiction or concurrent jurisdiction is likely to give rise to confusion and the risk of contradictory rulings.

345. Where jurisdiction is left unclear in legislation, a situation may arise in which an EDRB considers itself without jurisdiction to hear a challenge that it has received, or considers the challenge inadmissible. If a challenge is presented to the 'wrong' EDRB in this way, it is good practice for that EDRB to transfer it to the EDRB that does have jurisdiction, and for the other EDRB to consider the respective electoral action or decision as having been properly challenged – even if there may be confusion over the means used to pursue the challenge.

346. The set of procedural rules that govern an EDR system should be consistent and complete, drafted in clear language that eliminates the risk of arbitrary interpretations, and consistently followed by the EDRB.

347. Electoral law should clearly establish which electoral decisions are final and which are subject to review or challenge. In those cases in which a challenge is allowed the electoral law should expressly state which organ has jurisdiction to review any relevant challenge.

348. As part of civic education campaigns, wide dissemination of the constitutional, statutory and regulatory provisions on elections in the language of the community in which the election is to be held is considered good practice. Where they exist, the criteria in the case law to be used by the EDRB for interpreting legal provisions or establishing precedent should be published. Producing and distributing manuals on electoral challenges each time the relevant laws or regulations are amended is also good practice. It is desirable for EDRB staff to provide training not only for the officials and staff of the EMB, but in addition for all political parties and the media personnel in charge of covering election news.

Box 6.12. Bhutan: introducing a new system to the people

Deki Pema

Parliamentary elections under the Constitution were held for the first time in 2008. Voter education and awareness-raising were, and remain, of crucial importance in Bhutan. For over a year before the election the Election Commission of Bhutan implemented a multi-pronged public awareness and education strategy which used the print, audio and visual media as well as one-to-one classroom sessions in the villages. Songs, brochures and DVDs were distributed free of charge, and material was aired regularly

(cont.)

on radio and television to inform the people of the changes to the political and electoral systems and remind voters of their responsibilities throughout the process.

Through these campaigns the public were also informed about the dispute resolution process which had been put in place, and the candidates and parties were given detailed briefings in separate sessions conducted by the Election Commission. At the sessions each representative was reminded of his or her rights within the dispute resolution process, including the right to appeal.

349. The EDRB should provide voter education to explain the requirements of both substance and procedure to people who wish to exercise their right to an effective legal remedy. People who wish to make a challenge should be aware of the evidence required if they are to back up their arguments and claims with sufficient factual and legal material. They should also be aware that only the EDRB can make the actual decision on any particular case.

350. *Publicity* for the decisions of the EDRB and for the sessions in which they are announced, and *access to the record* for anyone interested once a decision is handed down, contribute to the transparency of the EDR system and the transparency of electoral matters.

b) Access to complete and effective electoral justice

351. Electoral dispute resolution procedures should be *accessible* in terms of time, distance and cost, and *inclusive* so that citizens, candidates, political parties and political groupings can make their challenges without discrimination based on gender or ethnic origin. It should be possible to obtain a ruling on the merits of a dispute effectively and promptly without unwarranted procedural prerequisites, requirements or obstacles. No one who believes that their rights within the electoral process have been infringed should find themselves without protection or be defenceless when their interests recognized in electoral law are detrimentally affected by the action of an authority or any other actor.

352. The human right to an effective remedy before an established independent court in the light of any impairment of a person's rights is enshrined in several international human rights instruments and in the vast majority of the constitutions of democratic countries. In addition, if the fundamental right of access to electoral justice is not sufficiently guaranteed domestically in a particular state, recourse is possible to the international bodies provided for in the international human rights instruments and conventions to which the state is a party, on the basis of the principles of subsidiarity and complementarity (see paragraph 407).

353. One essential characteristic of an EDR system is that it offers an integral defence of electoral rights and a guarantee that every action and decision related to the electoral process complies with the legal framework.

354. Access to justice should be guaranteed not only for the person, political party or other claimant bringing the challenge, but also for anyone who upholds a contrary interest – such as an interested third party – so that the latter is afforded a guaranteed hearing. In this way, the system will comply with the principles of due process related to the right to a defence, by virtue of which all parties have the right to engage in the process with an equal opportunity to plead and argue as befits their interests.

355. In addition, it is fundamental that there is a judicial mechanism to defend the *constitutionality*, and not just the legality, of electoral actions and decisions related to an electoral process, which the persons and entities affected – political parties, voters, candidates – can turn to in order to argue that specific provisions of the law are unconstitutional. This should also enable the EDR system to provide an integral defence of the principles of the constitutionality as well as the legality of electoral actions and decisions. Given the short time frames for resolving electoral challenges under pressure from the timetable of the electoral process, it is advisable for the EDRB to have the jurisdiction to review not only the legality but also the constitutionality of electoral actions and decisions.

356. To facilitate access to the EDR system, the procedure for bringing electoral challenges should be simple. Filing a complaint brief with the appropriate authority (the EMB), for example, should be sufficient to commence the procedure, open a case and, subsequently, have it forwarded to the appropriate decision-making authority (the EDRB) without the person or entity bringing the challenge having to travel from their place of residence in order to file it directly with the EDRB. This can guarantee the *geographical accessibility* of electoral justice without requiring a wide network of decentralized presences of the EDRB to be established. For example, in France, all challenges relating to national elections are dealt with by the Constitutional Council in Paris, but may be submitted through the Prefect of the *département.*

357. It is also important to minimize the formalities required for a challenge to be deemed to have been properly filed. Some EDR systems provide for different kinds of electoral challenge, depending for example on the nature of the action challenged, the organ before which it is brought, the person who brings it or their claim. This can lead to the exclusion of challenges that may be valid in substance on technical or procedural grounds, which does not promote the credibility of the EDR system. It is good practice for EDRBs to consider a challenge properly filed if it identifies the action challenged and the reason why it is considered unsatisfactory, even if a mistake has been made regarding the use or name of the means of challenge, jurisdiction or forum.

358. Moreover, the electoral law should expressly establish when and how irregularities related to electoral criminal offences or administrative infractions could have consequences for or impact on the electoral process and its outcomes.

359. While it is fundamental to guarantee access to electoral justice, it is equally important to avoid distortion of the EDR system's function. A relevant factor in EDR system design is how to respond to challenges that are frivolous, vexatious or intended merely to delegitimize the electoral process without inhibiting access generally.

c) Free electoral justice, or a service at a reasonable cost

360. There is free access to electoral justice when there is no need to put up any bond or guarantee in order to go before the EDRB, and its services do not involve any financial cost for the complainants or their representatives. This promotes access to justice regardless of a complainant's financial situation.

361. The electoral justice service does carry a cost. Many countries have established free use of the electoral justice service as a human right in their respective constitutions, in which case the cost is covered by the state from the public treasury and paid for out of tax. The use of the EDR system is thus free of charge as part of the fundamental right to complete and effective judicial protection. Electoral disputes which involve matters of public interest are also sometimes supported by non-governmental organizations (NGOs) and civil society organizations.

362. Where a specific charge or cost is made to users of the electoral justice system, this should be at a reasonable price that takes account of criteria such as necessity and proportionality. It should not become an obstacle to access to electoral justice (see, for example, box 6.13). In Peru, for example, a sum of money must be deposited when challenging the nomination of a candidate, which is returned only in the event that the dispute is declared to have been well-founded, that is, if the challenged candidate is excluded from the election. For this reason, although many systems provide that access to the EDRS should be free of charge, some require a charge as a prerequisite for access to the EDRS in the form of a judicial bond, a deposit or a non-recoverable sum. Still others provide that costs be paid or for a fine to be imposed on a party that argues frivolously or from an obviously unfounded position.

Box 6.13. The possible effect of fees on the amount of petitions: the case of Japan

Maiko Shimizu

In Japan the number of EDR cases is higher in municipal elections than in national elections. One reason for this could be that first instance petitions at the municipal level (administrative) do not require the payment of a fee while petitions at the national level (court petition) do. Administrative petitions are also dealt with much faster than those petitions submitted to a judicial process. It can also be assumed that competition in municipal elections tends to be higher, resulting in more disputes. Public awareness of EDR is not very high in Japan, possibly as a result of the complicated nature of the EDR system and the low level of interest in elections among the general public.

Number of complaints filed at the first instance

	Disputes related to challenges to the validity of the election itself		Disputes related to the legitimacy of the elected person	
	Prefecture Assembly elections/ Prefecture Governor elections	Municipality Assembly elections/ mayoral elections	Prefecture Assembly elections/ Prefecture Governor elections	Municipality Assembly elections/ mayoral elections
1999	9	38	5	41
2000	0	25	0	16
2001	0	23	1	12
2002	2	34	0	13
2003	16	57	9	35

Note: The number of election disputes is particularly high in 1999 and 2003 because there were nationwide local elections in both years.

363. In the UK, within three days of presenting an election petition the complainant must provide an amount not exceeding GBP 5000 as security (in the case of a parliamentary election) or an amount the High Court directs for all costs, which may become payable to any witness summoned on behalf of the complainant or to any respondent.

364. Some countries provide for the possibility of ordering that costs be paid when a complainant puts forward a clearly unfounded position that suggests malice, or that a fine be imposed on anyone who files frivolous or mischievous challenges.

Box 6.14. The 'Richmond Case': the United Kingdom

Andrew Ellis

Under the British system, a complaint heard by an election court is treated under civil processes and legal costs can be awarded against the loser. In the case of a challenge to the successful candidate in an election to the Greater London Council in Richmond,

(cont.)

London, in the 1980s, the successful candidate and his election agent had left out a bill for GBP 19 from the return of election expenses. This would have taken the cost of the campaign slightly over the legal limit. They had also failed to complete the official expenses return form correctly. The court refused to unseat the candidate but, as these errors had been proved, he had to pay all his own legal costs and three-quarters of the legal costs of the losing candidate who had brought the case – even though many other errors the loser had alleged in the expenses return were rejected. The bill was in the region of GBP 50,000.

This system in relation to costs of electoral cases applies generally in systems with UK-inspired legislation (see for example section 28 of the Election Petitions Act of Jamaica). It can clearly inhibit people from bringing cases or defending them, but finding an alternative may be difficult. Unrestricted payment of legal costs out of public funds could lead to many more cases of vexatious litigation. Another related issue is right of audience – who is entitled to argue a case in the court hearing? Costs increase if representation in court by a qualified legal practitioner of some kind is required.

d) Timeliness

365. Electoral judicial proceedings should be *timely,* that is, a decision should be reached promptly and expeditiously within the legally established periods or stages of the electoral process. A decision taken outside this time frame may be unfair, and would make it impossible to correct the damage done to some electoral rights.

366. Reasonable deadlines should be provided for bringing challenges (generally shorter than those for civil litigation and other branches of administrative law). These need to balance the time required by the person alleging harm by a particular electoral act or decision to take stock of its content and scope and to gather the evidence, on the one hand, against the need to obtain a timely resolution, given that electoral processes proceed in stages that cannot be changed or interrupted. Accordingly, the system should take into account the extremely short time periods of the various stages of the electoral process and the need for each to be completed before it is possible to move on to the subsequent ones. To give the EDRB time to process, hear and resolve the respective challenges correctly, a balance must be struck between the short electoral time frames, the right to a defence of the person or body against whom the complaint is made, and the imperatives related to the timely administration of justice. This requires efficiency in imparting electoral justice and satisfactory relations between the EDRBs and EMBs. In addition, it is in general a healthy practice of legal process to provide for short timescales for resolving the challenges that have been filed.

367. Many EDR systems adopt the principle of irrevocability of all those acts and decisions of the electoral authority that have not been challenged in a timely fashion within a period specified in law (see paragraph 217). It makes it impossible to question the validity of a particular electoral action or decision at a later stage once it has become firm. For example, in several countries, like Mexico, it is not legally permissible for an irregularity committed during the election campaign to be raised as grounds for annulling the election during the stage of announcing the results if it was not opposed by the person or party affected during the stage of preparing the election.

368. It is important to note that this principle only operates when the alleged irregularity was susceptible to challenge at the time. If no means of challenge is provided for at that earlier stage there would be grounds for considering it proper to challenge it, for example, at the results stage. Hence, the election laws should establish specific and systematic deadlines for challenges to certain actions or decisions (e.g. those related to the electoral register or the nomination of candidates), and for the EDRBs to issue their decisions on these challenges.

369. Once started, an electoral process cannot, in general, be halted because timely renewal of the representative organs of government depends on it. It is good practice not only that all challenges must be resolved in a timely fashion, but also that the fact of a challenge having been filed does not suspend the effects of the electoral action or decision challenged. This helps avoid the EDR system being used as a mechanism for blocking the proper unfolding of an electoral process. An alternative is to defer all challenges to the electoral results period, in order to ensure that the electoral process is not interrupted or encumbered by long judicial procedures. The potential disadvantage of this approach is that any very serious irregularity during the electoral process that affected the result could only be rectified by annulment of the election, because it would be too late for any other corrective measure to have any effect.

370. There is a distinction between those acts and decisions that have an impact on the unfolding of the electoral process and those which, strictly speaking, fall outside its scope, in which case the time periods for filing a challenge and resolving it may vary. Some types of challenge are more complex and so may require more time to collect the information needed for their processing, consideration and resolution (for example those related to oversight of political parties' resources). To the extent that they do not have an impact on the electoral process itself, the time periods for hearing these can be longer. The possibility may be considered of establishing by law that the respective decisions, administrative and judicial, should not be made during the electoral process so as not to 'contaminate' it.

371. In the case of alleged electoral crimes or offences, care should be taken to ensure that the investigation and any criminal prosecution are undertaken

in an objective, expeditious and impartial manner by the authority tasked to do it. It would be advisable to consider conferring technical autonomy on the body entrusted with prosecuting electoral crimes and offences, and it should enjoy the support of the various political forces. This is the experience in Panama, which has an Attorney General for Electoral Crimes provided for in the constitution as an autonomous position appointed by the legislature.

372. Usually there is no urgency to determine criminal or administrative liability for an alleged crime or an infraction during the period of the electoral campaign or before the declaration of the results. However, the dynamic for the hearing and resolution of electoral challenges which need to be resolved in the course of the electoral process is a separate one. If an alleged electoral offence is (if proven) also grounds for the annulment of an election, the evidence must be produced and the facts taken before an EDRB to hear the challenge so that it can rule accordingly – regardless of the conclusion reached subsequently through the procedures for determining criminal or administrative liability.

373. The determinations of the EDRB should be issued without unwarranted delay, always seeking to reach and issue a decision before the possible infringement of an electoral right becomes irreparable. The judgement should also be issued before the elected person or body is installed into office. It is thus common for EDRBs to meet continuously and for very long hours during key periods.

374. Some EDR systems do however provide for the possibility of the final decision being issued subsequently. There have even been cases of a decision being issued after the term of the official challenged is up, which means that its effects are exclusively financial (the payment of the salary of the elected member). This applies both in EDR systems that come under legislative bodies, as in the United States, and also, in some cases, in EDR systems entrusted to judicial bodies, as in Colombia. Conversely, in Nigeria a gubernatorial candidate in Anambra State, Peter Obi, who had successfully challenged the re-election of the incumbent governor, Emeka Ngige, in 2007, and was installed in office in his place, was granted a full five-year term of office by the court instead of the remainder of the term. This situation could be regarded as the restoration of Obi's electoral rights in full instead of monetary compensation.

375. Where an EDRB does not resolve a challenge within the time frames legally provided for as a result of its own inefficiencies or behaviour, this may in itself give rise to some kind of liability.

e) The right to a defence or a hearing and due process of law

376. The EDRS should guarantee the right to a defence or to a hearing on a challenge both to the complainant and to the person or body complained against. This includes both the opportunity to make their arguments and the obligation on the EDRB to hear and study them. The EDRS must ensure that evidence supporting or refuting the challenge is offered and produced by the two sides to the case, and that the EDRB has a corresponding obligation to weigh that evidence and explain why it considers that it is or is not relevant or effective at establishing the facts (see chapter 7, section 5). All procedures should be guided by the principle of equality of the parties. In general, a distinction is drawn between: (a) the party that files the challenge, which has the standing, or is entitled, to do so (see chapter 7, section 3); (b) the respondent, which, because it is generally an action or decision of the EMB that is being challenged, is the authority in charge of the EMB (other possibilities include a political party whose leadership issued a decision); and (c) third parties, if they have a right to be heard. Several systems provide for an interested third party – another political party or candidate who has an interest that is incompatible with that of the party bringing the challenge but is interested in the outcome – to bring a challenge. In some EDRSs (and in most common law countries) the contention is directly between the political parties or candidates, and not between the party affected and the administrative agency (generally the EMB) whose act or decision is being challenged.

377. The electoral law should expressly establish the requirements, including on standing and legal status, for a challenge to be admissible. Frivolous, vexatious or malicious challenges may thus be excluded and possibly even sanctioned. The EDRB should notify all interested parties in writing of its decision on whether the challenge is or is not admissible, and its reasons should be well founded and well reasoned.

Box 6.15. Challenges to the results of national-level elections and referendums: France

Andrew Ellis

In France, challenges to the results of national-level elections and of referendums are dealt with by the Constitutional Council. When a complaint is received, the Council assigns the case to one of its sections. If the complaint is found to be inadmissible or the alleged irregularities cannot change the result of the election, the case is dismissed.

Otherwise, in the case of elections, the Council asks the person elected to respond to the complaint. In addition, the responsible section of the Council may itself demand documents and conduct further investigations. When this process is completed, the

(cont.)

rapporteur of the responsible section drafts a report, which will form the basis for the Council to determine the complaint in a private hearing. The Council may unseat the person elected, or annul the result of a referendum in whole or in part.

Challenges to the results of local, regional and European elections are handled by the administrative courts, with appeal allowed only on a point of law. Challenges on electoral registration questions are handled by the ordinary courts, with no provision for appeal.

378. Several systems provide that challenges must be made through the authority in charge (generally the EMB), in order to make electoral justice more geographically accessible (see paragraph 356). The EMB thus has the background information on the action that is being challenged. It will be necessary for the EDRB to provide that it is the duty of the EMB to collaborate effectively to ensure that the case file is properly made up. Contending parties and candidates should have the right to full access to EMB material. Some EDR systems establish that if an EMB fails to remit all the electoral information related to the case that should be in its possession, it may be found administratively liable. The EDRB may not then be able to uphold the validity of the EMB's actions, thus making them subject to annulment or modification.

379. The electoral legislation should expressly state which legal remedies can be granted as a result of a challenge to the election results. In particular, it should specify the mechanisms, specific causes, and evidence needed for a total or partial recount to be ordered or to invalidate totally or in part the election results, and specify which EDRB has jurisdiction to decree it (see chapter 7, section 6).

Box 6.16. Essential features of EDR proceedings

Ensuring that EDR proceedings comply with the requirements of due process involves:

- electoral proceedings which take place before an EDRB that is predetermined in law, independent, impartial and accessible;
- rules for access to the dispute system and process which are clearly spelled out;
- the guarantee of a hearing and the principle of the right to a defence under equal conditions;
- full access in equal conditions to EDR proceedings and the relevant files and material;
- an expeditious and public process of decision with any remedy granted being effective and timely;

(cont.)

- decisions should be set out and justified in reasoned and fair reports, concluding with judgements that are handed down in keeping with the facts proven in the proceeding (the principle of congruence) and that assess each of the parties' claims (the principle of exhaustiveness); and
- the full enforcement of the judgement guaranteed.

f) Full and timely enforcement of judgements and rulings

380. The full and timely enforcement of the judgements and rulings handed down in response to challenges is of the utmost importance in any EDR system. Enforcement of the judgements handed down by the authority with jurisdiction is a public policy question, and all the authorities are duty bound to contribute to their full enforcement. It would be of no use for an EDRB to acknowledge that a particular political party or citizen is correct on a given matter and grant a specific remedy if it does not have effective means of ensuring the full and timely enforcement of its ruling and of the remedy or correction ordered.

381. Once the judgement or decision in an electoral dispute has been handed down, rules should be observed with a view to its full enforcement. For example, when the obligation consists of carrying out a certain action, the person or body under this obligation should be subject to a realistic time frame for doing so, depending on the circumstances. This time frame should be set out in the judgement or ruling. If after that time has passed the action has not been carried out, the EDRB should be authorized to impose some measures to compel the person or entity under the obligation to do so. It may consider an array of possible sanctions that take account of the seriousness and, where applicable, any repetition of the omission (e.g. fine, arrest, use of government force, and even beginning the process of removal, in the case of a public servant; or the procedure for suspending or cancelling the candidacy, or the concession in the case of a broadcast media outlet).

382. When the person or entity under the obligation refuses to carry out what is ordered in a judgement, it is advisable for the EDRB to have the power to replace him, her or it in order to ensure compliance. The EDRB should have the powers to order whatever is necessary to attain full enforcement of the judgement and to repair the violation committed in order to ensure restoration of their electoral rights to the citizens, candidates, citizens' organization, political groupings and political parties concerned.

383. It is often the case that national legislation does not provide for adequate sanctions (criminal or administrative) for failure by state institutions, public officials and media outlets, over which some EDRBs have no authority, to carry

out the judgements or rulings that result from electoral challenges. In addition, the sanctions of suspension or cancellation of the registration of political parties or candidates are vulnerable to abuse. The EDRB must act firmly and prudently to ensure the full enforcement of its judgements and rulings. However, it should consider refraining from ordering certain actions to be carried out by a person with respect to whom it does not have any mechanisms to ensure compliance. It is often preferable to recognize the lack of legal mechanisms to bind and order someone to engage in certain conduct rather than order it and then have the order ignored. The credibility of an EDRB would be seriously impaired if it were to hand down judgements or rulings that were ignored by those to whom they were directed. However, such situations would be likely to provide evidence of a need for reform of legislation.

384. Most electoral challenges originate directly or indirectly from an action, decision or omission by the EMB. The role of the EMB is thus especially important in carrying out the judgements or decisions, and electoral legislation must establish a duty of the EMB to assist EDRBs and allow full access for interested parties and candidates to the relevant EMB materials and files. It is therefore desirable that collaborative relations exist between the EDRB and the EMB, quite independent of the possibility of the EDRB imposing a measure that requires the EMB to act or lodging a complaint so that some type of liability can be attributed to the EMB.

g) Consistency in the interpretation and application of the electoral laws

385. One sign of the independence and impartiality of an EDRB is its consistency in the interpretation and application of the constitutional, statutory, regulatory and, where applicable, international provisions pertaining to elections, regardless of the political pressures and any other circumstances or actors involved. When dynamic and changing circumstances or new insights into the provisions applicable by the EDRB appear to demand a change in interpretation, special care should be taken to justify such changes fully and to ensure that they are truly exceptional. The predictability of the actions of EDRBs is fundamental to legal certainty and the credibility of the EDR system. Any change easily triggers suspicions of political bias.

386. In EDR systems that are entrusted to regular courts that are part of the judicial branch and are part of the common law tradition (for example Australia, Canada, India and the UK), under the doctrine of *stare decisis* an interpretation of the law previously embraced by a court becomes binding precedent for the same judicial body in future cases. Only by deciding that a later case is different can a court stray from a certain standard of interpretation previously upheld. It must conclude that the new case contains characteristics that are substantially different to make the precedent inapplicable.

387. In countries with a civil law tradition, the important function attributed to written law as the main source of law, combined with the principle of judicial independence which requires that a judge is generally subject only to the mandate of written law and not to rulings made by another judge, together mean that in most of these countries judicial precedent is not binding on future cases. This is the case, for example, in France. However, in some systems this is changing, and an increasing number of systems (judicial systems in general and EDR systems in particular) in this tradition provide that precedents established by certain judicial bodies are binding on lower courts.

388. Thus, for example, the Superior Chamber (Sala Superior) of the Electoral Court of the Judicial Branch of the Federation of Mexico is authorized to establish binding case law when it upholds the same standard for interpreting or filling gaps in the law in three judgements. Unlike other systems (both common law and civil law) in which precedent or case law is binding only on judicial bodies, in Mexico the case law established by the Superior Chamber of the Electoral Court binds all other electoral courts (both the lower-ranking ones of the federal judiciary and the state electoral courts) and also the EMBs (both the federal EMB and those that correspond to each state of the federation). The law also provides that the Superior Chamber may undo the binding nature of the case law by a majority of five of its seven members, specifying the reasons that justify the change in its interpretative criteria.

389. In general, the top-level organ of any EDR system should endeavour to establish clear and uniform criteria for interpreting the applicable constitutional and statutory provisions and for filling any possible legal gaps if it has the authority to do so. In addition, it should establish and disseminate the set of judicial precedents that may be binding on the lower EDRBs. It would also be desirable for the electoral legislation to establish that such precedent is binding on the EMBs, as differences in the application of criteria between different electoral authorities could pose a threat to legal certainty and imperil trust in the electoral process and its institutions. This is part of the so-called normative autonomy that characterizes the various EDR systems. It is advisable that each EDR system is regulated by clear and precise provisions.

Table 6.1. Advantages and disadvantages of the different types of electoral dispute resolution systems*

Type of EDRS	Advantages	Disadvantages
Legislative body	• Facilitates political solutions to deadlocks or serious conflicts • Promotes democratic governance through the support of the legislature to political representation • Safeguards independence among the three branches of government when it avoids the judiciary's involvement in partisan struggles	• Can encourage abuse by majorities in the legislature who tend to favour their own political interests • Affects legitimacy when decisions are not taken according to the rule of law but on the basis of political considerations • Encourages the resolution of electoral conflicts through negotiation or mobilization rather than through institutional channels and the law
Judicial body	• Contributes to legitimacy since it guarantees that electoral decisions are taken according to the rule of law, to the benefit of justice, legal certainty and political stability • Avoids abuse by legislative majorities, thus reinforcing minority rights • Acknowledges that electoral disputes, even if they have political content, are judicial in nature, and should be solved according to the constitution and the law	• Can encourage political forces who do not agree with its decisions to question the capacity or impartiality of the judicial body • Can encourage a dangerous involvement of judges in partisan political disputes • Risk of political forces controlling judicial appointments according to political criteria, instead of focusing on their professional capacity, independence and impartiality • Can undermine the high-ranked court involved when the losing political forces question its decisions
(a) Regular court of the judicial branch	• Reflects the judicial nature of electoral disputes and entrusts their resolution to a more experienced judicial body • Does not generate significant costs since no new institution is created	• Does not always provide the best and timely decision given the body's lack of specialization and/or enormous caseload • Can affect the image of the EJS in some emerging democracies whose judicial branch lacks prestige or independence • If the legislature does not participate in the selection of the members of the judicial body it could lack political consensus
(b) Constitutional court or council	• Contributes to the legitimacy and respectability of the EJS given the high rank, usual prestige and professional capacity of its members • Guarantees that electoral disputes are solved not just according to the law but according to the constitution as well	• If there is a prior decision from a different judicial body, there may be time constraints which could affect the quality of the new decision or render it inopportune • Affects the image of the EJS in some emerging democracies where the constitutional council plays a political role more than a judicial one

(cont.)

Type of EDRS	Advantages	Disadvantages
(c) Administrative court	• Reflects the judicial and administrative law nature of electoral disputes and entrusts their resolution to the most experienced administrative court • Does not generate related costs since no new institution is created	• Can undermine the administrative court involved when the losing political forces question its decisions • Does not always provide timely electoral decisions given the common enormous caseload • If the legislature does not participate in the selection of the members of the administrative court it could lack political consensus
(d) Specialized electoral court	• Contributes to the quality and appropriate timing of decisions • Centres the attention of the political forces in the selection of its members, helping to give them adequate guarantees for their independence and impartiality	• Can encourage conflicts between the EMB and the electoral court • Entails greater costs since it involves the creation of a new electoral court • Risk of selection of the electoral court members being based on their partisan convictions
Electoral management body with judicial powers	• Avoids possible discrepancies between the EMB and the body responsible for EDR • Contributes to identifying the body responsible for all of the electoral process, drawing attention to the selection of its members, their credentials and the esteem they are due • Reduces the usually high cost of elections	• Concentrates electoral power in one single body, creating the risk of eventual abuses without checks by a different body • Disregards the international human right to an effective remedy before an independent and impartial court
Ad hoc body, whether national or international	• Helps to establish institutional mechanisms for a return to democracy after serious political conflict or crisis • Guarantees, through international community involvement, that no group or sector will be excluded from the electoral process	• Risk of perpetuating the transitional regime • Risk of the defeated political forces disregarding electoral results • Can encourage the defeated political forces to question the participation of the international community

* When analysing the advantages and disadvantages of the different types of electoral justice systems, it should be noted that it is only possible to identify certain *trends*. The functioning of each country's EDRS is the result of a multiplicity of factors and, very commonly, the same type of system works differently from one country to another, since the historical, cultural and socio-political context makes a difference. Thus, there is no single institutional design of an EDRS that implies correctness or success. There is no single 'best system'.

CHAPTER 7

CHAPTER 7

Basic elements of EDR systems

1. Types of challenge

390. In general, as is noted in chapter 4, electoral challenges are intrinsically corrective as their effects include the annulment, modification or recognition of wrongful conduct in order to repair the violation that has been committed and restore the enjoyment of the electoral right involved.

391. Electoral challenges can be categorized as administrative, judicial, legislative and international. Given the difficulties that stem from the diversity of the electoral legal frameworks of different countries, and the ambiguity of some, this Handbook uses a formal criterion to determine whether a challenge is of an administrative, judicial, legislative or international kind. This criterion is based on the nature of the organ that hears and resolves the challenge. There may be other criteria for classifying the various electoral challenges, but the one adopted here is useful and illustrative of the varieties of challenge mechanisms in the various electoral dispute resolution systems.

392. It is most common for an EDRS to provide for either an administrative challenge before the EMB or a judicial challenge. On occasion it may also provide for legislative or even international challenges.

a) Administrative challenges

393. Administrative electoral challenges are those that are resolved by the EMB in charge of directing, organizing, administering and overseeing election procedures. Through such a challenge, those affected (political parties, candidates and ordinary citizens) may oppose an electoral action or decision using a procedure in which either the same organ of the EMB that issued the action or decision being challenged or another of a higher rank decides the dispute.

394. The vast majority of countries allow for administrative electoral challenges that are referred for resolution to one of the organs of the EMB. Some systems feature administrative challenges only, and some combine these with a subsequent challenge before a judicial and/or legislative body, thus constituting a mixed EDR system.

395. As is made clear in *Electoral Management Design: The International IDEA Handbook*, the various EMBs in the world can be distinguished by whether they adopt the Independent Model, the Governmental Model or the Mixed Model of electoral management. In general, EMBs have a pyramidal structure, with the highest-level body at the national level and other intermediate bodies subordinated to it – mainly reflecting the territorial, political, administrative and electoral division of the state – down to the level of the polling station. Administrative challenges filed against certain actions are heard by the electoral organs that carried out the action being challenged or by those to which they answer, until they reach the top of the hierarchy.

396. In those EMBs that are based on the Independent or Mixed Model, it is quite common for the composition of the highest-ranking organ to be determined by the public organs of the state (generally the legislative branch or the judicial branch, possibly with some participation by the executive branch). In these systems, it is common for some role also to be given to the political parties – generally a marginal one, with their representatives being given the right to vote but with independent experts constituting the majority of its members. Sometimes the independent experts are the only ones with a right to vote and the representatives of political parties only have the right to speak and oversight functions. In those EMBs that are made up of independent experts it is common for the political parties to play an important role in the selection of their members (see *Electoral Management Design: The International IDEA Handbook*).

b) Judicial challenges

397. Judicial means of bringing electoral challenges are those procedural legal instruments provided for by law by which two or more conflicting parties bring before a judicial body, that is, a judge or a court, whether or not as part of the judicial branch, a dispute over an alleged error, irregularity, instance of wrongful conduct, deficiency or illegality in a certain electoral action or decision. The judicial body, in its position as a superior third party and as an organ of the state, decides on the dispute in a final and impartial manner.

398. There is a growing tendency to establish mechanisms for judicial challenges in electoral frameworks. As is highlighted in chapter 5, these may be brought before regular courts, which constitute the judicial branch; a constitutional court or council; an administrative court; a specialized electoral court; or some combination of jurisdictions (see box 7.1).

Box 7.1. Types of court in charge of resolving judicial electoral challenges

- Regular court belonging to the judicial branch
- Constitutional court or council
- Administrative court
- Specialized electoral court

399. The various judicial electoral challenges can be classified, generally speaking, into trials and appeals. The latter, in turn, can be subdivided into regular remedies or appeals and special or exceptional remedies (see box 7.2).

Box 7.2. Classification of judicial electoral challenges

- Trials
- Appeals
  - Ordinary appeals
  - Extraordinary or exceptional appeals (e.g. writ of certiorari – see the Glossary)

(i) Trials

400. A trial is a formal judicial examination of evidence and a determination of legal claims. Electoral-administrative actions or decisions by an EMB or a political party can be challenged in such a trial. Judgement is entrusted to an impartial judicial body or court, which decides the dispute from a position of distance from the parties. The procedure is often adversarial, especially in countries with Anglo-American or Spanish traditions of jurisprudence. In common with French jurisprudence generally, a trial in a system with traditions of French jurisprudence may also include investigative elements of procedure.

(ii) Appeals

401. An appeal is a proceeding undertaken to have a decision reconsidered by a higher court for review and possible reversal. Appeals are hearings that can be invoked before a higher court on the merits of the judicial decision issued by the lower court, or against violations committed in the proceedings of the lower court. Appeals usually account for the largest share of judicial electoral dispute resolution mechanisms (EDRMs). They can be invoked either within or as a continuation of a judicial proceeding.

402. *Ordinary appeals* are regular proceedings by a higher court to review a judicial decision. After the appeal is submitted by the unsuccessful litigant, the appellate court, which generally has more than one member, examines

the entire record, both factual and legal, and any alleged procedural and substantive violations. The decision may be to affirm or reverse the ruling that is being challenged. The appellate court may accept the challenge to the original ruling, replacing the lower court's decision; reject the challenge, confirming the original ruling; or order that the process be annulled and that the original court should re-hear the case on the basis of legal rulings or guidance provided by the appellate court.

403. *Extraordinary or exceptional appeals* are those appeals, such as writ of certiorari, that can only be brought on grounds specifically set out in the procedural laws (an example could be a provision that an appeal is only admissible if the alleged violation could have had the effect of changing the result of the election). They only imply a review of the legality of the procedure or judicial decision being challenged and therefore cover only legal issues, since consideration of the facts is usually reserved for the lower court which handed down the judgement being challenged.

Box 7.3. The handling of electoral disputes in Russia (including appeal against inaction on the part of the EMB)

Sergueï Kouznetsov

According to Article 75 of the Law on Basic Guarantees of Electoral Rights and the Right of Citizens of the Russian Federation to Participate in a Referendum, electoral disputes are dealt with by the courts of general jurisdiction or electoral commissions in the following way:

a. an appeal against decisions, actions or omissions of the Central Election Commission (Tsentral'naia Izbiratel'naia Kommissiia) can be submitted to the Supreme Court (Verkhovnyi Sud) of the Russian Federation;
b. an appeal against decisions, actions or omissions of electoral commissions of the federal entities and regional commissions may be submitted to the respective supreme courts of the entities and courts of second instance (regional, territorial, courts of the cities with federal status, etc.); and
c. appeals against decisions of other commissions can be made in the courts of general jurisdiction.

Citizens and associations can complain against the decisions of an electoral commission to the commission at the level immediately above it. Appeals against decisions of municipal commissions can be made to a commission of a federal entity, and appeals against the decisions of the latter can be made to the Central Election Commission of Russia. Commissions at all levels are under the obligation to execute court decisions concerning violations of electoral rights.

The law on basic guarantees of electoral rights includes detailed procedures for dispute resolution.

(cont.)

One of the specific features of the complaints procedure in Russia is the possibility to complain not only against decisions or actions of electoral commissions and public officials that violate citizens' electoral rights but also against a *lack of action* by the competent authorities.

Complaints against decisions, actions or omissions of electoral commissions and public officials that violate citizens' electoral rights go to the electoral commission above in the hierarchy, as explained above, and it can take one of the following decisions:

a. to refuse the complaint after it has been examined;
b. to cancel the decision of the lower commission and examine the case on its merits; and
c. to cancel the decision of the lower commission and remit the case for a fresh examination (or take appropriate action).

c) Legislative challenges

404. Legislative electoral challenges are those legal instruments provided for in the constitution or statutes of some countries which grant powers to legislative bodies or other political assemblies to formally resolve certain electoral challenges or issue the certification or the final result of an election.

405. This type of electoral challenge is considered political, not only because of the political nature of the body in charge of resolving it, but also because of the lack of controls to ensure that the decision concerned is always in line with the constitution, the statute law and all other applicable provisions. It is often political interests or negotiations between those who constitute the majority in such assemblies that tend to prevail. The legislative organ or political assembly in charge of resolving the case is required to conform to the applicable constitutional and statutory framework but there may be no EDR mechanisms to guarantee this. However, this system can be accompanied by a judicial challenge mechanism – either as a prior remedy, as in Argentina, Italy, Switzerland and the United States, or as a subsequent remedy, as in Germany. This provides further guarantees that decisions are made in accordance with the constitution and the law.

406. The means for legislative electoral challenges have come to be seen as political, but the body responsible for resolving the challenge must operate within the terms of the constitution and the electoral laws regardless of whether there are mechanisms for challenging any unlawful decision before another body. Failure to ensure this has led to abuses by some legislatures (see paragraph 156 and box 5.3).

d) International challenges

407. Electoral rights are human rights and several have been enshrined in various international instruments (see chapter 2, section 2). Some of these universal or regional instruments have agencies and procedures for reinforcing, on the basis of *subsidiarity* and *complementarity*, means for protecting and defending that which is established domestically. The subsidiary nature of international challenges means that domestic means and mechanisms must be exhausted first before recourse is had to a universal or regional mechanism. In addition, the complementary nature of such challenges emphasizes the fact that international mechanisms do not replace but at best are additional to the means of protection provided for domestically. The jurisdiction of international bodies in charge of overseeing the implementation of electoral and human rights needs to be specifically recognized by the state party to the corresponding international instrument, treaty, covenant or convention.

408. The international means for bringing electoral challenges are those legal instruments provided for in international treaties and conventions by which those with the standing to do so may have recourse, on a subsidiary and complementary basis, to the competent body (for example the European Court of Human Rights or the Inter-American Court of Human Rights) after exhausting the domestic remedies provided. This enables a complainant to challenge an act or judgement that is alleged to violate either electoral rights or a right enshrined in the relevant international instrument. In due course, the international body with jurisdiction resolves the dispute. Its decision is binding if the state party has recognized its jurisdiction.

409. It should also be possible for another international organization to issue non-binding recommendations to a given state party to an international instrument, so long as the state recognizes its jurisdiction. For example, the United Nations Human Rights Council is made up of 47 member states, elected directly and individually by the members of the General Assembly, based on an equitable regional distribution. The Council addresses situations in which human rights, including political and electoral rights, have been violated (dealing in particular with grave and systematic violations), and makes recommendations on the promotion and protection of human rights. It maintains a system of special procedures and a complaints procedure and presents an annual report to the General Assembly.

410. At the regional level, the European Court of Human Rights may receive applications from any person, NGO or group of individuals claiming to be the victim of a violation by a state party of the rights, including electoral rights, set out in the 1950 European Convention for the Protection of Human Rights and Fundamental Freedoms. If the Court finds that there has been a

violation of the convention or its protocols, it shall afford just satisfaction. Its final judgement is transmitted to the Committee of Ministers, which supervises its execution.

411. Similarly, the Inter-American Commission on Human Rights has jurisdiction to hear complaints brought by any person, group of persons or non-governmental entity submitted within six months of receiving notice of the final domestic decision that the complainant considers causes some injury to her or his human rights, including electoral rights, established in the 1969 American Convention on Human Rights. The Commission limits itself to examining whether the fact alleged is a violation of the convention, and can make non-binding recommendations to the states party. In the event that the state party does not accept the Commission's recommendation, if the state in question has recognized its jurisdiction, the Commission is able to refer the case to the Inter-American Court of Human Rights. In such cases the judgements of the Court are binding.

412. The African Commission on Human and Peoples' Rights was established under the African Charter on Human and Peoples' Rights. In addition to the right and duty to interpret the Charter on request, the mandate of the Commission is to promote and protect human rights in Africa, including the electoral rights established in Article 13 of the Charter. The Commission receives and decides on complaints, called communications, from member states, individuals and NGOs. Anyone can bring a communication. Representation by legal counsel is not required and an NGO may complain on behalf of itself or others. The Commission can only state its findings and make recommendations to the Assembly of Heads of State and Government of the African Union. Enforcement of the Commission's decisions depends entirely on the goodwill of the offending state.

2. Actions that may be challenged

413. The electoral actions and decisions that are subject to challenge before an EDRB can be classified according to the nature of the body or entity whose action or decision is being challenged or according to the point in time when the challenge is set in motion, taking as a reference the periods of the electoral cycle. This classification is exclusively for analytical purposes and does not necessarily coincide with any given EDR system.

Box 7.4. Actions that can be challenged

a. Classified by the nature of the organ whose action or decision is challenged
   i. Actions by electoral authorities
   ii. Actions by political party organs
   iii. Actions by other persons or entities (candidates, media outlets, non-electoral authorities, etc.)
b. Classified by the moment when the challenge is brought
   i. Actions that occurred during the pre-electoral period
   ii. Actions that occurred during the electoral period
   iii. Actions that occurred during the post-electoral period

a) Actions that can be challenged classified by the nature of the entity whose action or decision is being challenged

414. Using this criterion for classification makes it possible to distinguish between those challenges that are brought against the actions of electoral authorities, and those that are brought against other entities such as political parties, candidates and media outlets. The EDR system of each country must determine which electoral actions are subject to challenge.

Box 7.5. Challenges to the decisions of bodies other than the electoral authorities

A significant number of EDR systems only allow for direct electoral challenges to be filed against official actions and decisions, that is, those of the EMB. There are, however, many other entities, such as political parties, media outlets, and so on, the actions of which may have a deleterious effect on an electoral process, and potentially a negative effect on electoral rights. Efforts are often made to link the action of the EMB with these other types of action. Once the EMB has ruled on the matter by accepting or rejecting the action of the other entity, the party affected may challenge the action of the EMB. In this way, such EDR systems provide only indirectly for the defence of electoral rights with respect to the actions of the other entities.

For example, in a political party's internal election to select candidates, citizen A, who is a member of the party, is negatively affected by a party organ because the party considers citizen B to have won and seeks to register B as the candidate before the EMB. Once the EMB registers or announces citizen B as the candidate, citizen A challenges the decision of the EMB before the EDRB in order to have the EDRB overturn the EMB's decision and order it to register her or him as the candidate. In this way, the EDRB would be indirectly restoring the right, which had been violated by the internal organ of a political party, of a citizen with an interest in the enjoyment of his or her electoral right to run for elective office.

415. Bearing in mind the complexity of pursuing the procedure described in box 7.5 for indirectly defending electoral rights against entities other than the EMB, several EDR systems now provide that actions taken by other entities can be challenged directly, especially in view of the risk of violations of certain rights being irreparable if such a lengthy and complex procedure were to be followed.

416. Ideally, no electoral action or decision should have the potential to cause injury to an electoral right that cannot be challenged by the interested person either directly or indirectly. Every electoral action should be subject to the provisions of the constitution and the law. As mentioned above, if the fundamental right to access electoral justice is not sufficiently guaranteed domestically in a particular state, there is a possibility of recourse, on a subsidiary and complementary basis, to the international mechanisms provided for in the international human rights instruments and conventions to which the state is party.

417. This section identifies the organs and entities whose actions may be challenged. The variety of electoral actions and decisions that are subject to challenge is analysed separately. The lists below are in no way exhaustive, and they simply highlight some types of cases.

i) Actions and decisions by EMB authorities

418. In general, electoral challenges are brought against actions by and the procedures and decisions of an EMB.

419. There are various types of EMBs around the world. It is possible to distinguish between the Independent or Autonomous Model of electoral management, the Governmental Model of electoral management, and the Mixed Model of electoral management (see paragraph 395). All EMBs carry out a series of electoral actions, procedures and decisions each of which is susceptible to challenge to the extent that it affects a holder of electoral rights. The challenges can be lodged at different periods of the electoral cycle.

ii) Actions and decisions of political party organs

420. Several EDR systems identify as subject to challenge directly before an EDRB those actions or decisions by political parties that are considered to violate an election-related constitutional or statutory provision, and possibly to violate an electoral right. Different situations can be identified based on whether the entity allegedly affected is a citizen affiliated with the political party whose action is being challenged or another political party, an opposition candidate or any other entity other than the party whose action is being challenged.

421. The possibility of bringing challenges against the actions and decisions of political parties is justified as part of the integral defence of fundamental electoral rights, including with respect to the actions of entities other than official authorities, such as political parties, which – given their dominant position with respect to their members, particularly in situations where they offer the only legal way in which candidates can be nominated for public office – are in a position to violate these electoral rights, for example, if a political party nominates a different candidate from the one who won an internal election.

422. An ever-growing number of EDR systems provide for the possibility, explicitly or implicitly, of the EDRB admitting a direct challenge against the actions or decisions of a political party which is alleged to have violated an electoral right of its members. This has helped to guarantee that the electoral actions and decisions of political parties are in line with the principles of constitutionality and legality, as well as the practice of internal democracy within the parties. In general, such challenges before the EDRB are subsidiary and complementary, as the internal possibilities for redress must be exhausted first.

423. Some EDR systems – often those entrusted to the regular courts of the judicial branch – provide for the possibility that a person can bring an action directly before an EDRB demanding that a certain party act in a particular way or refrain from an action that is considered to violate the electoral legal framework. In Poland, for example, in response to the publication of defamatory material, the EDRB is able to order the political party that committed the infraction to suspend dissemination of such publicity and even order it to be confiscated.

424. In the case of violations that could affect other political parties or opposing candidates, some EDR systems only provide for indirect means of ensuring that the electoral process complies with the legal framework and defending the electoral rights of political party members who allege that they are adversely affected by the action or decision of the EMB which validates or confers efficacy on the political party decision which has affected them.

425. Some systems provide for administrative procedures before the EMB which, without being electoral challenges in the proper sense of the term (as they would not be challenging the action or decision of a political party in a trial), enable the EMB to take into account alleged irregularities committed by the different political parties (particularly those linked to election campaigns). The EMB can then provide a legal remedy which is subject to judicial oversight by the EDRB. One example is the administrative procedure used in Mexico to analyse the content of material broadcast on radio and television that has been alleged to violate legal provisions. The remedy may entail an order to suspend the broadcasting of electoral publicity

prohibited by law. The important thing here is the corrective nature of the legal remedy granted, to clean up the electoral process in such a way that the harmful effects of an irregular action do not continue and reach the point of substantially affecting the results – regardless of any other administrative sanction imposed on the transgressor.

iii) Actions by other persons or entities

426. The actions of other persons or entities, such as candidates, media outlets, or non-electoral authorities, may also violate the legal provisions governing elections and possibly electoral rights. Thus some EDR systems – particularly those entrusted to the regular courts of the judicial branch – explicitly or implicitly provide for the possibility of the EDRB hearing direct challenges against the actions of those other persons or entities. As an example, a non-electoral authority could be alleged to have become improperly involved in the electoral process, trying to influence voters on behalf of a particular political force through institutional campaigns that call on people to vote.

427. Direct challenges of this sort are not common in EDR systems with a corrective function. Instead, in the case of alleged violations of electoral legal provisions or electoral rights, recourse is usually made by indirect means by challenging an action or decision of the EMB or other regulatory agency which validates or confers efficacy on the action of the other person or entity. The relevant provisions sometimes make it possible to bring an administrative case before the EMB or other regulatory agency in order to investigate whether those actors have committed an electoral administrative infraction or irregularity. If the provisions allow for this, the EMB or other agency may grant a legal remedy or punish the transgressor (e.g. someone who disseminates illegal publicity over the broadcast media, as in paragraph 425), in which case that decision of an administrative authority can usually be challenged before a judicial EDRB.

Box 7.6. Hungary: resolving disputes relating to the use of the media in election campaigns

Complaints regarding the role of the media in election campaigns in Hungary (especially with respect to violating the basic principles of electoral procedures, and the publication of political advertisements) are dealt with as follows:

a. regarding periodicals distributed locally or local provision of programmes, by the competent local election committee of the seat or address of the publisher or the programme provider;
b. regarding regional provision of programmes, by the competent regional election committee of the seat or address of the programme provider;

(cont.)

c. regarding periodicals distributed nationally, news agencies or nationwide provision of programmes, by the National Election Committee.

If the election committee finds the accused party guilty, it can, in addition to the general legal consequences, order the editorial staff of the periodical, the programme provider or the news agency to publish its decision or the operative clause thereof within three days (in the case of daily newspapers and news agencies), in the next issue (for periodicals), and (in the case of programme providers) within three days, at the same time of day and on as many occasions and as many times as the announcement violating the law was broadcast.

b) Actions that can be challenged classified by the moment when the challenge is brought

428. In general, electoral challenges may come up during any period of the electoral cycle (see chapter 2, section 3).

i) Challenges during the pre-electoral period

429. Before an election process begins, it is common for challenges to be filed related to the updating of the electoral registers, the registration of new political parties, or the delimitation of the electoral districts (the electoral geography). In addition, challenges may arise related to the internal democracy of political parties, and to the financing and oversight of the sources of political party funds and of regular expenditures.

The electoral register and voter registration cards

430. The electoral register is a fundamental instrument of representative democracy. It helps to give meaning to the legal and political principle expressed in the phrase 'one person one vote' in that it is designed to produce an accurate, verifiable, up-to-date and reliable public census of the persons who fall into the category of 'electors' and who are not in any way disqualified from exercising their right to vote.

431. Identifying and registering electors is a procedure that results from an action or decision of the EMB or other responsible authority. The register makes it possible to demonstrate one's status as an elector on election day, through the production of a voter registration card, where applicable, and inclusion on the electoral register. The register is a database with the names of and basic electoral information about all those who could potentially exercise their right to vote on election day. One of the principal foundations of representative democracy

is that the information contained in the register must be genuine, certain and reliable. The responsible authority must give assurances that the personal data that electors provide will not be disclosed to anyone without consent.

432. The actions subject to challenge associated with electoral registration include all those performed by the EMB or responsible authority in relation to setting up the voter registry, and the issuing or non-issuing to individuals of personal identification cards (where these are used for electoral purposes) or voter registration cards. Other possible actions subject to challenge are linked to whether errors have been corrected, whether there are any omissions from the lists, details of changes of residence, and adequate arrangements for publishing the lists open to inspection by the public. Access to the lists must be guaranteed for individuals, candidates and political parties.

Determinations on whether to grant, reject or cancel the registration of a political party and other political entities

433. The actions subject to challenge include those related to the establishment, operation or closure of political parties, those linked to the registration of parties or other political groupings, including decisions on their names, logos and symbols, and the rejection, suspension or cancellation of political party registrations.

Box 7.7. Opposition in Cambodia

The electoral law of Cambodia provides that no party may have a name the same as another party. A group of pro-government members left one of the opposition parties, the Khmer Nation Party, and announced that they remained the Khmer Nation Party. The ensuing legal case between the two Khmer Nation parties was decided in favour of the pro-government group.

Leader of the opposition Khmer Nation Party Sam Rainsy believed that this was likely to happen again, and that the same mechanism would be used to disqualify his party under whatever new name it chose. Consequently, he chose to rename his party the Sam Rainsy Party, a name which he thought could not be appropriated by a pro-government group. Up to 2010, his judgement has been proved right.

434. Several countries establish procedures for registering those political parties (and in some cases other political organizations or groupings) that meet legally established requirements. These procedures should not be designed to operate in such a way as to nullify the fundamental electoral right of association.

435. In addition to the dissolution of a political party by decision of its members – agreed for the causes and in keeping with the procedures provided for in its charter – the dissolution or abolition of a party and, where applicable, the

cancellation of its registration may only proceed by decision of the competent EDRB and in those circumstances provided for in the constitution or in law. These vary from country to country and include failure to comply with the requirements for obtaining registration, such as having the minimum number of members required by law; grievous and systematic breaches of the party's legal obligations; failure to participate or present candidates in a regular general election or over a certain period; failure to obtain a minimum percentage of the vote in a particular regular general election, or to achieve representation in the legislature; and failure to hold internal party elections over a certain period.

436. In Germany, the jurisdiction of the Constitutional Court to declare unconstitutional political parties, movements or other forms of organization whose objectives, actions or conduct do not respect the basic principles of democratic and constitutional government was established by the Fundamental Law of 1949. It was used, for example, in 1952 by the Federal Constitutional Court to prohibit the Socialist Party of the Reich and in 1956 to prohibit the Communist Party of Germany. Similar powers exist in Chile and Spain, vested in the constitutional court or another supreme judicial body.

437. In addition, some countries provide other grounds for the dissolution of political parties, such as their forming paramilitary organizations; actions that go against the democratic principles enshrined in the constitution, the electoral code, the Universal Declaration of Human Rights, and the international treaties to which the state is a party; and proven subordination to or dependence on foreign organizations or governments. Along the same lines, some countries consider participation in a coup d'état or sedition as grounds for cancelling the registration of a political party.

Delimitation of electoral districts

438. Decisions on the delimitation of electoral districts, or electoral geography, are made by the EMB or, as is the case in several countries, by the legislature based on technical studies prepared by the EMB or by a separate delimitation body. They are generally made during the pre-electoral period (although on occasion they are made during the post-electoral period). In general, they are inspired by the principle of one person, one vote and aim at more or less equal numbers of electors, so that each elected representative represents approximately the same number of electors. Accordingly, when the demographics shift in the different regions of a country, there is a need to make adjustments or changes to the way in which electoral district boundaries are drawn in order to preserve a more or less equal ratio of representatives to electors in each of the electoral districts.

439. The process of drawing boundaries between electoral districts can lend itself to a distortion in political representation known as gerrymandering if

it is based or influenced by a knowledge of which political party is generally favoured by voters in a particular area. Gerrymandering is the conscious manipulation of the geographic configuration of the electoral districts in order to benefit a particular political party. (The name comes from Governor Elbridge Gerry, who drew up an electoral district in the form of a salamander in Boston, Massachusetts, in order to promote victory for his supporters.)

440. Electoral laws (and/or precedents of the EDRBs) often establish additional requirements to be taken into account in drawing up electoral districts, such as the geographic continuity of each district or the principle that, unless there are justifiable objective reasons for doing otherwise, a single urban community – and even more so a single ethnic community – should not be divided.

441. Decisions on the delimitation of electoral districts were once normally considered political questions and therefore not justiciable. However, in 1962 the United States Supreme Court held that malapportionment of electoral districts was justiciable in the case of *Baker v. Carr*. The Court went on in 1964 to apply the standard of one person, one vote to state legislative elections; in 1973 it reaffirmed the requirement that districts be 'as mathematically equal as reasonably possible'; and in 1983 it held that congressional districting with a deviation of over 0.7 per cent from the target figure was unconstitutional. Today, more and more EDR systems have followed the US trend and provide for the possibility of delimitation decisions, even when adopted by the legislature, being challenged before the EDRB to review whether they meet the legal criteria.

Internal democracy of political parties

442. While some do not consider it appropriate for an EDRB or, as the case may be, an EMB to be involved in the internal life of political parties, more and more countries provide for judicial protection for the electoral right to association, and recognize the right of a political party member to have the party to which he or she belongs comply with its internal party rules. Some of the content of these rules may be laid down in, for example, a political party law, including democratic procedures for selecting party leaders and candidates, and means and procedures that members can use for their own defence within the party if they are subject to a party disciplinary sanction or to expulsion. Even where such provisions are not laid down in party legislation, they may be included in party rules.

443. This trend finds support in the historical trend worldwide to provide judicial protection for electoral rights. The theoretical and legal demands of the model of constitutional democracy under the rule of law are enshrined in the constitutional regimes of democratic governments and various

international human rights instruments. Political parties play an important role in fostering political participation and democratic life. They are in a very dominant position in relation to their members and the voters. If they were immune from judicial oversight of the constitutionality and legality of their actions and decisions this could nullify the exercise of electoral rights, especially in light of the monopoly or quasi-monopoly that parties have in many countries over the nomination of candidates to elective office. This is part of a general trend to protect human rights in relation to powerful private persons (e.g. through the doctrine related to the protection of human rights in private spheres).

444. In several countries constitutional and/or statutory provisions explicitly or implicitly state that the courts (regular, constitutional, administrative or electoral) should hear challenges to the actions of political parties related to their internal democracy or alleged violations of the electoral rights of their members. This should be done either directly, by a challenge to an internal party action, or indirectly by challenging the decision of the EMB that validates or confers efficacy on the action of the party concerned.

445. In general, the challenge faced by any body of constitutional or statutory law that seeks to regulate the internal democracy of political parties, and by any judicial body that has jurisdiction to guarantee it, is to strike a balance between two apparently conflicting principles or values. These are the right of members to democratic participation in determining the position of the party, on the one hand, and the right of political parties to organize themselves freely as part of the fundamental electoral right to association, on the other. The latter requires that a sphere be preserved in the internal organization and functioning of political parties that is free from interference by organs of the state. However, it may be argued that, unlike other types of association, in the case of political parties the right to self-organization is limited by the right of its members to democratic participation in the party's organization and functioning.

Oversight of political parties' charters or internal statutes

446. Several constitutional and/or statutory provisions provide for certain general bases and guidelines, or democratic requirements, to which political parties should adhere. At the same time, however, they delegate the power to establish the rules on their structure and internal democratic functioning to parties' own internal organs in the exercise of their organizational freedom. Such provisions generally include the obligation for parties to register their internal statutes as well as all amendments made to them with the competent authority (possibly the EMB), at which point this authority generally reviews them to ensure that they are in line with constitutional and statutory requirements.

447. Any dispute over the constitutionality or legality of internal party statutes or any amendment to them is generally within the jurisdiction of the EDRB (as in Costa Rica, Mexico and Panama). In those countries where its decisions are not final and therefore subject to appeal, they subsequently fall under the jurisdiction of the Supreme Court or Constitutional Court.

Selection of party leaders and candidates for elective office

448. Although political parties are often left to regulate the democratic procedures for selecting their own leaders or candidates for elective office in the exercise of their right to organize themselves, in many cases certain general rules by which they must abide in their statutes and specific actions are established by law. Among the general conditions laid down by law, intervention by the EMB is sometimes provided for in the internal party procedures for choosing leaders or candidates. Sometimes the law may provide only for the possibility of challenging actions and decisions before the EDRB.

449. Thus, for example, as regards parties' own governing bodies, the legislature often spells out the minimum internal procedures that each political party must have, or the need for these to exist at the national, state or provincial or departmental, and possibly municipal levels.

450. Exceptionally, the legislature may prescribe how some of these organs are to be constituted, the period of the term in office and limits on re-election; and impose an obligation to register the governing body with the EMB as well as an obligation to indicate, in parties' internal statutes, the grounds and procedures for recall or democratic oversight of leaders. However, the level of detail is often not very specific. The law in several countries provides that political party leaders and candidates for elective office must be selected by means of periodic elections (as in Argentina, Costa Rica, Nicaragua, Panama and Uruguay). It does not, however, always specify whether elections must be direct or indirect, or indeed establish the need for a free and secret ballot, or the direct, free, equal and secret vote of party members through either internal or primary elections.

451. In order to reduce de facto inequalities in practice, the law in some countries emphasizes equal opportunity for men and women to join party organs and stand for elective office, and proscribes any form of discrimination (as in Costa Rica and Ecuador). It may establish a quota either for women at all levels of a party's management and in the candidacies for representative positions, or only in respect of candidacies for elective office (as in Armenia, Burkina Faso, Indonesia, Panama and Paraguay). Some electoral laws provide for a system of proportional representation for distributing political party seats in the legislature in order to encourage the participation of different interests or minorities in the nomination of candidates for elective office (as in Honduras and Paraguay).

452. In some countries the law provides for intervention by the EMB in the procedures for selecting party leaders and candidates for elective office. In such cases the EMB cooperates with the political parties and movements as they choose their candidates for their national leadership bodies when this is done with the direct participation of their members, and in the choice of candidates for elective positions (as in Colombia). In some systems, the EMB has a representative on the intra-party organ in charge of organizing, directing and supervising the internal election of party authorities and candidates to elective office: in Honduras and the Dominican Republic, for example, it is the EMB that issues the call for internal elections to party organs. Other EMBs (as in Chile and Mexico) have powers to oversee the assemblies and conventions that political parties hold to elect their party leadership or select candidates for elective office and, at its own initiative or at the request of the party, to verify that they are held in line with the law, the regulations and parties' internal statutes. Without such verification, the internal elections would be null and void.

453. Special mention should be made of Uruguay. Under the 1998 reform, the Electoral Court hears all matters related to electoral actions and procedures connected with the political parties' internal elections for both candidates for the presidency and the members of political parties' own national decision-making bodies, which are held on the same day nationwide. It organizes these elections, issues the rules and requirements for holding them and judges all claims and appeals brought against electoral and party actions. The decisions of the Electoral Court are not subject to appeal.

454. In general, EMBs have jurisdiction to register the nominations by each political party of candidates for elective office. They check that the candidates meet the eligibility requirements and were selected in line with the procedure established by law and the party's internal statutes.

455. In addition, in the event of a dispute over the procedures for the political parties' internal (or primary) elections for leaders or candidates, a challenge may be submitted to the EDRB against the act of the electoral authority that led to the dispute or against the act of the electoral authority which validates or gives efficacy to the act of the party. A challenge may also test whether an action by a party is in violation of the constitutional or statutory provisions or violates the party's own rules. The procedures for such a challenge often require that all of the internal channels within the party for dispute resolution have been exhausted before the challenge can be accepted for hearing by the EDRB.

Expulsion of members and other sanctions

456. It is often provided, in general terms, that every member of a political party may, once internal remedies have been exhausted, bring a challenge

before the EDRB against any internal actions and decisions of that party that he or she considers illegal or by which a right has been denied – particularly the right to political association if a person has been expelled from membership. In several countries it is a legal requirement that internal party decisions on the expulsion of a member respect the member's right to a defence and the due process established either by law or in the party statutes.

457. There has been little research on the scope for judicial review of political parties' disciplinary acts, but it is thought to be extensive in the procedural or formal realm, although more limited in the material or substantive realm.

458. The disciplinary power that political parties have with respect to their members is part of their right to organize themselves, and in that sense part of the fundamental right to association. Each party regulates in its party statutes the grounds for which a member can be sanctioned with expulsion, as well as the procedure that must be followed for doing so. The main objective is to avoid any interference by public authorities, without implying that any party decisions of this kind are beyond the reach of judicial review.

459. Particularly in matters involving the exclusion of a member from an association, the fundamental electoral right to association includes the right of the member to remain in the organization so long as he or she does not engage in conduct that constitutes grounds or motive for expulsion as stated in the law or the internal statutes. This right may also be protected by the appropriate judicial bodies so as not to negate or diminish the exercise of a fundamental right of the member, especially as political parties, by constitutional mandate, have a dominant function as fundamental instruments for the political participation of citizens and the furtherance of democratic life (as in Spain).

460. In terms of procedural considerations, in order to prevent a member who is threatened with expulsion from being put in a defenceless position, an EDRB – once it has been verified that the party statutes are in line with the constitutional and statutory framework – should verify:

- whether the decision has been adopted by the correct organ;
- whether it has followed the procedure established in the party's internal rules;
- whether that procedure has been carried out in such a way as to guarantee rights such as such as a person's right to be informed of the charges brought against him or her, and the right to a defence (e.g. to be heard and produce evidence – in addition to the presumption of innocence); and
- in general, the right to due process as provided by law or in the party's internal statutes.

If a disciplinary proceeding did not embody these features the member would be defenceless in the face of the violation of his or her right not to be expelled from the party other than for a legal cause provided for in the party statutes and through a procedure that embodies full guarantees.

461. On the substance of internal party disputes, since political parties have freedom to organize themselves, the EDRB should limit itself to determining whether the events that are the basis of the decision to expel have actually occurred, and whether the decision of the party's governing body is reasonable – including the principle that its action should be proportional and not arbitrary – in the light of the provisions of the party's internal rules and the law. However, there could be exceptions to this limitation on the role of the judicial body. Given the dominant position of political parties, in those situations in which the decision to expel entails, for example, significant harm to or violation of a fundamental right of the member (for example, the right to accede to public positions in equal conditions, or other rights that are not electoral in nature, such as reputational or economic rights), the EDRB might be enabled to interpret and assess the facts.

Financing and oversight of the resources of political parties

462. In general, decisions by the relevant authorities (in some cases the EMB) on the allocation of public financing to political parties, and on oversight of funds and assets through rulings on the reports on the source of their financing and their regular expenditures, may also be subject to challenge. Oversight of parties' reports on campaign expenditures generally takes place in the post-electoral period. Also subject to challenge are the decisions of the relevant administrative authority on complaints lodged over alleged irregularities in the use and reporting of public funding, the imposition of a penalty if it is determined that someone has committed an infraction, or a decision by the electoral authority not to impose a sanction.

ii) Challenges during the electoral period

463. During the electoral period, the actions subject to challenge during the preparation stage may include the updating of the electoral register, the ordering and procurement of voter registration cards (where one is used), the nomination or registering of candidates, the location of polling stations, the selection of polling station officials, the registration of election observers where this is provided for, and actions related to the election campaigns.

464. Challenges to election results are often related to election day itself, particularly the voting procedure, the setting up, management and staffing of polling stations, the decisions of polling officials as to who is to be allowed to vote or prevented from voting, the freedom and secrecy of the ballot, and

so on. Other matters addressed in challenges include the procedures for counting and tallying the votes received, the distribution of elected seats, the declaration of the results, the certification of the validity of the election, and the publication of the election results.

Updating the electoral register

465. There is an increasing trend to secure the electoral rights of citizens to the full by making provision for the electoral register to be updated during the electoral period. In addition, it should be possible to challenge the improper inclusion or exclusion of a person on the register. In this respect, there are two issues which are intimately interrelated but constitute different actions during preparations for election day: challenges to the general publication of the electoral register and individual challenges to the list of electors. The right to make the first type of challenge is generally conferred on political parties, while voters with an interest in the matter are normally entitled to bring the second type of challenge.

Registration of candidacies, or nomination of candidates

466. Even though political parties play a central role in most electoral regimes, individual candidates are essential. (Some electoral systems provide for the possibility of independent candidates who are not nominated by political parties.) The registration of candidacies, or nomination of candidates, is thus an essential element of any election. Candidates must meet the eligibility requirements; this is reviewed by the EMB and, if its conclusion is challenged, by the EDRB.

Decisions on polling officials and the placement of polling stations

467. Decisions on the appointment of polling officials and the placement of polling stations, both of which are part of the remit of the EMB, are essential to the holding of elections and referendums. The purpose is to ensure that votes are cast and counted by an official body made up according to the requirements of the law and in a place or places fixed according to the law. In some systems citizens are chosen at random and provided with training to work as polling station officials. In others they are proposed by the political parties or are civil servants.

468. The composition of the polling station officials varies from system to system and reflects the tradition and specific experience of each country. In a number of countries, for example in Eastern Europe, political parties' representatives continue to be responsible for, or entrusted with, receiving and directly counting the votes. In other countries, their involvement is increasingly being reduced to overseeing these activities and ensuring that

they are carried out in keeping with the law. In such cases, the responsibility has been entrusted to public servants (as in Uruguay), or directly to citizens chosen randomly and provided with training (as in Indonesia and Mexico). Experience in some systems has shown that the involvement of public servants gives rise to suspicions that they may be biased in their actions in favour of the party in government. In some countries not being a public servant is a requirement for serving as a polling officer. Other arrangements include, but are not limited to, the EMB appointing the polling officials, and the involvement of civil society organizations.

469. Similarly, the procedure for the placement of polling stations seeks to ensure that the locations are determined according to clear and objective rules, that they are as geographically close to the voters as possible in order to encourage the greatest possible voter access and participation, and that their size and physical condition allows for normal operations and they can be subject to oversight on election day. The practical arrangements should be such as to impede any violation of the secret ballot and guarantee impartiality: the owners or those legally responsible for the building or premises may not have any political ties to parties or candidates or, in some countries, the government. In addition, some electoral laws establish that there must be adequate access for voters with special needs or disabilities, that the polling stations must be divided by gender, that account must be taken of the boundaries of electoral districts, that the area of a polling station must be fully within the limits of a single electoral district, and that no polling station serves a disproportionate number of voters such that it is impossible to process them all on election day.

470. The EMB's decisions on the composition of the polling station staff and the placement of polling stations are likely to be subject to review before the EDRB to ensure that they are in line with the constitutional and statutory framework.

Actions related to election campaigns

471. The various EDR systems offer different mechanisms for ensuring that electoral campaigns are in line with the constitutional and statutory legal framework, with regard to both the contenders (political parties and candidates) and third parties that may be involved (for example the media). The aim is to ensure a level playing field for the electoral contest. The actions of both contenders and others can give rise to electoral challenges.

472. Electoral campaigns can be times of high tension. They may give rise not only to electoral challenges and prosecution of allegations of electoral process-related offences or infractions but also to breaches of the general law, for example, in the field of public order. Offences of this kind are not dealt with in this Handbook.

473. Some EDR systems have mechanisms for challenges to be taken directly before the EDRB. In others, it is necessary to take an issue before the EMB first, usually without it formally being an administrative electoral challenge or a proceeding for attributing any administrative responsibility to the alleged transgressor. This sets in motion an administrative proceeding by which, after affording the parties involved (political parties, candidates and/or media outlets) the right to a hearing, the EMB decides on a corrective measure such as putting a stop to some irregularity in the electoral process (for example, by ordering that an illegal broadcast or promotional piece on the radio or television be suspended).

474. Judicial review by the EDRB is generally provided for in respect of any decision by the EMB related to the election campaign, including decisions related to the delivery of financial support for campaign expenses, the designation of places where campaign materials can be displayed, the distribution of official time for the broadcasting of campaign advertising in the public media, and so on. Clearly, EDRBs have to act within very short time frames to provide a timely and effective remedy in order to prevent any irregularity from substantially affecting the outcome of the election.

Election day and election results

475. Many of the issues relating to polling day, the counting and the declaration of results are listed in paragraph 464. In some countries, challenges to election results are substantiated and resolved before the competent body (usually the EMB and/or the EDRB) formally declares the result of an election and the names of the persons elected. However, in most EDR systems the actions or decisions challenged are those relating to the certification of the election (the declaration that the election was validly conducted and of its result, and where applicable the declaration of the names of the persons elected). These challenges are the responsibility of the EMB or the lower-level electoral judicial bodies, or even the highest-ranking officer of the EDRB.

476. In some systems, challenges are allowed, before either an organ of the legislature or a different judicial body, after the election has been certified and the results have been announced. In the UK, the result of an election is declared as soon as the count has been completed. A losing candidate may then bring a case (called an election petition) before an election court (see box 6.14 for an example). In France, a challenge to the result of a national election or a referendum may be submitted to the Constitutional Council by either a candidate or a registered elector.

iii) Challenges during the post-electoral period

477. Challenges made once the electoral process has concluded include those related to the oversight of the sources of political parties' resources and how

they were spent during the campaign. It is normally campaign expenditure that is reviewed rather than the regular expenditure of the political parties. Another issue that may arise is the final updating of the electoral register.

478. Challenges can be brought in respect of other types of electoral processes, local and supranational elections in addition to national elections and direct democracy instruments. It is also good practice to undertake a review of the applicable laws and regulations in this period in the light of experience of the recent election, and to propose possible reforms to the relevant legislation and the electoral regulations, including the framework of the EDR system.

Challenges with respect to other types of election and other matters

479. Some EDR systems give jurisdiction to the respective EDRB (particularly those entrusted to specialized electoral courts) to hear and resolve challenges to certain elections other than those for elective office, for example, internal political party elections (see paragraphs 442–445) and elections to professional associations and intermediate groups (Chile, Paraguay) and university positions (Paraguay, Uruguay). The Superior Chamber of the Electoral Court of the Judicial Branch of the Federation of Mexico has jurisdiction to hear and rule on labour disputes between the electoral authorities (EMB and EDRB) and their employees.

480. Many EDR systems establish the jurisdiction of the EDRB to hear challenges related to procedures of direct democracy, such as citizens' initiatives, referendums and recall votes, particularly where such procedures are under the jurisdiction of the EMB. For example, the Constitutional Council of France is empowered under the Constitution to hear challenges to the results of referendums. In general, direct democracy instruments may either be conducted at the same time as representative elections or at different times. A more detailed discussion about direct democracy instruments can be found in the *Direct Democracy: the International IDEA Handbook.*

3. Standing to bring challenges

481. The various EDR systems have different provisions regarding which persons or entities, for example, political parties, candidates, voters, citizens, authorities, observers, media outlets, and so on, can challenge the electoral actions and procedures that affect them. It is important for the EDR system to establish the fundamental right of every person to challenge any electoral action or decision he or she considers harms him or her before the EDRB. This is part of the human right to access to electoral justice, which is enshrined in several international human rights instruments. If a person who is negatively affected by an electoral action is denied this entitlement in a country that is a

party to any of those international or regional instruments, the international or regional mechanisms for protecting rights will have jurisdiction, on the basis of complementarity and subsidiarity (see paragraph 407).

482. Practically all EDR systems allow voters to file a challenge against their improper inclusion in or exclusion from the electoral register or a refusal to issue, as applicable, their national identification card or voter registration card. Some countries also allow political parties and candidates – and even the public prosecutor or electoral prosecutor – to challenge any decision related to the electoral register, even if it only involves an individual voter. Others reserve this entitlement to political parties in cases where there is a judicial challenge to the subsequent report of the electoral organ responsible, based on the observations made by those parties on the publication of the electoral register.

483. In addition, it is common for the decisions of the EMB or another competent authority concerning the registration of or refusal to register a new political party to be subject to challenge by the other political parties or by any individuals (in many countries these must be citizens) who are interested in forming it.

484. Although the standing to challenge political parties' internal statutes is usually vested in the members of that party or the other political parties (when the EMB approves or validates such statutes), in Colombia any citizen may bring a challenge before the National Electoral Council against those clauses of a party's statutes that are at odds with the constitution or the law. In some systems the EMB or other competent authorities can challenge a party's statutes as unconstitutional or illegal.

485. Practically all countries allow political parties to challenge any decisions of the EMB that affect them or which they consider to be illegal, as well as decisions of the EMB concerning preparations for elections and the election results or the ineligibility of persons elected. Often, other types of political organization may also do this.

486. Generally in EDR systems that are entrusted to a legislative body, in addition to the political parties, one or more legislators, whether incumbent or newly elected, are entitled to bring an electoral challenge before the legislative body (as in the case of legislative elections in Argentina, Germany or the United States).

487. In addition to cases in which EMBs are allowed to review the legality of election results on their own initiative, the vast majority of countries allow candidates to challenge the results before an EDRB. Some only accord candidates the status of third-party petitioner, while others do not expressly

give candidates any entitlement, although it could be considered implicit in some cases. It is clear that such standing for candidates is often related to the degree of evolution and the characteristics of the political party system, and therefore to the possibility of independent candidacies.

488. In addition, several countries provide for citizen action to challenge the results of an election or the eligibility of a candidate: not only the political parties and candidates but also citizens are entitled to present a challenge. This is an important and laudable factor in facilitating access to the EDR system, although the possible proliferation of challenges (e.g. this could be a political strategy used by a minority party or a losing party as a negotiating ploy) may impede the proper processing and resolution of challenges by the EDRBs – especially when they are given little time to do this. This might undermine the credibility and legitimacy of certain elections.

489. Some countries provide that when a certain kind of challenge is invoked, a hearing is held to hear from not only the political party concerned and/or any interested third parties, but also the electoral prosecutor and/or the attorney general or public ministry representing the interests of society.

4. Time periods for filing challenges and for their resolution

490. Because the representative bodies of government have to be renewed in a timely fashion and there is a trend towards shorter election campaigns, the time frames for filing and resolving electoral challenges are very brief – although those for resolving them are not expressly provided for in every case.

Table 7.1. Time limits for filing challenges to legislative election results: some examples

1 day after incident	2 days after incident	3 days after incident	10 days after incident	28–30 days after incident	30 days and more after incident
Armenia Czech Republic Lithuania Serbia	Albania Bolivia	Costa Rica Estonia Georgia Guatemala Hungary	Chile Honduras Russia	Canada Cyprus Guyana Iceland	Australia Azerbaijan Nepal Pakistan

Source: International IDEA Electoral Justice database, 17 May 2010, <http://www.idea.int/elections/ej/viewData.cfm>

491. There is a wide range of time frames for *bringing* challenges related to the electoral register. These vary from three to five days in most cases to longer periods of up to 30 days. In most cases, challenges related to acts that form part of the election preparations must be filed within three to five days, usually

calculated from either the date of the action or decision that gives rise to the challenge or the date when official notice is given to the interested person.

492. Some challenges to election results have to be filed immediately, that is, at the count being carried out at the polling station. Other claims, petitions and protests can be filed before higher-level electoral bodies, which also have a very brief filing period of two days (e.g. in Bosnia and Herzegovina). Several countries provide for a period of between three and five days to challenge election results, while some extend it to 15 or even 30 days. Table 7.1 gives some examples. In the UK, for example, the deadline is 21 days but if the case involves corrupt practices it is extended to 28 days. In Russia, challenges must be filed within 10 days of the results being declared. Others specify a specific occasion as the reference point, such as filing a challenge before the person elected is formally announced. This gives rise to some uncertainty, and such uncertainty can lead to the person elected being left without the possibility of a defence.

493. Some EDR systems also provide for a further mechanism for challenging election results within the EDRB, allowing a period of three days for the appeal to be filed. As indicated above, some systems include the possibility of a subsequent challenge before a non-electoral judicial body on constitutional or statutory grounds or before a legislative body.

494. Some countries have longer periods for bringing challenges related to certain decisions made outside the electoral period, such as those regarding the registration of political parties.

495. The time periods for *resolving* electoral challenges are not always expressly defined, and the provisions in this area are diverse. The most important principle is that challenges must be resolved before the harm becomes irreparable. It may be that even at the moment a challenge is made, the EDRB realizes that there is no time to resolve it satisfactorily. Or, if a challenge is upheld and a remedy of acknowledgement of fault is not sufficient, there needs to be time to publish a decision and implement a remedy which makes substantive reparation for the violation. If this cannot be done, the challenge may be declared inadmissible and dismissed – although this does not prevent or prejudge a subsequent action to establish criminal or administrative liability. However, the EDRB must always be alert, particularly during the key dates of the electoral process, and be in a position, if necessary, to hand down a decision even in a matter of hours so long as this does not affect the quality of its deliberation and decision making.

496. The time frame for resolving challenges to the electoral register is often between six and 10 days from the time they are submitted. The time frame for resolving a challenge to a decision regarding the establishment of a political party is often between three and 15 days. Challenges filed against actions

taken and decisions made during preparations for election day must usually be resolved within three to six days.

497. The time frame for EDRBs to rule on challenges to election results often varies from one day to 10 days from agreement that a challenge is admissible. For example, in Guatemala, the Supreme Court of Justice has three days to rule on an *amparo* petition, a judicial protection of an electoral right, and the Constitutional Court has five days to rule on an appeal. However, this period is 50 days in Colombia, and in some common law systems – for example in Bangladesh – there is no maximum time period for the resolution of electoral challenges. Some systems make reference to an event, stating for example that a challenge must be resolved before the outcome of the election is due to be declared, or prior to the swearing in or installation of the bodies elected.

498. Where challenges to election results are made before legislative bodies, as in Argentina and the United States, the regulations of the respective chambers do not provide for any limit. On the contrary, they expressly allow for the challenges to be resolved after the elected body has commenced its session. This means that some legislators may take their seats in the chamber provisionally, subject to the outcome of the respective challenge, and may later be unseated in favour of someone else.

499. This also happens in some EDR systems entrusted to judicial bodies, such as the responsible department (Section V) of the Council of State of Colombia, which has up to one year to annul an election – although in practice this period has been longer. In July 2009 it annulled the results of the election of senators in 2006 and ordered a recount in response to a challenge filed by the Attorney General of the Nation (Procurador General de la Nación), concluding that there had been various irregularities in several polling stations across the country affecting 33,000 votes, which could potentially have modified the results of the election of 102 members of the Senate, with some of them being unseated. In the same session, Section V of the Council of State, under Article 179, section 3, of the Constitution, voided the credentials of one Senator for having entered into contracts with the government within six months before the 2006 election. However, in January 2010, the Council of State in full bench revoked the earlier decision, finding that the contract was signed seven months before the election and that the constitutional provision had thus not been violated.

500. In some EDR systems entrusted to non-specialized electoral courts, such as those regular courts which are part of the judiciary and some constitutional or administrative courts (particularly those that deal with challenges or petitions related to the preparation of an election or challenges to electoral results), it is possible to prioritize electoral challenges in order to resolve them in a timely manner.

5. Evidence

501. Evidence includes any document, piece of testimony or tangible object that tends to prove or disprove an alleged fact. There are scant provisions in election codes about rules relating to evidence. In some cases the electoral law refers back to the codes of civil or administrative procedure. In countries in which a challenge is allowed before non-electoral judicial bodies, the rules of evidence are frequently governed by the procedural codes or laws applicable to the challenges that usually come before such bodies.

a) The burden of evidence

502. The burden of evidence is the duty of the party making the challenge to prove a disputed assertion or allegation and, in criminal cases, a charge or accusation. The burden of evidence includes not just the burden of production, which is the party's duty to introduce enough evidence on an issue to have it decided by the EDRB, but also the burden of persuasion, that is, the party's duty to convince the EDRB to view the facts in a way that favours that party. In civil cases, especially in common law systems, the verdict is usually reached 'on the balance of probabilities' or 'by a preponderance of the evidence', and in criminal cases the case must be made 'beyond reasonable doubt'.

503. The vast majority of electoral and/or procedural law incorporates, explicitly or implicitly, the general principle that the person or party who makes an allegation is under an obligation to prove it. Allegations may be of a positive type, claiming something as a fact, or negative, denying that something is a fact. Only disputed or controversial facts call for the production of evidence. The law itself is not subject to proof, nor are well-known facts or those which are impossible to prove.

504. These principles are generally accompanied by a presumption of the validity of administrative actions and decisions, that is, those carried out or made by the EMB. Accordingly, when an administrative electoral action is challenged as illegal or irregular, it is up to the party making the challenge to prove that the action challenged took place and is illegal or constitutes an irregularity. If the party making the challenge does not meet its burden of evidence, its claim is declared unfounded and the administrative electoral act by the EMB continues to be valid.

b) Means of proof

505. The means of proof are those elements which make evidence persuasive in the mind of the EDRB. The objective of defining means of proof is to help enable the EDRB to make a decision based on sufficient elements of certainty within the time frame required by the electoral timetable.

506. Some electoral or procedural laws (as in Colombia and Mexico) provide a definition of the means of proof so that litigants are aware of the types of evidence that they may offer in support of their factual and legal arguments and claims, and in some cases even of the effect or weight the EDRB should attribute to them. However, most procedural electoral codes and laws do not. Some provide that the codes of civil or administrative procedure may apply unless otherwise stated (for example, those of Bolivia, Guatemala and Paraguay). Many countries require that the relevant documentary evidence be attached to the petition, claim or complainant brief that puts forward the challenge and to the defendant's or respondent's plea (as in Chile, Costa Rica, Ecuador, Mexico and Peru).

507. While several systems expressly provide that the parties can offer any means of proof, some establish restrictions, allowing for example some or all of:

- electoral documents;
- public and private documents, including the official documents related to the action or decision that is being challenged;
- admissions, testimony, expert evidence and circumstantial evidence; and
- what is called legal and human presumption.

All these may be admitted with specified restrictions – for example, that the evidence should be pertinent to the case.

508. In most countries, the EDRB is authorized to demand the introduction of additional evidence in order better to understand the facts at issue, without implying any movement away from the principle that the party making an allegation is obliged to prove it.

509. Because of the short time frames for ruling on electoral challenges, where there are no laws or regulations relating to means of proof, EDRBs have had to develop criteria for admitting suitable or appropriate evidence in support of the parties' claims within the legal time limits for making a ruling. Witness testimony may for example be restricted, if not excluded, in cases where election results are contested.

c) Systems for weighing evidence

510. According to the predominant doctrine of procedural or evidence law, the systems for assessing evidence may be classified into four groups:

a. systems of legal or legally weighted evidence, in which the law indicates in advance the effect or weight that the EDRB should attribute to a means of proof;

b. free evidence systems, in which the EDRB can weigh the evidence offered, admitted and produced without any legal obstacle, so that the judge's opinion is formed freely without impediment of any kind, particularly legal impediment;
c. systems of logical and reasonable rules of evaluation and procedure for arriving at opinions or judgements (in Spanish, '*sana critica*'), in which the EDRB has the power to determine the efficacy of each of the elements in the record of the case in keeping with the rules of logic and the maxims of experience; and
d. mixed systems which combine elements of these three systems.

The *sana critica* system is midway between the first two in that the law does not specify the effect that should be assigned to a given piece of evidence, but nor is it left entirely to the free assessment of the EDRB. Instead, the EDRB must state the reasons or justify why it attributes probative value to each of the elements in the record.

511. Very few electoral codes and laws define the systems for weighing evidence that should be observed by the respective EDRBs in the cases that come before them. Some countries have adopted the free evidence system, several have established *sana critica* rules and a few more have a mixed system.

512. Among the greatest impacts of the introduction of electronic voting systems is their impact on the different EDRMs. The challenges that arise in this context relate to ascertaining and weighing the evidence, and to the mechanisms by which challenges will be resolved. In countries where the challenges are resolved by regular courts which are part of the judicial branch, these issues may need to be regulated by special provisions that require reform to the law. Investigating and assessing these aspects effectively may require special training for the staff of the EDRB. The rules for weighing electronic or digital evidence should be reviewed and, similarly, require the adoption of special measures or reforms.

Box 7.8. Electronic voting and electoral dispute resolution: California

Avery Davis-Roberts

Electronic voting in California is not subject to special mechanisms for the resolution of disputes that might arise from its implementation. Instead, e-voting disputes are resolved through existing channels.

The use of electronic voting and the resolution of disputes regarding the technology are widely reported in the press and through civil society organizations in California and in the United States more broadly. Despite recent controversies regarding voting technologies and widespread concern about their use, there remains a high degree

(cont.)

of trust in the institutions responsible for the resolution of disputes. In California in particular, the Secretary of State (SoS) is considered to be open to discussion and debate regarding e-voting, and campaigned on these issues while running for office.

Following the 2000 election, the federal government passed the Help America Vote Act (HAVA), which requires that each state review the voting technologies in use to ensure that some basic criteria are met (such as the ability of the voter to cast a blank or write-in ballot, accessibility for disabled voters, and that the technology notifies the voter if they have over-voted). While state legislation must be in line with HAVA, the details of implementation were left to the discretion of the state, so there are wide variations in practice among the 50 states.

A number of technologies produced by a number of suppliers are used by California's voters, including optical scan devices, auto-marking devices and direct recording equipment (DRE) or touch screen machines. All the technologies in use have a paper-based component, which is essential to transparency in the process as well as effective and meaningful dispute resolution. In California, DRE units must produce a voter-verifiable paper audit trail and, where budgets permit, every polling place must have one DRE to facilitate voting by disabled persons.

The SoS is the Chief Electoral Officer in the state of California. The SoS is responsible for ensuring that elections are conducted in accordance with the Electoral Code. The SoS is required to establish and maintain administrative complaints procedures in accordance with HAVA. The SoS is also responsible for certifying electronic voting systems that can be used by the counties. No devices may be purchased or used prior to approval by the SoS. S/he may adopt regulations regarding the source code, firmware, software and hardware of the electronic voting machines and devices. Importantly, s/he is also empowered to seek injunctive or administrative relief, such as monetary damages, or decertification of the technology in cases of unauthorized changes to the hardware, software or firmware of the voting machines once they have been conditionally certified by the SoS. S/he may also withdraw approval of technology previously approved.

The EDR mechanism in California, which includes e-voting-related disputes, is as follows.

Administrative complaints

The SoS must ensure that there are procedures in place for administrative complaints to be filed. Any person who is resident in the state of California may file a complaint if they think there has been a violation, is a violation or will be a violation of Title III of HAVA, for example, with regard to accessibility of the voting process for disabled voters. The complaint must be in writing, notarized and signed and sworn by the complainant on a form created by the SoS which is accessible to disabled voters and to voters using minority languages. The complaint must then be submitted to the SoS within 60 days of the occurrence or within 90 days of the complainant becoming aware of the occurrence.

(cont.)

The SoS may consolidate the complaints based on common events or points of law, and will send a notice to the respondents. A record of the complaint will be created. Between ten and 60 days after receiving the complaint, the SoS will hold a hearing, which, at his/her discretion, may be oral. Following the hearing, a determination regarding the complaint will be made by the SoS or his/her designee. Either a remedy will be granted (non-compensatory and non-punitive) or the complaint will be dismissed. In either event, the SoS will provide the reasoning behind the decision in writing to all concerned parties and post this on the website. Should the SoS or his/her designee fail to respond to the complaint within the 60-day deadline, the complaint will be subject to alternative dispute resolution – essentially an independent arbiter who serves as a Hearing Officer. The Hearing Officer will review the case, and will make a determination regarding the complaint within 60 days of the original deadline for determination by the SoS. The determination of the Hearing Officer is final and cannot include monetary compensation as reparation.

Challenges to election results

In such cases, the Courts of Appeal have appellate jurisdiction and the Superior Court has original jurisdiction. This includes cases where the results of an election are challenged. Challenges to the results of elections in California are of two categories: contestation of the results that do not require a recount, and challenges to the results that require a recount.

Contests without a recount An election may be contested in cases where the person who has won the election or has the most votes (the defendant) is not eligible for the office or has committed an offence against the collective franchise, or when such numbers of illegal or fraudulent votes were cast for the defendant that the results of the election would be different if they were not counted. The Superior Court has jurisdiction in such cases.

6. Remedies available from challenges to election results

513. The diversity of mechanisms among the various EDR systems stems from countries' different legal traditions and historical and socio-political contexts. The common thread between these mechanisms is that they are based on absolute respect for the popular will as expressed through the votes cast. In relation to challenges to election results, EDR systems can be categorized by looking at the legal remedies each offers. These will depend on the nature of the claim made by the political party or candidate that files the petition or complaint. For example, if a claim seeks to annul an entire vote, in theory the EDRB would not have any reason to order a recount.

514. The party or complainant making the challenge may be seeking one of a number of legal remedies:

a. the modification of the election result, with a consequent change of winner, through either a total or a partial recount of the votes, if the law provides for these, or by nullifying the votes received at a given number of polling stations due to irregularities;
b. the election being declared null and void where there has been either substantial wrongful conduct or widespread irregularities that affect the outcome, leading to the need for a complete re-run; or
c. the revocation of the declaration of the election of a particular representative for failure to meet the eligibility requirements.

Box 7.9. Remedies in challenges to election results

a. Modification of the electoral results (possible change in winner)
   i. Total or partial recount
   ii. Annulment of the vote received at some polling stations
b. Annulment of the election
c. Revoking the declaration of a candidate's victory for failure to meet eligibility requirements

515. It is important to remember that in some cases an EDRB will merely acknowledge or recognize that there has been wrongful conduct or an irregularity in the electoral process but that this did not substantially affect the results. In some such cases penalties may be imposed in the same or a separate judgement.

a) Modification of election results with a possible change in the winner

516. One of the remedies sought by a petitioner or complainant may be a change to the election result issued by the EMB. This may mean the result direct from the polling stations on election day, the result declared by the high-level organ that carried out the total vote tally immediately after the election, or the tally for a particular electoral district in relation to the vote received at a set of polling stations.

517. The ultimate objective of a challenge is a change to the candidate(s) declared elected by the EMB. To this end, it is possible to call for:

- a total or partial recount of the vote, within the terms provided for in law by each EDR system;

- the annulment of the votes received at a certain number of polling stations, based on a determination that there were substantial irregularities at those polling stations which affected the results; and/or
- in some systems, the deduction of any votes proved upon scrutiny to be invalid or void.

i) Total or partial recount

518. Electoral law treats full and partial recounts in diverse ways. There are four main trends:

a. to provide in the constitution or by statute for a total recount of the vote in any election, whether or not the result was close, as in Costa Rica before the September 2009 amendment and in the Netherlands;
b. to provide by law for a total recount in cases where the results are close, either automatically or at the request of an interested party, as in Canada, Hungary, Lithuania, Mexico since the 2007 reform, and some states of the United States;
c. to provide for a partial recount only at certain polling stations for which it is legally justified, as in the vast majority of EDR systems; and
d. not to provide expressly by law for total or partial recounts, as in Peru and at least three states in the USA.

Total recount of the vote in each and every election, regardless of the result

519. In the Netherlands and Costa Rica (before the 2009 amendment) the law has established that the EMB (respectively the Electoral Council, Kiesraad, and the Supreme Elections Tribunal) has the duty to carry out a new tally of the vote received at each and every polling station, regardless of whether the result is close or of whether it has been challenged. During the weeks following election day, the EMB carries out a total manual recount regardless of the circumstances. It is this count which, strictly speaking, is the official vote count. Even though this confers high levels of credibility and legitimacy on the result, it is clear that it is easier to implement in societies in which the electorate is not large.

520. In Costa Rica and the Netherlands everything done by the polling officers is subject to review and may be corrected by the highest-level EMB. It has powers to review the actions at the polling stations because they are subordinate organs. In Costa Rica, where the polling officers at local level are proposed by political parties, the Supreme Elections Tribunal has important guarantees of independence and impartiality and enjoys considerable prestige because of its honest and efficient performance over more than 60 years.

Total recount of the vote only in elections with tight results

521. Canada, some states in the USA, Hungary, Lithuania and Mexico provide by law for a total recount of the vote at the request of any of the parties. In Canada and the USA the petitioner must bear the cost if he or she is subsequently found to be mistaken. There is also provision for an automatic recount, called by the EMB itself, when the difference between first and second place is less than a specified percentage. For example, an automatic recount is triggered in Canada when the difference is less than 0.1 per cent of the votes cast; in the state of Washington, USA, when the difference is less than 0.5 per cent of the votes cast; in Lithuania when the difference is less than 50 votes; and in Hungary and Mexico when it is less than 1 per cent of the votes cast.

522. Although some US states provide for a total recount of the votes in elections for the House of Representatives and the Senate and for governors and state legislators, there is currently no provision in the USA for a total recount in presidential elections. Partial recounts are possible but at least three states (Alabama, Illinois and Kentucky) do not allow for any possibility of challenge or recount. In states other than those that provide for an automatic recount, there must first be a challenge or request by an interested party in the other states. In the various states of the United States polling officers are usually appointed on the proposal of the political parties. In most states the voting is computerized.

523. In the UK a losing candidate may submit an election petition challenging the election of a successful candidate by asking for scrutiny of the counted votes. The petitioner hopes to have individual votes excluded from or added to the count in order to change the result of the election. This scrutiny is not defined in the legislation, although its existence is recognized in several sections of the main piece of electoral legislation, the Representation of the People Act. This scrutiny procedure accompanies a polling system in which ballot papers are numbered and the polling number of the voter is recorded on a counterfoil to the ballot paper by the polling station staff, thus enabling the EDRB to identify and remove from the count ballot papers subsequently found to be ineligible. While this is broadly accepted in the UK, there are many countries in which such an approach would not command confidence because of secrecy of the ballot issues.

524. Similarly, in spite of the fact that there are no express statutory provisions in the EDR system, several EDRBs have established legal precedents upholding or ordering a total recount. For example, the Supreme Court of Taiwan (Zuì gaō fă yuàn) validated the total recount of the national vote ordered by the Taipei High (Appellate) Court after the 2004 presidential election. Other examples include the actions of the Higher Court of Namibia after the 2004

general elections, which ordered a recount after the opposition parties had filed a petition citing numerous irregularities in the vote count (the recount confirmed the earlier results), and those of Moldova's Constitutional Court (Curtea Constitutională) after the 2009 parliamentary elections.

Recount of the vote only with respect to those polling stations where it is legally justified

525. The vast majority of EDR systems provide legal justification for a partial recount, although the burden of proof required for this may be high. These EDR systems assume that the accuracy of the election results has been guaranteed by the multiple security measures established for appointing the polling station officials, identifying the voters, carrying out the voting itself, and counting and tallying the votes received at the polling stations. A return of the votes received is drawn up and signed by the officers at the polling station. Political parties may be represented at every polling station; they or their representatives have the right to file a protest in response to any irregularity or anomaly they may have noted on election day, and to receive a copy of the vote count protocols and tally as proof of the result obtained at the polling station.

526. Each political party, through its representative, is then able to compare their copy of the results from the polling station with the vote tally carried out by one of the organs of the EMB in the days immediately after election day. In several EDR systems, the law provides that a recount of the votes received at a polling station can be requested if during the tally by the EMB:

- the declaration of the counting and of tallying the vote received at a particular polling station shows signs that it has been altered;
- there are clear errors in the data it sets out;
- such a declaration does not exist; or
- the data it shows are not in agreement with the data in the copy that the political parties' representatives have.

These circumstances would indicate a partial recount of the vote received at a certain number of polling stations.

527. Political parties, and in several EDR systems candidates, have the right to challenge the results of the EMB's vote tally before the EDRB, either to uphold their right with respect to alleged irregularities committed on election day that were not corrected in the EMB's vote tally, or because the EMB has committed new irregularities. In the event of an improper omission by the EMB, the EDRB is able to conduct the recount of the vote received at the polling stations concerned.

Countries that do not provide for a total or partial recount

528. It should be noted that, as in three states of the United States (see paragraph 522), some countries, such as Bolivia and Peru, make no provision for either a partial or a total recount of the vote. These systems are based on the principle of preclusion, considering the vote count at the polling station at the end of election day to be an unrepeatable action or decision.

ii) Annulment of the vote received at some polling stations

529. There are three types of annulment:

- the annulment of a single ballot;
- the annulment of the votes received at a particular polling station; and
- the annulment of an entire election.

Annulment of a single ballot paper

530. Practically every electoral legal order establishes various conditions which, when met, lead to a determination that an individual ballot cast is null and void. In general, any ballot paper on which the voter's choice has been entered in a manner different from that which is required by law for it to be valid is considered null. The usual principle is that the vote is void if it is not possible to determine the voter's intentions in an unequivocal, clear and precise manner.

531. Null votes should be distinguished from cases in which the ballot paper is not marked, and it is considered blank. This distinction can be important in those systems that provide that a certain threshold must be reached for political parties to maintain their registration or to be allocated a seat under a proportional representation system, or as a criterion for access to public financing. It may also be relevant in referendums and recall votes where thresholds are included in the legislation. Nonetheless, some systems consider blank ballot papers to be null and void.

532. The vast majority of countries give a polling station or counting official the authority to consider and declare null an individual vote during the vote count without any possibility of challenge. On occasion, votes may be challenged, appealed against, or the subject of observations: these are all different cases in which there is doubt about the status or identity of the voter. In such cases, the higher-level organ of the EMB makes the determination.

533. In principle, annulment only applies to the individual vote of a particular voter, and thus does not affect the vote received at a polling station, or the declaration that results from that vote. Nonetheless, some electoral legal

frameworks associate a high number of null votes with the possibility of annulling the entire vote at a particular polling station, or even an election as a whole. For example, this could be the case if there are more null votes than valid ones at a given polling station, if the null votes account for more than half the votes cast in the respective election or if two-thirds of the votes cast are either null or blank.

Annulment of the votes received at a particular polling station

534. The grounds for nullifying the vote at a polling station can be classified according to the following three groups: (a) irregularities in the composition of the polling station officials; (b) irregularities in the voting process; and (c) irregularities in the vote count or in the protocols or minutes.

Irregularities in the composition of the polling station officials

535. In general, illegality in the setting up of the polling station staff is a ground for annulment. The composition of the polling station staff may be unlawful due to flaws in the selection or designation of the polling officers or because their members are not those officially appointed; due to their being appointed after the legally established time limits; or due to there being fewer members than the number allowed. Another cause of annulment of the vote received at a polling station is when it has been set up without justification at a location other than the one authorized.

536. In Colombia, if spouses or close relatives of the candidates have participated as polling officers in charge of the vote count, the votes cast for the candidate in question at that polling station are annulled.

Irregularities in the voting process at the polling station

537. Among the grounds for annulment due to irregularities in the voting process provided for in many legal frameworks, the following merit special mention:

- when the electoral register at the polling station turns out to be false, falsified or altered;
- when there are errors on the ballot papers related to the names of the candidates or the parties' emblems;
- when persons with the right to vote have been impeded from doing so;
- when a person who does not appear in the electoral register or whose identity is not verified has been allowed to vote;
- when multiple voting has been detected; and
- when monitoring by the political parties' representatives has not been allowed.

538. Other grounds for annulment include:

- coercive actions taken by the polling officials against voters that may have forced them to refrain from voting, or to vote against their will or without the proper legal guarantees;
- violence against the polling officials during the voting process;
- violence, coercion or threats against voters by candidates or other voters;
- fraud, bribery, 'treating', the exercise of undue influence, intimidation or violence used on behalf of any candidate;
- any generalized violence that impedes free and peaceful voting;
- violation of the principle of the secret ballot;
- campaign activities that are forbidden by law;
- financial interference or abuse of a position of authority in such a way as to limit the freedom of the vote;
- when the vote has been held on a date different from that indicated by the competent electoral organs, or during hours other than those provided for (except in the event of force majeure);
- when the polling station has opened late or closed early without justified cause, maliciously depriving voters of the right to vote; and
- when the vote has been held in a different place from the one authorized, or has been received by persons other than those authorized to do so, or, in general, when there have been grave irregularities that put the certainty of the vote in doubt.

Most EDR systems establish a requirement to void the vote received in any polling stations where the irregularity involved may have affected the overall result of the election.

Irregularities in the vote count or in the protocols

539. The following types of ground for annulment of the votes at a particular polling station are provided for:

- conducting the count in a place other than the one authorized;
- the use of violence against electoral officers as they conduct the vote count, to the extent that the result of the vote is affected;
- fraud or errors in computing the votes that benefit a particular candidate or slate of candidates to the extent that it has affected the outcome of the election;
- a difference of, for example, five or more between the number of voters and the number of ballot papers used;
- the number of votes cast is greater than the number of registered electors;
- there are more null votes than valid votes, or the number of ballot papers used is considerably more than the total number of electors registered at the particular polling station;

- any error in applying the electoral formula;
- other defects in the vote count, for example, arithmetical errors in or alterations to the tallying;
- the preparation or signing of protocols or certifications by persons not authorized to do so;
- the use of unauthorized forms;
- the absence, destruction or disappearance of electoral documentation;
- the lack of the signature of some or all polling officers;
- any tampering with the so-called electoral package or bag; and
- delivery of the electoral packages, petition forms or bags from the polling station to the next-highest level of the electoral machinery after the deadline for doing so has passed.

540. It is especially important to consider the effects of nullifying the vote at an entire polling station. In principle, such cases only affect the vote at that polling station, and not the entire electoral process. However, it is possible that annulling the vote at several polling stations will have an impact on the election as a whole. The immediate effect of nullifying a vote is that the votes at that polling station will be excluded from the general tally of the votes cast in the election in question; but this could result in a new tally that alters the overall winner. In some EDR systems, for example in Bangladesh, it means the possibility of a new vote at the polling stations affected if there are grounds for doing so. Almost all electoral legal frameworks establish the principle, formulated in either positive or negative terms, that if the annulment of the vote at a particular polling station or set of polling stations can affect the outcome or validity of the entire election, either a new vote or a new election will be required.

541. Some legal frameworks establish the principle in negative terms, prescribing that new elections shall *not* take place if it appears that the new vote (at the specific polling station) would *not* have any impact on the general outcome of the election. Others put it in positive terms, establishing that there should be a new election if the votes annulled *can* alter or affect the outcome of the election or are enough to decide whether a party will continue to enjoy legal standing.

542. While several countries allow for the possibility of the new vote being held only at those polling stations in which the vote has been annulled (or if an election was not held at a polling station), that is, a partial revote, some provide that new elections must be held in the whole country.

543. When there is a new tally of the votes cast, the certification issued to a slate or a candidate is revoked, and the candidate or slate that emerges as the winner as a result of the annulment of the votes cast at one or several polling stations is then certified.

b) Annulment of the election

544. In order to safeguard the legality of electoral actions and procedures, electoral legal frameworks establish various grounds for the annulment of an election. It should be noted that in electoral matters, as in any other field of public law, not every violation of an electoral legal provision has the same effect. In order to determine the degree of impact it is necessary to look at the legal consequences of the irregular actions or wrongful conduct.

545. Several electoral legal frameworks explicitly provide that annulment may only be decreed on grounds expressly set out in law, although some EDR systems grant the EDRB some discretion within the legal framework to declare the annulment of an election, for example, so long as the 'facts, defects, or irregularities … influence the general results of the election' (Uruguay).

546. In general, as an EDR principle, an annulment may only be declared when the irregularity affects the outcome of the election or causes clear bias. In addition, the filing of a challenge does not suspend the effects (even if they are provisional) of the decision or action challenged. Once the period provided for has lapsed without any challenge being filed, the corresponding action or decision becomes final. Also, in the event of doubt (as in Ecuador) or if the two electoral judges differ (as in the UK), the elections are judged valid. The reason for these provisions lies in the general principle in law which states that public actions validly carried out should be conserved. This is reflected in the aphorism 'the useful should not be vitiated by the useless', which has special relevance in electoral law, as several EDRBs have noted in their case law (for example Costa Rica, Mexico and Spain).

547. Often, the nullification of an election can only be declared by a judicial EDRB. On occasion, however, it results from an administrative challenge before an EMB (as in Azerbaijan, Croatia, Estonia, Hungary, Kyrgyzstan, Lithuania and Turkey) or a legislative challenge before a legislative EDRB (as in the Netherlands). The rule in judicial EDR systems is that EDRB decisions should be restricted to the issues raised and alleged, and must not address nullities other than those raised in a challenge or complaint. Moreover, based on the provisions of the legislation, annulment cannot be invoked by the person who has caused it, in keeping with another general principle of law that establishes that 'no one can allege the acts of his/her wrongful intent or clumsiness to his/her own benefit'.

548. Depending on the electoral legal framework, three grounds for the annulment of an election can be identified: (a) as a result of the annulment of the vote at various polling stations; (b) due to the ineligibility of a candidate or slate of candidates; and (c) when the election was not accompanied by the necessary guarantees.

i) As a consequence of the annulment of the vote at various polling stations

549. In situations as described in paragraphs 540–542, it is common for the electoral legal frameworks (or the case law) to set out assumptions that define when the annulment of the vote at a particular or several polling stations should be considered to be a reason to believe that the irregularities involved affect the overall election result, in which case a new election must be called. These include if the nullity of the votes affects more than half the polling stations, if the nullities in the voting affect more than half the votes cast or if they represent one-third of the valid votes cast nationally. In some countries the nullity of the votes at 20 per cent of the polling stations is the threshold established for annulment of the whole election.

ii) For reasons of ineligibility of a candidate or slate of candidates

550. A large number of electoral laws provide that there is ground for the annulment of an election if the candidate or the persons on a slate of candidates do not meet the eligibility requirements, or the candidate concerned has made fraudulent representations in this regard. Even in those countries that do not provide that this is a ground for annulling an election, when it subsequently turns out that a candidate elected is ineligible, the only possible measure is revocation of the declaration or certification.

iii) When the election is not accompanied by the necessary guarantees

551. Several electoral legal frameworks establish as grounds for annulment of the election that there have been sufficient acts of violence or coercion to alter the result, and thus that the election has been held without the necessary guarantees (e.g. Bolivia, Panama); that there has been widespread distortion of the vote count due to error, fraud or violence (e.g. Paraguay); that infractions have made it impossible to establish the genuine will of the voters (e.g. Russia); that corrupt or illegal practices for the purpose of promoting or procuring the election of any person have been so extensive that they may reasonably have affected the result (e.g. the UK); or that there have been actions that have vitiated the election in that they influence the general results (e.g. Uruguay).

552. The above instances involve various concepts, such as 'guarantees required', 'acts that vitiated the election', 'widespread distortion of the vote counts' or 'extensively prevailed', which do not give the EDRB complete discretion in terms of the power to decide freely and with care but instead require it to decide in a reasoned way on the technical application of indeterminate legal concepts and their adaptation for the purpose in hand. For this reason, in addition to being broadly bound by precedent, the

EDRB should provide reasons to justify its decisions. It is not sufficient to use expediency as an argument.

553. Finally, a small number of countries have established further grounds for annulment of the entire election, be it presidential and/or legislative, such as its having been held without being first being called by the appropriate organ, or its having been held on a day other than the day for which it was called.

c) Revoking a candidate's election because of a failure to meet the eligibility requirements

554. Another possible remedy that a complainant or petitioner might pursue is revoking the certification of a candidate or the declaration that he or she has been elected if it is shown that he or she does not meet the legally established eligibility requirements. This situation arises when annulment of the election is not a legal consequence of failure to meet the eligibility requirements, particularly when the ineligibility extends to only one of the candidates on a given slate (principal and alternate), or in the case of elections carried out using proportional representation. In the latter case, the most common consequence is the election of the next person on the list (where the party lists are closed). In other systems, a complementary or partial election is held, as for example in Thailand.

7. Principles of consistency and the exhaustiveness of judgements or decisions

555. It is important for every EDR system to provide for and respect the general principles of procedural law applicable to judgements and decisions in order to demonstrate the impartiality of the EDRBs. Accordingly, EDRBs should take care (unless there is a provision that expressly provides for a different outcome) that their judgements and decisions are consistent with the complaints of the parties and the issues debated. Decisions should not address matters different from those over which a challenge or complaint has been filed.

556. Similarly, it is important to note that some EDRBs have the power to make up for any deficiencies in the complaint or argument concerning the allegations contained in a challenge. This does not mean, however, that the EDRB can act on its own initiative. What such provisions do is to make up for any deficiency in the argument alleging harm to electoral rights. The EDRB cannot present allegations that are not contained in the original complaint itself.

557. The principle of the exhaustiveness of judgements and decisions requires an EDRB to address each and every one of the positions put forward by the

complainant and the person or entity responding to the complaint, in order to ensure that nothing relevant is omitted in reaching justice. This principle complements the principle of consistency between the relief sought and the decision reached.

CHAPTER 8

CHAPTER 8

Alternative EDR mechanisms

1. Introduction

558. Formal EDR systems are complemented by other means and mechanisms for managing electoral disputes. Such mechanisms are normally referred to as informal or alternative electoral dispute resolution (AEDR) mechanisms. Their primary purpose is not to replace formal EDR systems but to play a supportive role, especially in situations in which the formal systems face credibility, financial or time constraints linked to political or institutional crises or to their inadequate design. In contrast to EDR mechanisms, AEDR mechanisms provide for one or more parties in conflict to initiate a process to resolve it, which can be done unilaterally (by withdrawing its claims or response), bilaterally, or through a third party or agency.

559. Some AEDR mechanisms exist alongside formal EDR mechanisms and play a permanent supportive and complementary role. Others come into being on an ad hoc basis or in exceptional or extraordinary circumstances as a result of political crises or institutional failure in existing formal EDR mechanisms.

560. AEDR mechanisms with a complementary function are the most common. In those countries that provide for them, they are generally permanent and/or provided for before elections are held as an alternative means of resolving possible electoral disputes in a simpler and more informal manner, and are backed up by the established EDR system. A good example is the use of conciliation, mediation or arbitration as opposed to litigation through formal EDRBs. In such cases the use of AEDR mechanisms is not a sign of weakness in the formal EDR system, but a way to foster speedy and cost-effective dispute resolution. Both formal and informal dispute resolution systems coexist and complement each other.

561. Other AEDR mechanisms are employed to fill a credibility gap that exists in the formal EDR system because of either political conflict or institutional weaknesses. Such AEDR mechanisms come into play when a serious dispute arises in relation to the holding of an election, its unfolding or outcome. The resolution of the dispute or challenge is entrusted on an extraordinary and exceptional basis to an ad hoc body not originally provided for in the EDR system. Good examples are the use of negotiation and mediation in the cases of Kenya and Zimbabwe to create governments of national unity in order to resolve political-electoral conflicts that erupted following disputed elections in the two countries in 2008 and 2009 respectively.

2. The evolution of alternative dispute resolution

562. Resolving electoral disputes outside the normal courts is not new. Societies the world over have long used non-judicial, indigenous or informal methods to resolve electoral conflicts and other disputes. For example, in the USA, AEDR mechanisms were introduced in some states in the 1970s to resolve community-wide civil rights disputes through mediation and to address the increased delays in and expense of litigation arising from an overcrowded court system.

563. What is new, however, is the proliferation of AEDR mechanisms and their wider use and institutionalization around the world, especially in post-conflict societies, in recent years. The benefits of the use of AEDR mechanisms go beyond the political and electoral arena. They can be used, for example, to resolve complex problems at community level in circumstances when relationships between the disputants have to be maintained, community cooperation has to be strengthened and alternatives to violence or litigation are needed.

564. In South Africa, the advent of democracy in the 1990s saw large-scale experimentation with alternative dispute resolution (ADR) in areas such as labour disputes, access to justice, service delivery and, most importantly, the conduct of the first democratic elections, which were held in 1994. Various ADR structures were created to deal with the plethora of disputes during these contentious elections and relieve the tense political climate; they included community-based conflict management structures and political party liaison committees. These structures used AEDR mechanisms such as negotiation, mediation and arbitration to resolve conflicts at all levels of government, that is, national, provincial and local (see also paragraph 579 and box 8.1).

Box 8.1. South Africa's Independent Electoral Commission conflict management programme

Joram Rukambe

South Africa's Independent Electoral Commission established a conflict management programme in 1999. This programme operates only at election time and draws on

(cont.)

experts in conflict management, such as attorneys, teachers and religious leaders in the community, who are hired a few weeks before the election. They are given training in election law and can be called on as needed. The experts use their mediation and conciliation skills and submit reports to the EMB, on the basis of which they are paid. Their intervention can be by telephone or through public hearings in the community, where the parties to a dispute are heard from and a resolution is proposed. The programme has proved effective and the number of challenges coming before the courts, and electoral disputes in general, has diminished. There were, for example, 1113 disputes in the 1999 elections, including disputes over access for voters, candidates or political parties being impeded by intimidation and violence, or the destruction of campaign publicity. The number of such disputes fell to 314 in the 2000 elections and 253 in 2004.

565. AEDR mechanisms have since been widely and effectively used in most post-conflict countries, including Afghanistan, the Democratic Republic of the Congo, Indonesia, Malawi and Mozambique, as well as South Africa. In such cases, there has been widespread use of methods of negotiation and arbitration to manage electoral disputes through the assignment of adjudicative functions and powers to civic-based structures. These had the power to arbitrate and deliver decisions that were binding on the disputants. Such mediation and arbitration committees were set up under the auspices of the EMB at the national, provincial and municipal levels, served as the first ports of call on electoral disputes and helped to alleviate pressure on the formal courts.

566. Countries such as Ghana and Botswana, which are often cited as model democracies in Africa, use party liaison committees and other community-based structures to assist the EMBs in promoting transparent and credible elections through effective conflict mediation, management and resolution.

3. Permanent AEDR mechanisms that exist alongside EDR mechanisms

a) Key steps in the AEDR process

567. In general, AEDR mechanisms may be classified as *unilateral*, where the will of one of the parties in dispute is sufficient to resolve it or consider it concluded; *bilateral*, when the parties involved need to be in agreement before the dispute can be considered resolved; and those that require *third-party intervention* by a party other than an organ of state. Among the first group are renunciation or abandonment and admission or recognition. The second category involves compromise or give-and-take between two or more parties. Three options are available with third-party intervention: conciliation, mediation and arbitration (see box 8.2).

Box 8.2. Alternative EDR mechanisms

i. Unilateral: withdrawal by the petitioner or complainant and recognition or acceptance by the respondent
ii. Bilateral or multilateral: compromise (transaction) or peaceful settlement between the parties
iii. Third-party intervention (judicial equivalents):
   - Conciliation
   - Mediation
   - Arbitration

568. AEDR mechanisms are by nature voluntary and disputants are free to use them at will. Unless they agree to enter into conciliation, mediation or arbitration, they are not bound by the awards or decisions of the relevant bodies. In this they are different from EDR mechanisms, which are mandatory and have binding force even on actors that have opted not to engage with the process. AEDR mechanisms can under no circumstances be a substitute for EDR mechanisms, but the two are mutually reinforcing. Even where AEDR mechanisms are provided for, open recourse to EDR mechanisms must continue to be available.

569. In some countries provisions that regulate EDR systems expressly provide for the possibility of AEDR mechanisms. In some cases, except perhaps in cases of fraud (as legally defined), their decisions are given full legal effect and may even be binding on the parties involved. AEDR mechanisms used in different legal contexts, including in formal court systems in established democracies, range from facilitated pre-trial negotiations, in which disputants are encouraged to negotiate directly with each other prior to some other legal process, to arbitration systems or mini-trials that look very much like a court process.

570. Electoral disputes can be settled outside the EDRB by the withdrawal of an electoral petition or complaint by the petitioner or complainant. This action of withdrawal is tantamount to a renunciation or waiver of a right. Recognition or acceptance of guilt by the respondent can also lead to the dispute being resolved (see box 8.3). Both actions are unilateral, because the will of either the complainant or the respondent is sufficient for the dispute to be considered concluded – although sometimes the law requires consent from the other.

Box 8.3. The 'Winchester Case': the United Kingdom

Andrew Ellis

In the 1997 general election in the UK, the two leading candidates each polled over 20,000 votes in the single-member district of Winchester. The margin between them was two votes. Losing candidate Gerry Malone and his party believed that a few votes

(cont.)

had been wrongly excluded. He submitted an election petition – a complaint – for a review by an election court. Winning candidate Mark Oaten and his party were not sure how the case would be decided, and also knew that defending the case and losing could lead to a big bill for costs (see box 6.14). He therefore did not oppose the case in court, and a new election was declared. Part of Oaten's campaign platform was 'Malone is a sore loser who has forced an unnecessary election'. In the re-run election, Oaten defeated Malone by over 20,000 votes. Oaten's politician's judgement of the best way to protect his interest turned out to be correct.

571. *Compromise* is the peaceful settlement, either express or tacit, of a dispute, without recourse by the two disputants to a third person or agency to help settle the dispute. Compromise requires the bilateral or multilateral agreement of both or all the disputants involved.

572. *Mediation* and *conciliation* are similar insofar as in both the parties use an impartial third party to resolve their dispute. In mediation, the mediator sets out to bring the parties closer together while acting as a passive facilitator. In conciliation, the conciliator is an active participant in the negotiation, proposing possible solutions to the disputants in order to arrive at one that is acceptable to both or all disputants. Mediation is not subject to specific formulas or rules, whereas conciliation is legally regulated.

573. *Arbitration* arises from the parties' agreement to use an arbitrator. The final decision, normally called an 'award', is be handed down based on either the law or equity. Arbitration has characteristics similar to judicial decisions because, on its endorsement by a court, the award takes on the characteristics of a court decision or judgement, meaning that it is binding on the disputants and legally enforceable.

574. Although arbitration procedures are generally agreed beforehand by the disputants, they are expected to observe the due process of law. This requires a fair hearing including the right to a defence, the submission and examination of evidence and the cross-examination of facts before a final decision is taken.

575. Some countries provide for two methods of arbitration, depending on the nature of the dispute: *arbitration by institutions or agencies* established by law or *arbitration by individuals* freely appointed by the disputants themselves. Even where the law provides for institutionally-based arbitration, the parties to a dispute are free to choose whether they want to opt for arbitration or litigation through a normal court (in the electoral realm, examples are Indonesia in 2004 and Afghanistan in 2005).

576. AEDR mechanisms, with their more informal nature, offer advantages that can add immense value to efforts to foster electoral justice. These include:

- easier, faster and more cost-effective access to justice;
- a less threatening environment for the disputants;
- the possibility of win-win outcomes for all disputants; and
- the opportunity to circumvent the problems of discredited EDR mechanisms.

577. AEDR mechanisms also have some weaknesses. In particular, they are ineffectual in the presence of an extreme power imbalance between disputants, that is, at balancing the interests of a weak disputant with those of a stronger disputant, and may not work when one party is uncooperative – especially in a multiparty dispute.

b) Countries with extensive experience of permanent AEDR mechanisms

578. Alternative EDR mechanisms are not sufficiently developed, and there have been few studies of their effectiveness. However, many countries have some form of AEDR mechanisms: Afghanistan, related to local electoral bodies; Cambodia (see box 8.4); Ethiopia; Kenya; Lesotho; Malawi; Mexico, for certain local elections in indigenous or ethnic communities under the system of custom and practice; Samoa; South Africa; and Uganda.

Box 8.4. AEDR in Cambodia

Denis Truesdell

The official EDR institutions in Cambodia include the National Election Commission (NEC) and the Constitutional Council. The NEC is responsible for deciding all complaints and appeals through the holding of public hearings, except for cases that fall under the jurisdiction of the judiciary. Electoral disputes are addressed at the level where they occur, starting with polling station officials, the Commune Election Commission (CEC) and the Provincial Election Commission (PEC). Appeals can be made against all decisions taken by these commissions on electoral complaints at the next level above, up to the NEC and ultimately to the Constitutional Council.

Electoral disputes are therefore dealt with within electoral structures, outside the formal justice/court system which is out of the reach of the vast majority of the population, as well as being distrusted and associated with criminal matters. As a result, most Cambodians are accustomed to calling on local authorities, village chiefs, village elders and leaders of ethnic minorities, who make up informal bodies to arbitrate day-to-day disputes. However, there is no legal framework to guarantee people's rights, nor is there a definitive settlement when these informal mechanisms are employed for dispute resolution. These actors are not empowered to settle disputes in a judicial

(cont.)

sense, although the Law on Commune Administration empowers commune councils to conciliate disputes among citizens.

Alternative electoral dispute resolution mechanisms have been formalized in electoral regulations to resolve the majority of electoral disputes. Although these are designed to resolve minor electoral offences, the cultural tradition of extrajudicial mediation and conciliation makes AEDR mechanisms a powerful dispute resolution tool. More serious cases therefore tend to be 'reconciled' when they should have been referred to the higher electoral authority. The CEC implements the AEDR mechanisms, although it does not have the capacity to carry out the quasi-judicial formal hearing procedure that is required for all appeals and major breaches of the law. These are conducted by the PEC and the NEC. Parties who are not satisfied with the decision or refuse conciliation have the opportunity to pursue their complaint at the higher level. Nonetheless, the system is criticized because a large number of complaints are rejected at the entry point by low-level electoral officials who arbitrarily judge them to be frivolous, or based on no evidence or hearsay. Critics are also wary of AEDR mechanisms being imposed on parties who would prefer adjudication through the more formal quasi-judicial hearing procedure available at the higher PEC or NEC levels.

In spite of their limitations, AEDR mechanisms contribute to the quick resolution of most electoral disputes and have an important role in preventing conflicts through easy access to the electoral authority, providing guidance, answering questions and resolving issues before they develop into formal complaints.

579. South Africa and Lesotho, for example, have institutionalized a system of *party liaison committees*, which serve as vehicles for consultation and cooperation between the EMB and the registered parties on all electoral matters with the aim of delivering free, fair and genuine elections. These committees have been established nationally, provincially and locally, and are permanent. Each registered political party has the right to appoint two representatives to each committee. The committees meet frequently and their administration is entrusted to the EMB, which chairs them at all levels. They have made a significant contribution to identifying and resolving various electoral disputes and challenges, and their deliberations are regarded as open and honest. Such committees are the legally recognized structures for resolving electoral disputes and challenges. They take a consultative and constructive approach and seek to reach consensus among the political parties and their candidates. The tribunals appointed by South Africa's Electoral Court to resolve various electoral disputes and challenges generally endorse the conclusions of the committees, which are also respected and implemented by the organs and agencies involved.

580. Little has been written on the use of conciliation, mediation and arbitration in the electoral realm. Nonetheless, it would be efficient and effective for EMBs to enable such mechanisms for use in electoral disputes. It is common,

particularly in those EMBs that include representatives of political parties, for there to be extensive debate within the EMB in an effort to reach agreement on handling interests that are commonly disputed. This helps to alleviate the often heavy burden of EDR and to offer quicker and generally more cost-effective solutions, which are important in the light of the tight electoral time frames. Codes of conduct promoted by EMBs also provide for the establishment of ad hoc committees made up of representatives of all the political forces participating in an election, with a mandate to oversee compliance with all the clauses in the code. These are often effective means for resolving conflicts and reducing the number of challenges, especially during election campaigns, as was the case in Yemen in 2003 and the Palestinian Authority in 2006.

581. Many countries make it a requirement, before a complainant proceeds with a claim against an action or decision of an organ of the EMB, that he or she must first have appeared before the body or authority responsible in order to give it an opportunity to correct its alleged error or irregularity. Only after such a hearing can there be recourse to the court or the next instance. It should be noted that this prior exhaustion of administrative remedies is not a formal administrative challenge, and thus should be considered not an administrative electoral challenge but an AEDR mechanism.

582. Similarly, when political parties establish internal mechanisms for resolving internal disputes within the party, it is technically justified to consider them as AEDR mechanisms. It is a general rule that in order for a party member to have recourse to an EDRB in order to challenge an act of her or his party, s/he must first have exhausted the internal party mechanisms provided for in its by-laws. The rulings handed down by such internal party mechanisms are usually not challenged before an EDRB, which means that the decisions of the AEDR mechanism are final and binding.

4. Ad hoc AEDR bodies created as an extraordinary mechanism to resolve a specific electoral conflict

a) Ad hoc AEDR bodies established as an internal national solution

583. Through this type of AEDR, the competent body or bodies of a country (generally the legislature) entrust an ad hoc transitory body, which is judicial in nature, with a specific mandate to resolve the challenges related to an electoral process. This situation arises in exceptional and extremely serious cases in which significant disagreements arise among the political forces with respect to the conduct or results of an electoral process, and they opt to establish institutional mechanisms other than those originally provided for to resolve specific electoral disputes. Once a consensus is reached among the political forces involved and the relevant sectors of society, the legislative branch issues a regulation or a decree by which additional mechanisms

are created and/or an ad hoc body is entrusted with the final resolution of electoral disputes, against which there is no further appeal.

584. Such a situation arose during the 1876 presidential election in the United States. Challenges to the election results in three states (whose 19 members of the Electoral College were enough to affect the outcome) were entrusted to an ad hoc Electoral Commission not provided for in the US Constitution, but established through a legislative decree issued after the election. The commission was made up of five senators, five members of the House of Representatives and five Supreme Court judges who decided by eight votes to seven in favour of the Republican candidate, Rutherford B. Hayes, essentially by voting along party lines. The result originally reached by the three states was overturned and a different candidate was declared the winner.

Box 8.5. The USA: from decentralized to centralized EDR

Tracy Campbell

The United States is a federal constitutional republic where the constitutional framework delegates powers not expressly granted to the federal government to the 50 states. Such powers include the organization and conduct of both state and national elections. The US Constitution is explicit with regard to federal elections for the US Congress. Article I, Section 4 of the US Constitution states: 'The times, places and manner of holding elections for senators and representatives, shall be prescribed in each State by the legislature thereof; but the Congress may at any time by law make or alter such regulations, except as to the places of choosing senators'. Other portions of the Constitution and the legislative history of a variety of federally-enacted election legislation (e.g. the Federal Contested Elections Act of 1969) also provide the states with considerable latitude in resolving not only state but federal electoral disputes.

Because the regulatory framework for elections in the United States is decentralized, it varies substantially from state to state. Not only do states adopt different laws, regulations and procedures for carrying out these rules, but the states are free to delegate many of these procedures to their local governments – usually counties. It is the county that typically decides such things as the type of voting equipment to employ, the design of the ballot paper, and what procedures (if any) there will be for absentee and provisional voting. Most states have adopted statutory and administrative machinery for resolving electoral disputes, but this machinery varies across states.

As election law varies from state to state, the case law concerning electoral dispute resolution also varies. There are of course federal interests in the conduct of elections, particularly when the election at issue concerns federal office. The US Supreme Court's decision to enter and resolve the disputed 2000 presidential election in Florida is an example of this interest. All recounts were halted upon its decision.

Federal election disputes are sometimes resolved by a tribunal other than the Supreme Court. Article I, Section 5 of the US Constitution states that 'Each House of Congress

(cont.)

shall be the judge of the elections, returns, and qualifications of its own members'. The Federal Contested Election Act (FCEA) provides the means for this. Disputes regarding the election of candidates to seats in the US Congress may be resolved by the chamber affected; this happens by the hearing and investigating of the complaint by the Committee on House Administration. The Committee reports its findings to the full House, which then votes on a final resolution.

585. In this example, the established institutions were overwhelmed by the situation and there was a need to find an alternative solution. While ideally the political culture, the protagonists and wider society are committed to safeguarding and respecting the decisions of the established institutions and it would be better if such situations never arose, the reality is that from time to time existing systems are discredited or not robust enough to resolve disputes with credibility. However, the institutional harm that results may be greater than the benefits provided by the supposed solution. The adoption of such an alternative solution should be considered very carefully, not least because it could set a dangerous precedent that could be invoked by any future losing contender who opts to question an election result and challenge the electoral authority in the expectation that the alternative solution could benefit him or her.

b) International ad hoc AEDR bodies

586. In Kenya, in the aftermath of the post-election violence in 2007, the African Union through the former United Nations Secretary-General, Kofi Annan, intervened to mediate an agreement and created a coalition government. In 2009, the Southern African Development Community (SADC) appointed former South African President Thabo Mbeki to mediate in the conflict in Zimbabwe which followed the 2008 election. This process led to the signing of a power-sharing agreement by the belligerent parties and the formation of a government of national unity.

587. These two examples of extra-constitutional measures to resolve an electoral dispute required that the two respective parliaments ratify the agreements as a way of operationalizing the peace agreement and making them binding on all parties to the dispute. The use of external actors to negotiate and mediate during the post-election conflict in the two countries, and the subsequent decision to subject the peace agreements to parliamentary endorsement in order to make them legally binding, qualifies these initiatives as AEDR mechanisms.

Endnote

588. Both EDR and AEDR systems ultimately have value when they are trusted and if necessary used when complaints arise. Even when this trust is broadly present, they are still part of an overall electoral process in which the participants are political actors. Politicians make political judgements – and the electoral justice system has to be an attractive enough option to encourage them to use it.

ANNEXES

ANNEXES

Annex A

Glossary

Ad hoc EDR system	An *EDR system* that involves an ad hoc body derived from a provisional or transitional arrangement. This might be created either with international involvement, or as an internal national institutional solution. The key characteristic of this type of *EDR system* is its provisional or transitional nature: the ad hoc body is tasked with the resolution of the challenges arising from a specific election or series of elections held over a given period. The body itself may be legislative, judicial or administrative in nature.
Adjudication	The legal process of resolving a dispute. The formal giving or pronouncement of a *judgement* or decree in a court proceeding, which also includes the *judgement* or decision given. The entry of a decree by a court in respect to the parties in a case. It implies a hearing by a court, after notice, of legal *evidence* on the factual issue(s) involved.
Administrative challenges	Those challenges that are resolved by the EMB in charge of directing, organizing, administering and overseeing election procedures. Through such a challenge, those affected may oppose an electoral action or decision using a procedure in which either the same organ of the EMB that issued the action or decision being challenged or another of a higher rank decides the dispute.
Alternative dispute resolution (ADR)	A means for disputing parties to come to an agreement short of *litigation*. ADR is generally classified into at least four types: negotiation, *mediation*, collaborative law and *arbitration*. (Sometimes a fifth type, *conciliation*, is included as well, but for the present purposes it can be regarded as a form of *mediation*.) ADR can be used alongside existing legal systems, or as a result of mistrust in the conventional system.

Alternative electoral dispute resolution mechanism (AEDR mechanism)	AEDR mechanisms may exist alongside formal EDR mechanisms or come into being on an ad hoc basis or during exceptional circumstances. They provide for one or more parties to a *conflict* to initiate a process to resolve it, unilaterally, bilaterally, or through a third party or agency. In the latter case, the equivalent judicial mechanisms are *conciliation*, *mediation* and *arbitration*.
Alternative electoral dispute resolution (AEDR)	Bodies/institutions and/or mechanisms that operate outside the legally established *EDRBs* and/or system which handle, deal with and/or settle disputes related to *electoral processes*. These are usually informal/traditional bodies and/or mechanisms, such as ad hoc committees for the supervision of compliance with codes of conduct, traditional dispute resolution mechanisms, non-governmental/civil society organizations, etc.
Annulment	Making void. There are three types of annulment: the annulment of a single ballot; the annulment of the votes received at a particular *polling station*; and the annulment of an entire election.
Appeal	A request made to a higher *EDRB* to confirm, reverse or modify a decision made by a lower *EDRB*.
Arbitration	*Binding voluntary arbitration*: A process in which the disputing parties choose and agree a neutral person to hear their dispute and resolve it by making a final and binding decision or award. Arbitration is an adversarial, adjudicative process designed to resolve the specific issues submitted by the parties. Arbitration differs significantly from *litigation* in that (1) it does not require conformity with the legal rules of *evidence* and procedure, (2) there is flexibility in timing and choice of decision makers, and (3) the proceeding is conducted in private rather than in a public forum. Binding arbitration awards are usually enforceable by courts, so long as there are no defects in the arbitration procedure. *Mandatory non-binding arbitration*: This form of arbitration follows from court proceedings. Court-appointed *arbitrators* hear cases subject to jurisdictional limits set out in the relevant *legislation* and regulations. The losing party has the right to a new *trial* (trial de novo) in the trial court.
Arbitrator	An attorney or other person selected to hear a case and settle a dispute without a formal *trial*, through a process of *arbitration*.
Boundary delimitation	The process for determining the way in which constituency or electoral area boundaries are drawn; it deals with the division of a country into electoral districts and the allocation of electors to electoral districts and *polling sites*. Sometimes called districting or boundary demarcation. Also known as delimitation.

Campaign (electoral)	Any form of political activity aimed to promote support for a *candidate*, political party or choice available to voters in preparation for an election or a *direct democracy instrument* during a defined campaign period, including meetings, rallies, speeches, parades, broadcasts, debates and other events, and the use of the media, the Internet or any other form of communication.
Campaign financing	Funding of a political *campaign* (with monies received through fundraising, contributions, etc.).
Candidate	A person who is nominated to contest an election either as a political party representative or independent of any political party's support.
Certification of results	The formal endorsement and confirmation of the announcement of electoral results.
Civic education	An information and/or educational programme which is designed to increase the comprehension and knowledge of citizens' rights and responsibilities.
Civil law	Law based primarily on codified legislative texts found in constitutions or statutes. The secondary part of civil law is the legal approaches that are part of custom.
Civil law system	A legal system based on *civil law* and derived from the principles of the legal code of ancient Rome. In civil law *jurisdictions*, judges do not generally have the power to make law by setting legal *precedent*.
Code of conduct	A set of general rules of behaviour, for example for *members* and/or staff of an EMB, or for political parties, with respect to participation in an *electoral process*.
Common law	Law developed by judges through decisions of courts and similar tribunals (also called case law), rather than through legislative statutes or executive branch action. These decisions stand as *precedents* and the principle of *stare decisis* applies.
Common law system	A legal system that gives precedential weight to *common law* on the principle that it is unfair to treat similar facts differently on different occasions.
Complaint	The first document filed with the court by a person or entity claiming legal rights against another.
Conciliation	A method of dispute resolution by means of discussion and settlement without going to court.

Conflict	Competition between opposing forces, reflecting a diversity of opinions, preferences, needs or interests.
Constitutional court	A court concerned with constitutional issues, which may include the constitutionality of laws, procedures and outcomes related to *electoral processes*.
Corrective measure	*Electoral challenges* are intrinsically corrective as their effects include the *annulment*, modification or recognition of wrongful conduct in order to repair the violation that has been committed and restore the enjoyment of the electoral right involved. A corrective measure is taken to clean up the *electoral process* in such a way that the harmful effects of an irregular action do not continue and reach the point of substantially affecting the results – regardless of any other administrative *sanction* imposed on the transgressor.
Declaration of results	Oral or written formal public communication of the result of an electoral event. This may consist of the number of votes received by each *candidate* or political party contesting an election, and of the candidate(s) and/or party(ies) entitled to sit as/seat an elected member(s) under the provisions of the *electoral law*; or of the number of votes recorded for each of two or more options presented in the use of a *direct democracy instrument*.
Direct democracy instrument	Instrument which gives citizens the right to be directly involved in the political decision-making process. It may take one of four forms: *referendum*; citizens' initiative, agenda initiative or a *recall* vote.
Elector	A person who is qualified and registered to vote in an election or under a *direct democracy instrument*.
Electoral administration	The measures necessary for conducting or implementing any aspect of an *electoral process*.
Electoral administrative infraction	An act or omission by an electoral body or official which contravenes or fails to meet the requirements of *electoral laws* or procedures but which is not defined by law as a criminal offence.
Electoral challenge	A *complaint* lodged by an electoral participant or stakeholder who believes that his or her *electoral rights* have been violated.
Electoral commission	A title often given to an *Independent Model EMB* or the non-governmental component of a *Mixed Model EMB*.

Electoral court	Court of justice or other body before which an electoral actor may dispute the validity of an election, or challenge the conduct of candidates, political parties or the EMB. See also *electoral tribunal*.
Electoral crime	An act or omission defined as a criminal offence, usually through electoral *legislation* or general criminal *legislation*. Examples include electoral fraud, voter coercion, impeding or falsifying *voter registration*, and violations of *campaign financing* provisions.
Electoral cycle	The full series of steps involved in the preparation and implementation of an election or *direct democracy instrument*, viewed as one event in a continuing series. In addition to the steps involved in a particular *electoral process*, it includes post-election evaluation and/or audit, the maintenance of institutional memory, and the process of consultation and planning of the forthcoming *electoral process*.
Electoral dispute	Any *complaint*, challenge, claim or contest relating to any stage of the *electoral process*.
Electoral dispute resolution (EDR)	The process of hearing and *adjudication* of any *complaint*, *electoral challenge*, claim or contest relating to any stage of the *electoral process*.
Electoral dispute resolution body (EDRB)	The body entrusted with defending *electoral rights* and resolving *electoral disputes*. These may be entrusted to administrative bodies, judicial bodies, legislative bodies, international bodies or, exceptionally, as a provincial or transitional arrangement, to ad hoc bodies.
EDR legislative system	An *EDR system* that vests the power of final decision on the validity of elections, including any challenges brought, to the legislature, one of its committees or some other political assembly.
EDR system	The legal framework within an *electoral justice system* that specifies the mechanisms established for resolving *electoral disputes* and protecting *electoral rights*. These may be entrusted to administrative bodies, judicial bodies, legislative bodies, international bodies or ad hoc bodies. See also *electoral dispute resolution body (EDRB)*.
Electoral justice	In this Handbook, electoral justice refers to the various means and mechanisms for ensuring that every action, procedure and decision related to the *electoral process* is in line with the law (the constitution, statute law, international instruments or treaties and all other provisions in force in a country), as well as those for protecting or restoring the enjoyment of *electoral rights*. Electoral justice gives people who believe their *electoral rights* to have been violated the ability to make a *complaint*, get a hearing and receive an *adjudication*.

Electoral justice mechanism (also EDR mechanism)	All of the means in place for ensuring that *electoral processes* are not marred by irregularities, and for defending *electoral rights*. Among the mechanisms, a distinction should be made between: (a) those that provide a formal remedy or are *corrective* in nature (b) those that are *punitive* in nature; and (c) *alternative electoral dispute resolution* mechanisms.
Electoral justice system (EJS)	The set of means or mechanisms available in a country (sometimes, in a local community or in a regional or international context) to ensure and verify that electoral actions, procedures and decisions comply with the legal framework, and to protect or restore the enjoyment of *electoral rights*. An EJS is a key instrument of the *rule of law* and the ultimate *guarantee* of compliance with the democratic principle of holding *free, fair and genuine elections.*
Electoral law	One or more pieces of *legislation* governing all aspects of the process for electing the political institutions defined in a country's constitution or institutional framework.
Electoral legal framework	The collection of legal structural elements defining or influencing an *electoral process*, the major elements being constitutional provisions, *electoral laws*, other *legislation* impacting on *electoral processes*, such as political party laws and laws structuring legislative bodies, subsidiary electoral rules and regulations, and codes of conduct.
Electoral management	The process of execution of the activities, tasks and functions of *electoral administration.*
Electoral management body (EMB)	An EMB is an organization or body which has been founded for the purpose of, and is legally responsible for, managing some or all of the essential (or core) elements for the conduct of elections, and of *direct democracy instruments*. These essential (or core) elements include determining who is eligible to vote, receiving and validating the nominations of electoral participants (for elections, political parties and/or candidates), conducting balloting, counting votes, and *tabulation* of votes.
EMB-entrusted EDR system	Under this type of system, responsibility is entrusted to an independent *electoral management body* which, in addition to taking charge of organizing and administering *electoral processes*, has judicial powers to resolve challenges and issue a final ruling as to the validity of the *electoral process.*
Electoral offence	See *electoral crime.*

Electoral penalty	A *punitive measure* following an *electoral offence/crime*, imposed on the perpetrator, entity or person responsible for the irregularity. An electoral penalty can be either criminal (by conventional punishment) or administrative (usually through financial means) in nature. A criminal penalty is always imposed by a court. An administrative penalty can in some *electoral justice systems* be imposed by the *EMB*.
Electoral process	The series of steps involved in the preparation and carrying out of a specific election or *direct democracy instrument*. The electoral process usually includes the enactment of the *electoral law*, electoral registration, the nomination of candidates and/or political parties or the registration of proposals, the *campaign*, the voting, the counting and *tabulation* of votes, the resolution of *electoral disputes* and the announcement of results.
Electoral regulations	Rules subsidiary to *legislation* made, often by the *EMB* or the ministry within which an *EMB* is located, under powers contained in the *electoral law* which govern aspects of the organization and administration of an election.
Electoral rights	Political rights which are enshrined in the basic or fundamental provisions of a particular legal order (generally in the constitution), in general relating to the political right to participate in the conduct of public affairs, directly or by means of freely elected representatives. The main electoral rights include the right to vote and to run for elective office, freedom of association, *freedom of expression* and freedom of assembly.
Electoral system	A set of rules and procedures which provides for the electorate to cast their votes and which translate these votes into seats for parties and *candidates* in the parliament or the legislature.
Electoral tribunal	A judicial institution with specific competence to hear contests and disputes on electoral matters.
Eligible voter	A person eligible to register and to vote in an election or direct democracy instrument.
Evidence	Evidence includes any document, piece of testimony or tangible object presented at a hearing by an *EDRB* in line with accepted rules of admissibility that tends to prove or disprove an alleged fact.
Filing fee	A legal requirement to pay any fee or deposit as a condition for the submission of a *complaint*.

Freedom of expression	A universal right protected by the Universal Declaration of Human Rights. Article 19 provides that 'Everyone has the right to freedom of opinion and expression; this right includes freedom to hold opinions without interference and to seek, receive, and impart information and ideas through any media regardless of frontiers'.
Free, fair and genuine elections	A free, fair and genuine election emanates from an *electoral process* which is a real contest where there is full enjoyment of fundamental freedoms and political rights related to elections: *freedom of expression*, freedom of association, freedom of assembly and freedom of movement. This *electoral process* is supervised by an impartial electoral administration to ensure that the election is conducted fairly, impartially and in accordance with laws. Opportunities exist for independent scrutiny and access to independent review. There is a legal framework and electors are fully informed of their rights.
Governmental Model EMB	An *EMB* model where elections are organized and managed by the executive branch of government through a ministry, such as the Ministry of the Interior, and/or through local authorities.
Guarantee	Any legal means or instruments, which are both structural and procedural, by which values, rights or institutions that are protected or established by the legal order on behalf of the voter are assured, protected, supported, defended or safeguarded.
Incompatibility	A limitation in *legislation* of candidacy for or election to a representative position based on the perceived undesirability of a person who already holds one public position gaining access to or holding another.
Independent Model EMB	An *EMB* model where elections are organized and managed by an EMB which is institutionally independent and autonomous of the executive branch of government, and which has and manages its own budget.
Infraction	The act or an instance of infringing a legal or administrative provision or regulation.
International challenge	Those legal instruments provided for in international treaties and conventions by which those with the standing to do so may have recourse, on a subsidiary and complementary basis, to the competent body after exhausting the domestic remedies provided.

Judicial challenge	Those procedural legal instruments provided for by law by which two or more conflicting parties bring before a judicial body, that is, a judge or a court, whether or not as part of the judicial branch, a dispute over an alleged error, irregularity, instance of wrongful conduct, deficiency or illegality in a certain electoral action or decision. The judicial body, in its position as a superior third party and as an organ of the state, decides on the dispute in a final and impartial manner. Generally speaking, the various judicial *electoral challenges* can be classified into *trials* and *appeals*.
Judicial EDR system	An *EDR system* that entrusts the authority to make the final decision on a challenge to a particular election to a judicial body. The body in question might be: (a) regular court of the judicial branch; (b) *a constitutional court or council*; (c) an administrative court; or (d) *a specialized electoral court*.
Judgement	The decision reached and promulgated by a judicial body and/ or an *EDRB*.
Jurisdiction	The competence and geographic scope of a court or other judicial body in direction-making, decision-making and implementation powers. The power or authority of a court to act. The court must have jurisdiction both over the subject matter and geographic area of the *complaint* and over the person or body against whom relief is sought.
Legislation	The body of law made by the legislative process, also called statute law. Written laws passed by a Parliament, Congress or other legislative body at national or local level.
Legislative challenge	Those legal instruments provided for in the constitution or statutes of some countries which grant powers to legislative bodies or other political assemblies to formally resolve certain *electoral challenges* or issue the *certification* or the final result of an election.
Legitimacy	The perceived fairness of a dispute resolution process.
Liability	Obligations under law arising from civil actions (torts) or under contract. Legal liability can only be decided by courts even if the settlement is made out of the court by mutual agreement.
Litigation	A judicial contest which seeks a decision from a court.
Lower-level EMB	An *EMB* formed at any sub-national level, for example a province, region, district or commune.

Mediation	A process in which the disputing parties use a third party to assist them in reaching a settlement of a dispute though a process which is private, informal and non-binding. The mediator has no power to impose a settlement, but attempts to assist the disputants in reaching consensus and agreement on a mutually acceptable resolution to the dispute.
Member (of an EDRB or EMB)	A person appointed or elected to serve on the body or committee which directs the conduct and implementation of the powers and functions of the *EDRB* or *EMB*.
Mixed legislative-administrative EDR system	A system that combines features of the administrative *EDR* and the legislative *EDR systems*, usually through stating that challenges are first heard by the administrative body, and subsequent challenges are heard by the legislative body in question.
Mixed Model EMB	An *EMB* with a dual structure, which has a policy, monitoring or supervisory component that is independent of the executive branch of government (as for the *Independent Model EMB*) and with an implementation component located within a department of state and/or local government (as for the *Governmental Model EMB*).
Observer	A person accredited to witness and assess, but not intervene in, the proceedings of an *electoral process*.
Offence	A breach of a law or rule; an illegal act.
Party registration	The act of enrolling political parties to participate in elections on the basis of eligibility criteria and submitted signatures and deposits.
Personation	The fraudulent casting of the vote of a registered elector by another person by a person pretending to be the registered elector.
Polling station (or polling site)	A venue established for the purpose of polling and controlled by staff of the *EMB*. Also called a voting station.
Precedent	A legal principle which future courts of law are bound to follow in making decisions. The law is based on the principle of precedent and *stare decisis*. Thus if a court, particularly a lower court, comes across a similar fact or situation it is obliged to follow the legal principles established in the earlier case when making a decision on the case currently before it.

Punitive measure	A punitive measure does not correct or annul the effect of an electoral irregularity. It punishes either the person who committed the violation or the person responsible for ensuring that the violation does not happen, through either the electoral administrative law, which imposes the *sanctions*, or the electoral criminal law.
Recall	A *direct democracy instrument* that allows a specified number of citizens to demand a vote of the electorate on whether an elected holder of public office should be removed from that office before the end of his/her term of office.
Recount	A recalculation, in full or in part, of the votes cast in an election or *direct democracy instrument.*
Referendum	A *direct democracy instrument* consisting of a vote of the electorate on an issue of public policy such as a constitutional amendment or a bill. The consequences of the vote may be either binding or consultative.
Registered voter	An *eligible voter* inscribed in an official list or register of *electors.*
Registration of political parties and candidates	The act of reviewing the validity of applications to participate in an election of political parties and *candidates* and accepting those that meet defined criteria.
Registration of voters	The act of entering the names of eligible *electors* and other relevant information in a register or list of electors.
Rule of law	Rule of law generally entails equal protection of the human rights of individuals and groups as well as equal punishment under the law. It reigns over government and protects citizens against arbitrary state action, ensuring citizens are subject to the rule of law, not the arbitrary rule of men. It encompasses three institutions: the security or law enforcement institution, the court system and judiciary, and the correction system. The principle that law should 'rule' in the sense that it establishes a framework within which all conduct or behaviour takes place.
Sanction	Measures taken by an institution in response to non-compliant or unacceptable behaviour.
Seat allocation	The process of distributing the seats of a legislative assembly to the political parties or *candidates* on the basis of the number of votes they have obtained.

Specialized electoral court	A court that specializes in electoral matters. The authority of this court varies depending on the *EDR system* in the country in question.
Stare decisis	A principle of legal decision making that provides that a previous judicial decision must be followed in identical circumstances.
Statute	See *legislation*.
Tabulation	The process of compiling the result of counting of votes cast in an *electoral process*. Also known as amalgamation of results.
Transitional EMB	An EMB which is set up temporarily to facilitate transitional elections. It is normally set up under the auspices of the international community, such as the UN, and may consist of or include international experts as members.
Trial	In law, judicial examination or hearing of the facts and reaching judgement in a civil or criminal case.
Universal suffrage	The extension of the right to vote or participate in a democratically elected government to all adults, without distinction as to race, sex, belief, intelligence, or economic or social status.
Voter education	A process by which people are made aware of the *electoral process*, including the particulars and procedures for *voter registration* and voting.
Voter registration	The process of establishing the eligibility of individuals to cast a ballot in an *electoral process* or direct democracy instrument and inscribing eligible individuals on a register. As one of the more costly, time-consuming and complex aspects of the electoral process, it often accounts for a considerable portion of the budget, staff time and resources of an election authority.
Writ of certiorari	A writ that a superior appellate court issues at its discretion to an inferior court, ordering it to produce a certified record of a particular case it has tried in order to determine whether any irregularities or errors occurred that justify a review of the case.

Annex B

References and further reading

General

ACE Knowledge Network <http://www.aceproject.org>
The ACE Knowledge Network offers a wide range of services related to electoral knowledge, assistance and capacity development through an online knowledge repository that provides comprehensive information and customized advice on electoral processes.

ConstitutionNet <http://www.constitutionnet.org>
ConstitutionNet is a web-based resource centre, developed by International IDEA in partnership with Interpeace, with funding from the government of Norway, for those participating in constitution building. It aims to assist constitution builders and their collaborators in designing context-specific solutions to common problems by giving them access to specifically designed, well-targeted, need-based and clearly communicated comparative knowledge tools.

International IDEA Unified Database <http://www.idea.int/uid/>
International IDEA has created a unified database which incorporates data from previously separate databases and resources covering topics such as electoral justice, voter turnout, electoral system design, gender quotas, direct democracy and many more.

International Institute for Democracy and Electoral Assistance (International IDEA), *Direct Democracy: The International IDEA Handbook* (Stockholm: International IDEA, 2008), available at <http://www.idea.int/publications/direct_democracy/index.cfm>

—, *Electoral Management Design: The International IDEA Handbook* (Stockholm: International IDEA, 2006), available at <http://www.idea.int/publications/emd/index.cfm>
—, *Code of Conduct for Political Parties Campaigning in Democratic Elections* (Stockholm: International IDEA, 1999), available at <http://www.idea.int/publications/coc_campaigning/index.cfm>
—, *Code of Conduct for the Ethical and Professional Administration of Elections* (Stockholm: International IDEA, 1997), available at <http://www.idea.int/publications/conduct_admin/index.cfm>

Orozco Henríquez, Jesús, 'Sistemas de justicia electoral en el derecho comparado' [EJ systems in comparative law], in *Sistemas de justicia electoral: Evaluación y perspectivas* [Electoral Justice Systems: Assesment and Prospects] (Mexico City: IFE, UNDP, IIJ-UNAM, IFES, IDEA and TEPJF, 2001)
United Nations, *Global Declaration of Principles for International Election Observation and Code of Conduct for International Election Observers*, 15 October 2005, available at <http://www.idea.int/resources/analysis/observation_coc.cfm>
Weinberg, Barry H., *The Resolution of Election Disputes: Legal Principles that Control Election Challenges, 2nd Edition* (Washington: IFES, 2008), available at <http://www.ifes.org/Content/Publications/Books/2008/The-Resolution-of-Election-Disputes.aspx>

Bosnia and Herzegovina

Election Law of Bosnia and Herzegovina, *Official Gazette of Bosnia and Herzegovina*, 23/01, 7/02, 9/02, 20/02, 25/02, 4/04, 25/05, 52/05, 65/05, 77/05, 11/06 and 24/06
Law on Court of Bosnia and Herzegovina, *Official Gazette of Bosnia and Herzegovina*, 29/00, 16/02, 24/02, 3/03, 37/03, 42/03, 4/04, 9/04, 35/04 and 61/04

Bhutan

Election Commission of Bhutan, *Learning from Experience Programme*, vols 1 and 2 (Thimphu: Election Commission of Bhutan, 2008)
—, *Action Plan for the Implementation of the Learning from Experience Programme* (Thimphu: Election Commission of Bhutan, 2008)
European Parliament, Final Report of the EU Election Observation Report of the Kingdom of Bhutan, EU/EOM, Brussels, May 2008
Keynote Speech by Mr Robert Dahl, IFES Legal Policy Adviser, Paper presented at the Seminar on Legal Solutions to Disputes Related to Election Results during the General Assembly of the Association of Asian Election Authorities (AAEA), 21–25 July 2008, Taipei, Taiwan, available at <http://aaeasec.org/d_6.html>

Report by the Election Commission of Bhutan, Paper presented at the Seminar on Legal Solutions to Disputes Related to Election Results during the General Assembly of the Association of Asian Election Authorities (AAEA), 21–25 July 2008, Taipei, Taiwan, available at <http://aaeasec.org/d_6.html>

Burkina Faso

International Institute for Democracy and Electoral Assistance (International IDEA), *La réforme du système électoral au Burkina Faso* [The Reform of the Electoral System in Burkina Faso], (Stockholm: International IDEA, 1999)

—, *La démocratie au Burkina Faso* [Democracy in Burkina Faso], (Stockholm: International IDEA, 1998)

Cambodia

Committee for Free and Fair Elections in Cambodia (COMFREL) in cooperation with the Neutral and Impartial Committee for Free and Fair Elections in Cambodia (NICFEC) and the Youth Council of Cambodia (YCC), *Final Joint Assessment Report: Findings and Conclusions on Cooling Day, Polling/Ballot Counting and Immediate Post-Election Period for the Second Mandate of Commune Council Elections, 2007*, April 2007, available at <http://www.com.comfrel.org>

United Nations Development Programme (UNDP), Country report, 'National Assembly election in Cambodia', 27 July 2003, available at <http://www.un.org.kh/undp/?url=/undp/resources/publications/&page=5>

Germany

Beyme, Klaus von, *Das politische System der Bundesrepublik Deutschland: Eine Einführung* [The Political System of Germany: An Introduction] (Wiesbaden: VS-Verlag, 2004)

Graßhoff, Karin and Klein, Hans H., 'Verschleppte Wahlprüfung' [Protracted scrutiny of election], *Frankfurter Allgemeine Zeitung*, 11 September 2006

Hey, Arnulf von, *Wahlfreiheit und Wahlprüfung* [Electoral Freedom and Scrutiny of Election] (Berlin: Dunker & Humblot, 1975)

Lindner, Ralf and Schultze, Rainer-Olaf, 'Germany', in Dieter Nohlen, Matthias Catón and Philip Stöver (eds), *Elections in Europe: A Data Handbook* (Oxford: Oxford University Press, 2007)

Nohlen, Dieter, *Wahlrecht und Parteiensystem: Zur Theorie und Empirie der Wahlsysteme* [Electoral Law and Party System: Theory of and Empirical Evidence on Electoral Systems] (Opladen: Budrich, 2007)

Nohlen, Dieter, 'Wahlrecht/Wahlsystem/Wahlprüfung' [Electoral law/electoral system/scrutiny of election], in Uwe Andersen and Wichard

Woyke (eds), *Handwörterbuch des politischen Systems der Bundesrepublik Deutschland* (Opladen: Leske&Budrich, 2003), pp. 582–89

Rauber, David N., *Wahlprüfung in Deutschland: materiell-rechtliche Maßstäbe für die Wahlprüfung bei Parlamentswahlen und Wahlen auf kommunaler Ebene* [Scrutiny of Elections in Germany: Substantive Standards on Scrutinizing Parliamentary Elections and Local Elections] (Baden-Baden: Nomos, 2005)

Rudzio, Wolfgang, *Das Politische System der Bundesrepublik Deutschland* [The Political System of Germany](Wiesbaden: VS-Verlag, 2006)

Schreiber, Wolfgang, *Handbuch des Wahlrechts zum deutschen Bundestag* [Compendium on the Electoral Law to Germany's First Chamber in the Legislature] (Köln: Heymann, 2002)

Japan

Jin, Horie (ed.), *Seiji Kaikaku to Senkyo Seido* [Political Reform and Electoral Systems] (Tokyo: Ashi Shobou, 1993), pp. 292–96

Russia

Demidov, B., 'Russia: integrity assessment', Global Integrity Country Report 2004, available at <http://www.globalintegrity.org>

European Court of Human Rights, Chamber judgement in the case of the Russian Conservative Party of Entrepreneurs v. Russia (application no. 55066/00), Press release issued by the Registrar on 11 January 2007, available at <http://www.coe.int/press>

Fogelklou, A., 'Interpretation and accommodation in the Russian Constitutional Court', in Ferdinand Feldbrugge (ed.), *Russia, Europe and the Rule of Law* (Leiden, Boston: Martinus Nijhoff, 2006)

Interfax, 'President Putin signs law banning Duma deputies from changing party and approves removal of "Against All" option in voting ballots', 14 July 2006

Lukin, A., 'A short history of Russian elections' short life', *Moscow Times*, 17 March 2004

Mendras, M., *Comment fonctionne la Russie? Le politique, le bureaucrate et l'oligarque* [How Does Russia Work? The Politician, the Bureaucrat and the Oligarch] (Paris: CERI Autrement, 2003)

Morschakova, T., 'The principle of independence vs the mechanism of dependence', *GazetaRU*, 31 March 2005

Mosnews, 'Russian Supreme Court refuses to review parliamentary election results', *Mosnews*, 16 December 2004

Popova, M., 'Russian courts and the CEC in electoral disputes', *Europe-Asia Studies*, 58/3 (May 2006), p. 397

Reports by the Organization for Security and Co-operation in Europe, Office for Democratic Institutions and Human Rights, on the election observation missions to Russia in 2003 and 2004 are available at <http://www.osce.org/odihr-elections/14519.html>

Information on the relevant national legislation, court decisions and international recommendations and observations can be found on the Vota database of the Venice Commission, <http://www.venice.coe/vota>; the official website of the Central Electoral Commission of the Russian Federation, <http://www.cikrf.ru/cikrf/eng/law/>; the official website of the Constitutional Court of the Russian Federation, <http://ks.rfnet.ru> and the official website of the OSCE/ODIHR, <http://www.osce.org/odihr-elections/item_12_14342.html>.

United Kingdom

Schofield's Election Law, <http://www.sweetandmaxwell.co.uk/Catalogue/ProductDetails.aspx?recordid=4143&productid=433945>

United States

Campbell, Tracy, *Deliver the Vote: A History of Election Fraud, an American Political Tradition, 1742–2004* (New York: Basic Books, 2006)

Morris, Roy, *Fraud of the Century: Rutherford B. Hayes, Samuel Tilden, and the Stolen Election of 1876* (New York: Simon & Schuster, 2001)

Robinson, Lloyd, *The Stolen Election: Hayes Versus Tilden, 1876* (New York: Forge Books, 2001)

E-justice

Carrington, Paul, 'Virtual civil litigation: a visit to John Bunyan's Celestial City', available at <http://www.iapl2010.hu>

Cerrillo, Agusti and Fabra, Pere, *E-Justice: Using Information Communication Technologies in the Court System* (London: Information Science Reference, 2009)

Digital Interview Recording Project of the Cumbria Constabulary, available at <http://www.lcjb.cjsonline.gov.uk>

Oskamp, Anja, Lodder, Arno R. and Apistola, Martin, *IT Support of the Judiciary: Australia, Singapore, Venezuela, Norway, The Netherlands and Italy* (Cambridge: T-M-C Asser Press, 2004)

Preparatory works of the Colloquium of the International Association of Procedural Law, 'Electronic Justice, Present and Future', University of Pecs, 23–25 September 2010, available at <http://www.iapl2010.hu>

For more information about the mandate and powers of the TSE see <http://www.tse.jus.br/institucional/biblioteca/site_novo/historia_das_eleicoes/capitulos/justca_eleitoral/justica_eleitoral.htm>; an example of the TSE online services available can be found at <http://www.tse.jus.br/internet/home/push.htm>.

E-voting in the United States

American Association of People with Disabilities v. Shelley (2004) 324 F.Supp.2d 1120

Americans for Safe Access v. Alameda County (2009) A121390, A122619 (Alameda County Super. Ct. No. RG04-192053), available at <http://www.courthousenews.com/2009/06/17/Court_Upholds_Injunction_in_Voting_Machine_Case.htm> (accessed 18 June 2009)

California Judicial Branch, 'Factsheet', available at <http://www.courtinfo.ca.gov/about/aboutjb.htm> (accessed 18 June 2009)

Election Administration Research Center, 'What is election administration?', available at <http://earc.berkeley.edu/faq.php> (accessed 18 June 2009)

Help America Vote Act (HAVA) (2002)

San Diego County v Bowen, available at <http://www.verifiedvotingfoundation.org/article.php?id=6545>

'Secretary of state and four counties sued for denying access to voters with disabilities', available at <http://www.accessiblesociety.org/topics/voting/cavotesuit0304bkgd.html> (accessed 18 June 2009)

Secretary of state of the State of California, Text of Proposed Recount Regulations, available at <http://www.sos.ca.gov/elections/elections_recountregs.htm> (accessed 19 June 2009)

Secretary of state of the State of California, Frequently asked questions about the top-to-bottom review, available at <http://www.sos.ca.gov/elections/elections_vsr.htm> (accessed 18 June 2009)

Secretary of state of the State of California, California complaint procedures per Help America Vote Act (HAVA) of 2002, Title IV, section 402, available at <http://www.sos.ca.gov/elections/hava-complaint-procedure.htm>

Annex C

About the authors

Adhy Aman is Programme Officer within International IDEA's Electoral Processes Global Programme working primarily on electoral justice and participatory democracy issues. Simultaneously, he is also a staff member of the Asia Pacific Regional Programme responsible for regional and country-level initiatives on political and electoral reform issues. For the first reform era general elections in Indonesia (1999), Adhy served as First Secretary of the National Election Supervisory Committee, a body tasked with supervising the elections and resolving disputes. Through subsequent years, he worked on electoral dispute resolution reform in Asian countries. Adhy holds a master of laws degree from Georgetown University, Washington, DC.

Ayman Ayoub is a Spanish lawyer of Syrian origin who specializes in programmes of development assistance, including electoral and legal reform. His work for over 17 years has primarily focused on the provision of professional assistance services for democratization processes in transitional and post-conflict countries in the Middle East, West Africa, Eastern Europe and South-East Asia. He has worked as a senior expert and in leading managerial capacities for the European Commission, the United Nations and the United States Agency for International Development (USAID), as well as other donors and international organizations. From 2005 to 2007 he worked as Senior Programme Officer at International IDEA (Stockholm) and continued to work as a senior consultant for IDEA thereafter. He co-authored *Electoral Management Design: The International IDEA Handbook* (2006) and produced its Arabic version as well as the Arabic version of *Electoral System Design: The New International IDEA Handbook* (2005). In addition, Mr Ayoub has written a number of election-related articles and reports, and translated a number of the ACE electoral Encyclopaedia topic areas into Arabic. He continues to work as a senior expert for development assistance projects globally.

Tracy Campbell specializes in 20th century United States political and social history. He has written three books: *The Politics of Despair: Power and Resistance in the Tobacco Wars* (Kentucky, 1993); *Short of the Glory: The Fall and Redemption of Edward F. Prichard, Jr* (Kentucky, 1998), which was nominated for a Pulitzer Prize; and *Deliver the Vote: A History of Election Fraud, an American Political Tradition, 1742–2004* (Basic Books, 2006). He has lectured widely on issues of election integrity and political history, and has written a fourth grade history text on Kentucky. In 2008, he served as George McGovern Visiting Professor of Public Leadership at Dakota Wesleyan University. In addition to serving as Director of Undergraduate Studies in the History Department at the University of Kentucky, USA, he is Co-Director of the Wendell H. Ford Public Policy Research Center.

Avery Davis-Roberts joined The Carter Center in 2003 and is a Senior Program Associate in the Democracy Program. She currently manages the Center's Democratic Election Standards Project, which seeks to develop the criteria by which observers assess a democratic process. In addition, she manages the Center's work on methodologies for observing electronic voting technology. She has worked in Carter Center election observation missions in Asia, Africa, South America and the Middle East. Before joining the Center, Avery worked as a research consultant in London. She gained a joint honours degree in Arabic and law in 2001 and a master of laws degree (LL.M) in international human rights law, both from the School of Oriental and African Studies at the University of London, UK.

Zoran Dokovic works as Migration/Freedom of Movement Adviser in the OSCE Office for Democratic Institutions and Human Rights (ODIHR) assisting OSCE participating states in implementing OSCE commitments on freedom of movement through reform of the population registration system. Previously, Mr Dokovic worked in the Election Department of the OSCE Mission to Bosnia and Herzegovina and eventually joined the Central Election Commission of Bosnia and Herzegovina, first as Head of Voter Registration and later as Secretary General of the Commission. He also took part in a number of the ODIHR election observation missions in Eastern Europe and Central Asia.

Andrew Ellis is Director of International IDEA's Asia Pacific Programme, having previously been the Director of Operations and head of the Electoral Processes Programme at the Institute. From 1999 to 2003 he acted as Senior Adviser for the National Democratic Institute (NDI) in Indonesia, working on constitutional reform, and electoral process and decentralization issues. He is the co-author of International IDEA's *Electoral System Design: The New International IDEA Handbook* (2005) and *Electoral Management Design: The International IDEA Handbook* (2006) as well as *Direct Democracy: The International IDEA Handbook* (2008). He has written numerous papers on issues of institutional framework design. Other major assignments include acting as Chief Technical Adviser to the Palestinian Election Commission in 1996, and designing and planning the European Commission's electoral assistance programme in Cambodia for the 1998 elections. He is a former Vice-chair and Secretary General of the Liberal Party in the United Kingdom and a former Chief Executive of the Liberal Democrats in the UK.

Sergueï Kouznetsov practised as a lawyer in Russia before joining the Council of Europe in 1995. He joined the Venice Commission in 1998 as a legal officer in the elections and referendums division. Mr Kouznetsov has acquired extensive experience in South-Eastern Europe and in the countries of the Commonwealth of Independent States through his involvement in the preparation of Venice Commission opinions on constitutional and electoral issues and on legislation on political parties in Azerbaijan, Bosnia and Herzegovina, Kyrgyzstan, Serbia and Ukraine. He has participated in teams of legal advisors in several election observation missions of the Parliamentary Assembly of the Council of Europe, most notably in Azerbaijan (2006, 2008), Bosnia and Herzegovina (2006), Palestine (2005), Russia (1993), Serbia (2007 and 2008) and Ukraine (2004, 2006, 2007).

Ralf Lindner is a Senior Researcher at the Fraunhofer Institute for Systems and Innovation Research in Karlsruhe, Germany. He holds a PhD in political science from the University of Augsburg, Germany. His research interests include electoral behaviour and party systems in Europe and North America, the theory and practice of policy advice, and innovation, science and technology studies. Lindner's publications include contributions to *Elections in the Americas* (ed. D. Nohlen, Oxford, 2005), *Elections in Europe* (eds D. Nohlen and P. Stöver, Baden-Baden, 2010) and a book analysing the impact of the Internet on political parties and interest groups (*Politischer Wandel durch digitale Netzwerkkommunikation?*, Wiesbaden, 2007).

Augustin Loada is a Professor from Burkina Faso. He graduated in France and has been Professor of Public Law and Political Science at the University of Ouagadougou, Burkina Faso, since 1995. He was a Fulbright Visiting Scholar in 2000 at Boston University, United States. He was also Dean of the Faculty of Law and Political Science at the University of Ouagadougou. He is currently Director of the Center for Democratic Governance (CGD), a Burkina Faso-based research centre that conducts studies in the fields of governance and democratization and contributes to strengthening the capacities of political actors (civil society, political parties, local authorities etc.) in democratic governance.

Jesús Orozco-Henríquez is currently a Professor at the Legal Research Institute of the National Autonomous University of Mexico (UNAM) and has been elected by the General Assembly of the Organization of American

States as Commissioner at the Inter-American Commission on Human Rights (2010–2013). He served as a judge at the highest electoral judicial authority in Mexico, the Central Chamber of the Federal Electoral Court (1990–96) and the Higher Chamber of the Electoral Court of the Federal Judiciary (1996–2006). He has published widely on electoral law, human rights, constitutional law and comparative law. He holds a doctorate in law, with honours, from UNAM as well as a master's in comparative law from the University of California at Los Angeles, United States.

Deki Pema has been an Election Commissioner with the Election Commission of Bhutan (ECB) since 2006. During that time she has been involved in the establishment of the electoral system, including the drafting of the new electoral laws and the institutional set-up of the ECB. She has also been involved in education campaigns for the electorate and for election officials and in the registration processes for the elections held in 2008. Before her work with the ECB, Deki Pema worked as a Senior Planning Officer in the Policy and Planning Division of the Ministry of Agriculture. She has an MSc in Agricultural Economics from the University of London, UK.

Joram Rukambe is the Regional Electoral Advisor for the United Nations Development Programme (UNDP) in Johannesburg. Prior to this he was a Programme Manager for International IDEA's Africa and Middle East Programme (AMEP) and Director of Elections and Chief Executive of the Electoral Commission of Namibia. He also served as consultant and technical advisor to various EMBs in Southern Africa, including South Africa and Zambia between 1994 and 2001 and has observed elections in many Southern African countries. Mr Rukambe holds a master of arts degree in media and cultural studies from the University of Natal, South Africa.

Maiko Shimizu has been involved in electoral observation activities in Pakistan, Cambodia, Indonesia and Taiwan as an election observer as well as an observation mission coordinator with the Asian Network for Free Elections (ANFREL) and the Japanese NGO InterBand. From November 2005 to December 2006 she worked in the Electoral Processes Team at International IDEA assisting the Electoral Justice Project and in voter turnout workshops. She was a researcher in the Political and Economic Affairs team at the Japanese Embassy in Timor-Leste from 2007 to 2010. She holds a master's degree in international studies (peace and conflict resolution) from the University of Queensland, Australia, which she attended on a Rotary World Peace Fellowship.

Denis Truesdell is an international electoral consultant. He worked as a legal advisor in Cambodia from 2001 to 2007, carrying out a wide-ranging United Nations Development Programme (UNDP) electoral assistance programme for the Cambodian National Electoral Committee. He has since served with

International Foundation for Electoral Systems (IFES) in Haiti and the UNMIS Electoral Assistance Division in Sudan. Previously, Mr Truesdell worked in several peacekeeping missions such as UNTAC, UNPROFOR, UNCRO and UNMIBH until returning to Canada as a legal advisor to the Directeur Général des Élections du Québec and later as a consultant to the Canadian International Development Agency (CIDA) in its Peace-Building Unit. Mr. Truesdell is a member of the Quebec Bar and has an LL.M from the London School of Economics, UK.

Domenico Tuccinardi is Director of NEEDS, the training programme for EU observers conducted by a consortium led by International IDEA. He specializes in electoral legislation and management. In 1999–2000 he directed the OSCE external registration and voting services for Bosnia and Herzegovina. As OSCE Deputy Director of Elections in 2001–2002 he designed the digitalization of the voter register and organized the transfer of election administration functions to the new Election Commission of Bosnia and Herzegovina. Mr Tuccinardi served as Election Administration Specialist in the Planning Team for the Iraq transitional elections of 2005 and led the European Union (EU) project in support of the same elections. More recently, he was Special Adviser to the EU on the Independence Referendum in Montenegro and managed the establishment of the Practitioners' Network of the ACE Electoral Knowledge Network. Mr Tuccinardi served as Deputy Chief Observer for the EU election observation missions in Venezuela and Nicaragua and participated in several other electoral assistance and elections observation processes around the world. He is one of the authors of the EU Methodological Guide on Electoral Assistance and the EC-UNDP-IDEA Training Course on Effective Electoral Assistance, and has collaborated on other publications in the fields of electoral management, voter registration and technology.

Annex D

International IDEA at a glance

Our mission

In a world where democracy cannot be taken for granted, the mission of the International Institute for Democracy and Electoral Assistance (International IDEA) is:

to support sustainable democratic change through providing comparative knowledge, and assisting in democratic reform, and influencing policies and politics.

In addressing our mission we focus on the ability of democratic institutions to deliver a political system marked by public participation and inclusion, representative and accountable government, responsiveness to citizens' needs and aspirations, and the rule of law and equal rights for all citizens.

We undertake our work through **three activity areas:**

- providing comparative knowledge and experience derived from practical experience on democracy building processes from diverse contexts around the world;
- assisting political actors in reforming democratic institutions and processes, and engaging in political processes when invited to do so; and
- influencing democracy building policies through the provision of our comparative knowledge resources and assistance to political actors.

Our work encapsulates **two key principles:**

- We are exponents of democratic change. The very nature of democracy is about evolving and adapting governance systems to address the needs of an ever changing society.
- We are supporters of change. The drivers of change must come from within societies themselves.

Our programme

Democracy cannot be imported or exported, but it can be supported. And because democratic actors can be inspired by what others are doing elsewhere around the world, International IDEA plays an instrumental role in supporting their initiatives by:

Providing comparative knowledge and experience in:

- elections and referendums;
- constitutions;
- political parties;
- gender in democracy and women's political empowerment;
- democracy self-assessments; and
- democracy and development.

Assisting political actors in national reform processes:

As democratic change ultimately happens among citizens at the national and local levels, we support, upon request and within our programme areas, national reform processes in countries located in:

- Latin America;
- Africa and the Middle East; and
- Asia and the Pacific.

Influencing democracy-building policies:

A fundamental feature of strengthening democracy-building processes is the exchange of knowledge and experience among political actors. We support such exchange through:

- dialogues;
- seminars and conferences; and
- capacity building.

Seeking to develop and mainstream understanding of key issues:

Since democratic institutions and processes operate in national and international political contexts we are developing and mainstreaming the understanding of how democracy interplays with:

- development;
- conflict and security;
- gender; and
- diversity.

Our approach

Democracy grows from within societies and is a dynamic and constantly evolving process; it never reaches a state of final consolidation. This is reflected in our work: in supporting our partners' efforts to make continuous advances in democratic processes we work step by step with them with a long-term perspective.

We develop synergies with those involved in driving democratic processes – regional political entities (the European Union (EU), the Organization of American States (OAS), and the African Union (AU), for example), policymakers, politicians, political parties, electoral management bodies, civil society organizations – and strategic partnerships with the key regional, international and multi/bilateral agencies supporting democratic change and different United Nations bodies.

Quintessentially, we bring experience and options to the table but do not prescribe solutions – true to the principle that the decision makers in a democracy are the citizens and their chosen representatives.

International IDEA is an intergovernmental organization that supports sustainable democracy worldwide. International IDEA's Member States are all democracies and provide both political and financial support to the work of the institute. The Member States include Australia, Barbados, Belgium, Botswana, Canada, Cape Verde, Chile, Costa Rica, Denmark, Finland, Germany, Ghana, India, Mauritius, Mexico, Namibia, the Netherlands, Norway, Peru, Portugal, South Africa, Spain, Sweden, Switzerland and Uruguay. Japan has observer status.

Index

A

B

C

D

E

F

G

H

I

J

K

L

M

N

O

P

Q

R

S

T

U

V

W

Y

Z